● 本书为闽江学院2022年社科项目（翻译专业硕士点培育专项）"中国文化英译探索"（项目编号：YWZ2002）的主要成果

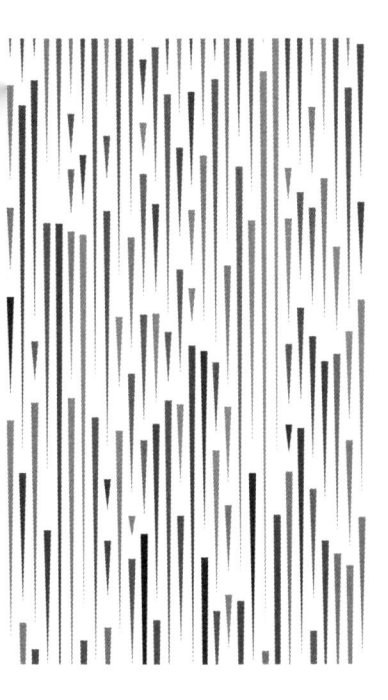

张雅卿　著

# 中国文化英译探索

厦门大学出版社
XIAMEN UNIVERSITY PRESS
国家一级出版社
全国百佳图书出版单位

**图书在版编目（CIP）数据**

中国文化英译探索 / 张雅卿著. -- 厦门：厦门大学出版社，2024.12. -- ISBN 978-7-5615-9523-7

Ⅰ. G122；H315.9

中国国家版本馆 CIP 数据核字第 2024ML2275 号

---

责任编辑　王扬帆
美术编辑　李夏凌
技术编辑　许克华

---

出版发行　厦门大学出版社
社　　址　厦门市软件园二期望海路 39 号
邮政编码　361008
总　　机　0592-2181111　0592-2181406（传真）
营销中心　0592-2184458　0592-2181365
网　　址　http：//www.xmupress.com
邮　　箱　xmup@xmupress.com
印　　刷　厦门市明亮彩印有限公司

---

开本　720 mm×1 020 mm　1/16
印张　16
插页　2
字数　310 千字
版次　2024 年 12 月第 1 版
印次　2024 年 12 月第 1 次印刷
定价　79.00 元

本书如有印装质量问题请直接寄承印厂调换

# 序

　　2018年秋至2024年春,我先后受聘为闽江学院"闽都学者"讲座教授和卓越教授,指导该校外语学科、翻译硕士点建设,组建外国语学院青年教师团队,张雅卿博士为团队成员,这段因缘让我有机会见证了他在学术上的一路成长:他不停地提交各个层次社科基金项目申请书,虽然屡战屡败,却从不气馁。功夫不负有心人,终于在2022年获得闽江学院社科项目立项(翻译硕士点建设专项),历时三年完成了项目研究和成果撰写。前不久在校园偶遇雅卿,他请我为其学术专著《中国文化英译探索》作序。考虑到他有近20年的中国文化英文课程教学经验,博士论文研究方向为汉学翻译,这和我的学术兴趣和研究领域比较相近,同时我对他的项目缘起和研究框架也比较熟悉,遂欣然同意。只是苦于近来烦事缠身,静不下心。这两日应内蒙古大学外国语学院院长李满亮教授邀请来内蒙古大学讲学和筹办2024年度全国语言服务研究高端论坛,得空提笔为他的作品写几句话。

　　雅卿虽然是外国语学院的英语教师,却似乎更热爱中文,尤其是先秦诸子百家的作品。通览全书,可以看到他所讨论的中国文化主要集中在中国古代文化部分,特别是秦汉以前的文史哲语料。他的讨论涉及孔、孟、老、庄、荀、墨等先秦诸子中比较有影响力的儒、道、法、墨各家,有一定的代表性。虽然受到篇幅限制,这本书的选材有一定局限,但是所选文本的确是讨论中国文化绕不开的,就这一点来说,其选材还是值得肯定的。从具体研究方法来说,雅卿采用的是比较研究方法,围绕某一个具体中国文本对不同英文译本进行平行并置(juxaposition)比较分析。我对他引用的译本做了粗略统计，发现仅仅《论语》和《道德经》的英译讨论就涉及40多个译本。这倒是与他平日给我的手不释卷、勤勉好学、博览群书的印象相吻合。

从研究的导向来说，雅卿的探索立足于选择中国好故事并讲好中国故事，让中国文化的对外传播行稳致远。他的探索包含了对什么是中国文化的思考，以及对如何译好中国文化的尝试。他从文本功能、翻译目的、翻译策略、读者接受难易程度、译文本身是否优美、译文是否容易被读者记住等多个角度对不同译本展开评论，同时，对于名家译作大胆质疑，对于相对边缘的译本或译者也没有偏见，如实地给予正面评价。

风乍起，吹皱一池春水。从大的角度来说，雅卿的探索为中国文化翻译研究带来一股新风，有可能在未来引起更多学者的共鸣。从小的角度来说，对于闽江学院翻译硕士点建设有学术助力作用，对于新文科背景下闽江学院应用型人才培养具有现实意义。

是为序。

司显柱
2024年3月22日于青城呼和浩特

子曰:"知之者不如好之者,好之者不如乐之者。"

——《论语·雍也》

西方有其历史悠久的雄辩传统、论辩实践、劝说模式。这些传统、实践、模式决定什么样的说法是"在理"的,如何使用修辞资源才能收到最大效果而又不逾矩,某一种特定场合下劝说对象一般对劝说者抱有什么样的期望,论辩者之间的关系怎么确定,哪一方应负举证责任,等等。只有增强对这一具有深层规范功能的传统的研究了解,才能从根本上避免在确定外宣方略时流于浮浅或盲目。

——刘亚猛[①]

---

① 刘亚猛.追求象征的力量:关于西方修辞思想的思考.北京:生活·读书·新知三联书店,2004:19.

# 目 录

绪 论 /001/
    第一节 中国文化走出去背景下的典籍筛选与英译策略 /001/
    第二节 研究思路及意义 /011/

第一章 《论语》英译比较与评析 /014/

第二章 《孟子》英译比较与评析 /053/

第三章 《道德经》英译比较与评析 /087/

第四章 《庄子》英译比较与评析 /106/

第五章 《荀子》英译比较与评析 /135/

第六章 《墨子》英译比较与评析 /164/

第七章 《韩非子》英译比较与评析 /185/

第八章 《孙子兵法》英译比较与评析 /202/

第九章 典故与成语英译比较与评析 /222/
    第一节 《世说新语》典故英译比较与评析 /222/
    第二节 《韩非子》典故与成语英译比较与评析 /227/
    第三节 其他来源的典故与成语英译比较与评析 /241/

后 记 /248/

# 绪 论

## 第一节 中国文化走出去背景下的典籍筛选与英译策略

### 一、中国文化与中国好故事

中国文化源远流长,中华典籍浩如烟海,置身于其中的学者在倍感骄傲的同时,却又常常对阅读书目或章节的选择与对外推广方面觉得无所适从。当前正值中国文化走出去的关键时期,对于要讲好中国故事这一点,学术界早已达成共识,相关论著更是汗牛充栋。但是对于什么是中国好故事(即什么是中国文化精华)、对谁讲述中国故事(即中国文化外译的目标受众是谁)、如何讲好中国故事(即该如何呈现中国文化)这几个关键问题都还缺乏准确定位与系统思考。"一个民族的文化,往往凝聚着这个民族对世界和生命的历史认知和现实感受,也往往积淀着这个民族最深层的精神追求和行为准则。"[①]如果以内嵌在中华民族灵魂深处的世界观、人生观与价值观为参照点,则以《论语》、《孟子》、《道德经》和《庄子》为代表的中国轴心时代的先秦典籍当为不二选择。以孔子、孟子、老子、庄子为代表的先秦诸子及其著作在中国文化界与学术圈可谓无人不知,无人不晓(尽管了解的广度与深度存在个体差异)。先秦典籍,尤其是《论语》,确保了中国读书人和文化人在思想交流与学术论辩中永远能够处于"同一页面上"(on the same page)。照理来说,以《论语》为代表的诸子典籍堪称宏观意义上的"中国好故事",成为中国文化对外传播的首选似乎是顺理成章的事情。但是就微观层面而言,由于作者的时代局限,这些作品难免

---

① 中共中央文献研究室.十六大以来重要文献选编(下).北京:中央文献出版社,2008:431.

存在这样或那样的观念瑕疵,并不适合照单全收或对外进行全面"文化传真"。比如,孔子的论断"唯女子与小人难养也"①就使得很多中国先秦文化入门级的本土年轻女性读者耿耿于怀,从而拒《论语》于千里之外。很难想象将这样的论述进行完全忠实的直译会得到身处英语语言文化背景中的西方读者的正面评价,遑论引发他们对中国文化的追慕之情。因此,我们主张对中国经典进行再审视与评估,提炼出真正的中国好故事(适合对外传播的作品或片段)进行英译。

## 二、中国故事的西方受众

要讲好中国故事,不能不对目标受众②进行画像。与一般的以传达信息为主的语言翻译不同,文化翻译主要是价值观的输出、交流、论辩乃至博弈的过程。面对来自不同文化的作品,读者最基本的心态有两种:一种是好奇,另一种则是抵触。

对于与其基本价值观一致的事物或现象,读者会因为获得局部新知识、新体验③而欣然接纳。

但是读者对于任何事物的新鲜感总是有时效性的。译者如果长期迎合读者的阅读趣味与预期,久而久之,故事成了套路,读者就不再有好奇心了。那样的话,"江郎才尽"的同质化文化故事讲述者将面临失去受众的巨大风险。即便是就译者所承担的中国价值观输出的使命而言,如果一味迁就受众、处处

---

① 在当代读者看来,孔子在这句话中(至少是字面上)通过一个不恰当的类比对女性进行了负面评价。这句话究竟该做何解,学界尚无定论。不少学者认为它使得孔子的修辞人格蒙上了一层阴影,出于为尊者讳的文化心理,极力撇清孔子与男性沙文主义者的关联。在现有《论语》英译本中,但凡稍具读者意识的译者对此都会附上详细乃至冗长的注解以便为这句话的可接受性进行辩护。本书无意加入这一争论,提及这句话只是为了说明不加鉴别地推广或翻译文化经典是不无风险的。

② 帕尔曼和奥尔布莱希特-泰特卡在他们的《新修辞学》中把受众定义为"说者有意通过自己的论辩加以影响的所有那些人构成的一个组合"(the ensemble of those whom the speaker wishes to influence by his argumentation)。参见 Perelman Ch., L. Olbrechts-Tyteca. The New Rhetoric. Notre Dame: University of Notre Dame Press, 1969:19.

③ 所谓局部新知识、新体验指的是那些基本原理或运作机理大同小异,但是具体表现因地域、种族、语言差异而有具体细节差异的文化现象,比如中国"梁祝"与西方"罗密欧与朱丽叶"的故事,大体属于爱情这一人类永恒的话题,具体情节的差异改变不了读者或观众对"有情人终成眷属"的祝福与期许。这类"人同此心、心同此理"的文化现象,往往只有程度的差别,没有范畴的差异,不会从根本上挑战乃至更新受众观念。

以受众趣味为行事标准,则其翻译行为必定不具备可持续性。主观上,译者会因为长期未能达到影响及改变目标读者思想、感情、态度、行为的预期目标而失去自身翻译动力(缺乏学术成就感)。客观上,译者长期"有辱使命",自然会失去外部机构赞助①,从而使得文化翻译事业难以为继。长远看来,这一修辞情势必然促使文化译者走上一条"不无挑战同时也不乏可行性"的翻译之路。那就是适度挑战读者的文化价值观与阅读习惯,尝试在有限范围内改变或引导读者的这条路,这意味着无论是译者还是读者都要走出自己的舒适区。作为寻求改变现状而主动发起挑战的译者一方,自然是要扛起证明自己所选的新语料、推送的新价值具有正当性的举证责任(burden of proof)②,征用一切可能的话语手段去努力说服并改变抵触的、高度警觉的,也就是"不合作"③的目标读者。

---

① 在项目立项、资源倾斜等方面得不到应有扶持,失去自我更新的动力与能力。

② 举证责任是一个源于法律话语但是又不限于法律话语的话语修辞概念,熟稔法律修辞理论与实践的西方修辞学者帕尔曼指出,"意义是不能没来由地随意改变的。当我们重申大家都已经接受的意义时固然无须出示任何理由,可是当我们试图改变这种意义时,情况就恰恰相反。举证责任总是落在对现成意义持不同看法的人头上"(But this change of meaning cannot take place without reason, for contrary to the generally granted meaning, the change in meaning must be justified. The burden of proof befalls the opponent to the customary meaning).参见 Chaim Perelman. From Metaphysics to Rhetoric//Michel Meyer. Formal Logic and Informal Logic. Dordrecht: Kluwer Academic Publishers, 1989: 12-13.

③ 关于不合作原则,刘亚猛等有过原创性论述。刘亚猛在其《修辞作为语用的对应学科——在语言使用研究中开展竞争性合作》一文中将 NCP(principle of non-cooperation),也就是不合作原则定义为:在与对方交流或谈话时,总是预设听话人不会自愿与你合作以产生预期的效果或结果;在听他人说话时,总是预设说话人不会主动与你合作,协助你从自己的角度看待当前的问题或按你自己的方式做出决定。(When engaging and addressing another party, always proceed without assuming that the addressee would voluntarily cooperate with you in producing the effect or result you desire. When being engaged and addressed, always respond without assuming that the addressor would voluntarily cooperate with you in your effort to see the matter concerned from your own perspective or to reach a decision about it on your own terms.)刘亚猛原文参见 Liu Yameng, Zhu Chunshen. Rhetoric as the Antistrophos of Pragmatics: Toward a "Competition of Cooperation" in the Study of Language Use. *Journal of Pragmatics*, 2011(43): 3403-3415. 译文参见张雅卿.合作与抵抗——对《修辞作为语用的对应学科》的评介与思考.东北农业大学学报(社会科学版),2014(4):55-61.

### 三、如何讲好中国故事

根据上文的分析,不难发现讲好中国故事需要研究受众,顺应或挑战受众的既有观念和价值体系,进而采用合适的话语策略去影响或说服受众接纳中国故事译本、赞许中国价值、爱慕中国文化。所有这一切均指向了作为翻译观念母体的西方修辞①。作为一个有着两千多年历史的人文学科,西方修辞②一向致力于理解、开发和运用以言语为代表的象征手段所蕴含的力量,包括学术活动在内的几乎所有西方社会实践活动都深受修辞的影响。同时,由于修辞在西方人文教育传统中十分普及,"学术是一种修辞实践"几乎已经成为学界共识。将修辞作为学术研究中的一种视角和解读工具更是司空见惯。从修辞视角重新审视和界定翻译实践这种独特的学术活动,了解修辞在其中的作用及运作机理,这是我们与西方友好相处并讲好中国故事的重要前提,也是新时代中国在国际话语秩序中占据一席之地的重要途径。

为了讲好中国故事,尤其是做好中国文化对外翻译,我们有必要形成以下几个新认识:

#### (一)翻译具有修辞说服性

在传统的语言中心翻译观看来,翻译只是文本之间抽象的对应,译事无非是"信""达""雅"或"异化""归化"这些基于文本的技术与伦理的问题;当代翻译学则明显转向了对"人"的考察③,不再视翻译为一种简单的语言转换行为,

---

① 参见刘亚猛.修辞是翻译思想的观念母体.当代修辞学,2014(3):1-7.

② 当代学术界关于西方修辞(rhetoric)的主流定义为:"通过象征手段影响人们的思想、情感、态度、行为的一门实践"(The practice of influencing thought, feelings, attitude and behavior through symbolic means)。需要说明的是:中文语境中从先秦以来关于"修辞"一词的理解固然不乏修辞格等与西方对应的部分(counterpart),但目前仍然存在着较大差别,比较典型的区别就是大部分汉语修辞领域学者依然坚持认为修辞是语言学科下辖的一个以美化文辞为主业的分支学科,而英语语言学界大部分学者则比较容易认同修辞以说服与论辩为主要研究方向。虽然"修辞"一向是"rhetoric"的标准译名,鉴于中西"修辞"内涵的巨大差异,本书将"rhetoric"译为"西方修辞",以便与"汉语修辞"区分开来。同时,考虑到本书主要谈论翻译中涉及的西方修辞技巧(少量涉及汉语修辞的地方已经标明),为节约篇幅,继续使用"修辞"作为"rhetoric"的译名简称。

③ 陈小慰认为翻译是"面对人、作用人、影响人的跨语言、跨文化活动"。参见陈小慰.翻译与修辞新论.北京:外语教学与研究出版社,2013:151.

而是以译者翻译动因、译文对读者所产生的效果为核心关注点,换言之,修辞视角正逐渐切入乃至取代传统翻译观。翻译与修辞的关联性首先体现在翻译本质上的修辞性(即说服的目的性)这一方面。陈小慰从修辞角度把翻译定义为"在特定译语社会文化环境中,跨越语言文化边界,有效运用象征手段,影响特定译语受众的对话过程"①。刘亚猛指出,由于翻译话语的特殊性质,被写入译文的核心思想情趣也必然部分或全部落在目标读者的期待视野之外,或者说必然带有某种读者一时还难以接受的新异性;译者为了使自己的观点及论证得到认真听取的机会,在信息构筑及传输的每一个环节都竭尽全力从异己语言文化中发掘出说服手段向读者推介其中包含的旨趣。因此,翻译不仅是一种修辞,而且是一种被施加了尤其严苛的约束因而特别富有挑战性的修辞。② 由于翻译始终包括意图和效果的问题,译者总是关注目标读者读了译文有何反应,译文对既有观念有何冲击,是否促进译语文化的更新与变化。因此,翻译应该被视为从异己语言文化发掘出最佳说服手段并产生宏观社会政治效果的一种不折不扣的修辞行为。

### (二)翻译是一种选择与诠释

翻译过程不可避免要涉及选择与诠释。翻译并非仅仅是把一种语言的字面意义用超然于阐释的另外一种语言表达出来的话语实践。任何翻译实践都必然不是对原作内容信息原原本本、巨细靡遗的所谓忠实"传达",这在客观上来说是"不可能的",在主观上说则是"不必要的"。翻译是一种决策过程(decision-making process),取舍的过程本身就包含主观性。对那些有利于实现预期翻译目的的事实,译者需有意识地"提及、强调,赋予它们在场(presence)"③的特质;而对那些无助于有效影响受众,甚至起反作用的事实,则应该"刻意回避、掩盖,甚或压制",④做必要的淡化或删减处理。正如汉斯·格奥尔格·加达默尔(Hans Georg Gadamer)所说的那样,"如果我们在

---

① 陈小慰.翻译与修辞新论.北京:外语教学与研究出版社,2013:152.
② 刘亚猛.修辞是翻译思想的观念母体.当代修辞学,2014(3):1-7.
③ 凸显是一种重要的翻译说服策略,正如西方修辞学泰斗肯尼斯·伯克(Kenneth Burke)所指出的那样:见即有所不见(a way of seeing is a way of not seeing),译者通过凸显译文某个维度,必然相应淡化了其他(或许同样重要)的维度。就此而言,读者所看到的,正是译者愿意让他们看到的。这再次确认了翻译活动的修辞说服属性。
④ 详见刘亚猛.追求象征的力量:关于西方修辞思想的思考.北京:生活·读书·新知三联书店,2004:76.

翻译时想从原文中突出一种对我们很重要的性质,那么我们只有让这同一原文中的其他性质不显现出来或者完全压制下去才能实现。这种行为恰好就是我们称为解释的行为。正如所有的解释一样,翻译也是一种突出重点的活动,谁要翻译,谁就必须进行这种重点突出的活动"。① 翻译与诠释二者总是交织在一起,一些阐释会在翻译时对某一个词语结构的处理中显示出来,而某些特殊的处理又会在翻译的过程中影响到它的阐释。西方修辞思想中最早由公元前五世纪希腊哲辩师普罗泰戈拉(Protagoras)提出的一个基本认定,即"针对任何一个争议都可以提出完全相反的两个论点"(On every issue there are two arguments opposed to each other.)②,显然也适用于解释翻译过程中译者的选择与诠释。因此,诠释是翻译的一个重要维度,翻译与诠释的关系进一步体现了翻译的修辞本质。

(三)翻译带有修辞隐蔽性

当代学者们关于翻译的标准固然见仁见智,乃至于大相径庭,有一点却是毋庸置疑的,那就是翻译的译文与原文相关,这一基本预设并未被颠覆。虽然诸如"翻译就是背叛"这样的说法几乎已经成为老生常谈,但大多数读者对于译文依然具备起码的信任,相信译者是在努力如实地传达原文思想。相对于公开论辩等说服手段,翻译由于披着"忠实"的外衣而具有较高的修辞隐蔽性。由于翻译经常以叙事的方式而非以论辩的名义不留痕迹地改变受众的既有认知,成功的翻译往往在很大程度上影响、改变受众的原有认识而不为受众所察觉。翻译由于具有与生俱来的隐蔽性而颇受文化学者的青睐,经常被用作一种参与学术论辩的手段。古典修辞一向十分注重韬晦(self-effacement or "sprezzatura"),也就是一种努力不使人觉察到自己修辞动作的艺术。③ 就此而言,翻译可以被视为一种自我韬晦的宏观学术修辞手段。不仅翻译本身具有高度的修辞隐蔽性,在具体的翻译过程中,为了让翻译取得预期效果,译者

---

① 加达默尔.哲学解释学.夏镇平,宋建平,译.上海:上海译文出版社,2004:498-499.
② 参见刘亚猛.追求象征的力量:关于西方修辞思想的思考.北京:生活・读书・新知三联书店,2004:124.
③ 据刘亚猛考证,修辞艺术必须自我掩饰的观念起源于古希腊与古罗马。亚里士多德曾经说过,"修辞只有在不被人看成是修辞的时候才能真正发挥其效力"。昆提利安也要求学生避免在演说中做"任何可以使人感觉到[你们的]巧妙设计"的事。以上这些关于修辞必须自我掩饰的讨论详见刘亚猛.追求象征的力量:关于西方修辞思想的思考.北京:生活・读书・新知三联书店,2004:23-25.

常常想方设法采用种种文本手段掩盖译文的争议性,从而使修辞者(即译者)的观点、态度、论辩等获得受众的信服和认同。刘亚猛在《一言以论之:浓缩作为论辩的变形手段》一文中提出了论辩"变形"(transfiguring)和"缩微"(miniaturizing or condensation)这两个概念,指出缩微因为具有使论辩"隐形化"的功能而成为跨文化论辩中经常被使用的一个重要技术手段。所谓缩微,便是将传统的普通论辩基本单位,即文本的基本结构成分压缩成一个语言单位,通过这样的浓缩手段产生的微型论辩结构因为十分"微观",论辩对手很难察觉其中竟然包含着一个论辩,因此往往能够取得出其不意的论辩效果。[1] 作为典型的跨文化行为,典籍翻译中这种论辩策略更是频繁被使用。众所周知,关键术语的定义体现着哲学论辩各方的基本立场。任何一个哲学家一旦放弃自己给这些术语下的定义,转而接受对立方对它们做出的解释,就形同放弃自己的立场和观点。诠释的多样性使得任何学者在给核心概念下定义之时总是获得伦理授权,亦即每个人都可以对同一事物有自己不同的理解,一旦下了定义,则有了进一步阐释发挥的立足之地,乃至辩驳的"根据地"。在以翻译为手段的跨文化论辩实践中,译者为了拥有诠释主体性,往往从自己的诠释立场出发,将关键词以翻译的名义界定成为己所用的"工作定义"。由于下定义这一行为本身看起来只是在陈述一个观点,因而无可厚非。实际上,一旦"工作定义"以翻译的名义出现,往往会被披上客观性的外衣,便于在"忠实翻译"的名义下展开一系列修辞运作。像下定义或对关键词进行翻译这种将推理过程巧妙压缩进个别词语的微型论辩结构具有得天独厚的优势,它不像一个正式的标准论辩那样容易引发受众的警觉与抵制。同时,它还因其短小精悍而能够对受众进行预构筑,为即将提出的主要论点铺垫与开路。因此,下定义是很难察觉的一种修辞动作。

基于这些认识,在翻译操作层面要注意以下原则与策略。

(一)遵从"认同"原则

伯克曾经阐释并强调过认同原则的重要话语功能:只有当我们能够讲另外一个人的话,在言辞、姿势、声调、语序、形象、态度、思想等方面做到和他并无二致,也就是说,只有当我们认同这个人的言谈方式时,我们才能说得动他。通过奉承进行说服虽说只不过是一般意义上的说服的一个特例,但是我们可以完全

---

[1] Liu Yameng. Argument in a Nutshell: Condensation as a Transfiguring Mechanism in Argumentative Discourse. *Argumentation*, 2004(18):43-59.

放心地将它当作一个范式。通过系统地扩展它的意义,我们可以窥探到它背后隐藏着的使我们得以实现认同或达致"一体"(consubstantiality)的各个条件。通过遵从受众的"意见",我们就能显露出和他们一体的"征象"(signs)。①

就中国文化对外传播翻译实践而言,"讲另外一个人的话"就是秉承相近的价值观(至少是显露出共享一套价值观)的"征象"。在具体操作层面,意味着翻译作品在涉及价值观的选材方面要遵循循序渐进的原则,刚开始向目标读者输出中国文化时,应尽量选择价值观一致或相近的内容,让读者尽量不产生"非我族类,其心必异"的排斥感。就以"爱他人"这个文化价值为例,一开始就向西方读者输出孔子的"孝道"观念,必然令友邦人士"莫名惊诧"。不妨先选译墨子的"兼爱"思想,获得西方读者共鸣,②然后逐步介绍孔子(有等差的)的仁爱思想,在获得读者认可之后,再适时推出不无争议却又很难绕开的"孝"的话题。到了这个阶段,读者或许已经不在意所谓儒家价值在某些维度上与现代社会格格不入的问题,而是对诸子百家思想乃至中国哲学思想整体产生浓厚兴趣。

另外,在数字化与读图时代,浸淫于信息海洋中的读者(无论东西方)能够且愿意分配给阅读的时间与耐心都是非常有限的,大部分的阅读时间都是碎片化的。充满学术注解(如理雅各、安乐哲的典籍译本时常出现注解多于原文的情况)的大部头译作往往令读者望而却步。对于西方读者而言,作为他者的中国经典往往被认为是神秘、玄奥且晦涩的(比如《道德经》),即便会去翻看,往往也会由于内容生涩而难以读完。鉴于这一情况,译者应该充分考虑读者的阅读习惯,主动顺应读者需求,化整为零。这同时意味着译者不能不加选择

---

① 原文为:"You persuade a man only insofar as you can talk his language by speech, gesture, tonality, order, image, attitude, idea, identifying your ways with his. Persuasion by flattery is but a special case of persuasion in general. But flattery can safely serve as our paradigm if we systematically widen its meaning, to see behind it the conditions of identification or consubstantiality in general. And you give the 'signs' of such consubstantiality by deference to an audience's 'opinions'. For the orator … will seek to display the appropriate 'signs' of character needed to earn the audience's good will. True, the rhetorician may have to change an audience's opinion in one respect; but he succeed only insofar as he yields to that audience's opinions in other respects. Some of their opinions are needed to support the fulcrum by which he would move other opinions."。参见 Kenneth Burke. A Rhetoric of Motives. Berkeley: University of California Press,1969:55-56.

② 西方也有类似思想,只是往往有较强的宗教烙印,这一点译者不仅需要注意,更应该保持足够警觉。

而一味追求大而全。为了吸引读者并获得认同,译者要替读者筛选中国本土文化阐释权威认为最有价值、最接近读者价值观的原文,以尽可能通俗易懂的方式进行翻译并在必要的地方辅以解说。

(二)建构译者人格威信以影响目标读者

人格威信(ethos)指修辞者由于个人品德、声誉(personal character and fame)或所属机构赋予他的身份、地位(institutional identity and status),也就是"势",而享有的权威和感召力。译者通过确立自己在智力、道义、专业等方面相对于受众的"优势"而享有的信用和权威,对任何说服工作的成败都具有举足轻重的意义。文化翻译者对自己所从事的翻译工作应该具备的修辞人格必须胸有成竹,尤其要熟悉这些人格的外在表象,并且能按照需要有选择地"显露"出某些人格特征的"样子"(displaying the tokens)。① 这样才能通过自己的译文构筑和投射出理想的人格形象并取信于读者。理想的译者人格既包括专业人格也包括伦理人格。就专业人格而言,在对双语的掌握能力方面,译者是受众心中理所当然的"英雄"与话语权威。② 译者应该通过逻辑严密、措辞精准、行文优美的译文展现或建构熟稔源语与译语语言文化的专家修辞人格。就伦理人格而言,首先要以不偏不倚、不弄虚作假的学术作风建构伦理人格。不偏不倚,就是译文尽量不带译者个人倾向性;不弄虚作假,就是译者要做个诚实的代言人,③ 不能够利用信息差蒙蔽读者。当译者的智力、道义、专业知识等为受众/读者所认可之后,作为修辞者的译者与读者之间足以产生一种"势效应"④的差别,读者完全有可能由于对译者的见识、智慧、操守、知识等的服膺而在逻辑与事实核查方面降低标准,对译者的材料选择、核心概念界定、文本解读等最富有争议空间的事项在心理层面给予"授权"并最终认可其选择。

---

① 文化翻译修辞者在说服目标受众时所呈现的仅仅"像是"自己的人格,它未必是修辞者真实为人的自然流露,而是服务于一定修辞目的的一种特意的构筑。

② 参见陈小慰.翻译与修辞新论.北京:外语教学与研究出版社,2013:161.

③ 也就是说,理想的翻译是一种委托发言,一种代理人的讲话。有关这一观点的论述参见陈小慰.翻译与修辞新论.北京:外语教学与研究出版社,2013:164.

④ 刘亚猛对"势"这一修辞核心概念有系统梳理和独到见解:"当代法国著名汉学家弗朗索瓦·朱利安(François Jullien)在他研究'势'的专著 *La propension des choses/The Propensity of Things* 中用法语单词 disposition 和 dispositif 来翻译'势':前者取其'排列''处置''支配'等义,后者则取其'用于产生一定效果的手段'等义。朱利安的翻译策略表明他将'势'理解为可以产生一定'效果'的某种'排列'。"参见刘亚猛.追求象征的力量:关于西方修辞思想的思考.北京:生活·读书·新知三联书店,2004:161.

### (三)开发语言本身所具有的劝说潜能,用好"辞屏"工具

伯克受摄影师使用不同滤色镜(color filters, lens or screen)拍摄同一个物体获得大不相同的照片这一现象的启发,将人们所使用的各种象征系统或词语(terms)集合称为"辞屏"(terministic screen①)。正如任何一个镜头都无法忠实还原拍摄对象所有特征并且往往只能有选择地凸显某些特征一样,作为观察和理解世界的工具,每一套词语或符号构成的独特"镜头"或"荧屏"(我们不妨称其为"辞屏")所得到的世界图像并非原原本本的"现实",而只是所用的那一套语言符号允许我们看到的那一"相"(维度),因而难免会突出某些特征,掩盖其他特征,乃至于歪曲某些形象。用伯克自己的话说,即便我们说任何词汇都是对现实的某种反射(反映),词汇的本质决定了这一反射(反映)必然是选择性的,因此它同时也是对现实的折射(偏离)②。辞屏的应用固然会对我们的观察和理解造成扭曲,但是离开词语我们无法讨论任何事物。无论我们使用哪一套词语,它们必然构成一个相应的"屏"。③ "辞屏"的折射性从认识论的角度看是人类只能无可奈何地深陷其中的一个困境,从修辞的角度看却是人类进行象征行动的一个使能条件(enabling condition)。刘亚猛指出,正因为词汇具有内在的"选择性反射"或"折射"功能,其应用才必然具有"劝勉性"和"说服性",才使得目的和动机能够在象征行动中得以体现和实现。辞屏这种"歪打正着"的修辞功用可以说正是它的"短处之长处"(the qualities of its defects)。辞屏的"劝勉性"使得译者在构思译文文本时可以依据自己的修辞目的选择或凸显某些词汇,为目标读者构筑起一个有利于接受其说辞的辞屏。译者在进行中国文化翻译时,一方面要避开辞屏的陷阱(比如使用充满西方神学色彩的 God 翻译中国的"天"),一方面则要开发语言本身所具有的劝说潜能,用好"辞屏"工具。

---

① 伯克还使用了"nomenclature""terminology""vocabulary""perspective""viewpoint""frame of acceptance"等不同的近义词来指称"terministic screen"。

② Kenneth Burke. Language as Symbolic Action. Berkeley:University of California Press,1966:44-45.

③ Kenneth Burke. Language as Symbolic Action. Berkeley:University of California Press,1966:50.

## 第二节　研究思路及意义

### 一、讲西方读者喜闻乐见的中国古典哲辩故事

从宏观角度而言,本书将讨论焦点放在中国古典的精华作家的代表性作品上,致力于选取具有代表性的、能够体现中国人积极向上、乐观豁达、兼容并包、明理通达、兼济天下的思想、情感、态度的语料。从微观角度而言,将焦点放在经典中能够体现中国哲辩思维与实践的具体段落,无论是一篇(如韩非子《说难》)、一段(如《世说新语》"管宁割席"),还是一句(如"父母唯其疾之忧"),只要有助于构筑、投射中国人格乃至整体中国人性格,只要有助于增进友邦人士对中国的了解或理解的,都在讨论之列。①

从选择的倾向性而言,本书较多关注了那些能够体现中国人整体世界观、人生观的哲学论辩素材。其原因有二:一是假如能够将这些语料以西方英语读者易于理解且喜闻乐见的方式推送出去,必然有助于改变西方人关于中国哲学碎片化、思辨性不强的固有观念。二是这些语料多数以对话形式存在,更准确地说,多数是以唇枪舌剑、剑拔弩张的修辞论辩话语的形式表达作者的观点和立场。即便中国学者不特意加以说明,只要能够将这一独特的话语形式及其相关争议点有效地传达给西方,浸淫于西方修辞传统的西方读者必然不会忽略其中所包含的中国修辞论辩因素。无论是其中所体现的被论辩参与者默认的论辩话语规则,还是白纸黑字的论辩话语本身,都是中国具有独特且高度发达的修辞论辩理论与实践的雄辩证明。这些语料的成功推送,将使得中国思辨传统在事实上不仅存在而且高度发达这一论点不证自明,还对于提升中国学术界的整体修辞人格、提升中国在国际学术圈的话语地位有着不容忽视的作用。

另外一点则是尊重历史的原则。真诚地面对自己的文化历史,是文化国格修辞建构不可或缺的一个维度。正如鲁迅先生所言:"真的猛士,敢于直面惨淡的人生,敢于正视淋漓的鲜血。"能够直面自身文化糟粕,同时旗帜鲜明地反对糟粕,在反思中进步,这不仅是有勇气的行为,同时也是明智的行为。因

---

① 因时间、空间等客观条件约束,即便是本书选定的书目与篇章,也还有不少被迫搁置的选文。

此本书如果全部选用正能量、高大上的语料,反而会因为太完美而显得虚假,难以取信于目标读者。恰恰是一些不尽完美的语料从不同的侧面一起形塑了中国文化立体而真实的修辞人格。基于这一考虑,在局部讨论中也选择了部分不无争议的中国价值观①。

## 二、修辞地比较中国典籍英译平行文本

为了讨论方便,首先选择篇幅相对较短的先秦思想家具有奠基地位的代表性话语以及中国文化中比较突出的典故与成语,在此基础上,尽可能地寻找不同时期具有代表性的不同英语翻译版本②进行对比分析。分析的视角是以受众为核心的西方修辞研究方法,主要关注原文解读的争议性、译文是否对目标读者产生预期的修辞效果、译者在翻译过程中所选用的话语修辞策略等。这本质上是一种比较研究,更准确地说,是进行修辞的比较。

所选译文多数为名家名作,但是不同译本往往有不同的诠释倾向,有的甚至有截然相反的理解与翻译,这就为修辞解读与批评营造了足够的话语空间。当两个以上的权威观点交锋时,只能让一个更大的权威来仲裁,那就是理性与实践。本书将译文话语重新语境化,思考并评估它在特定目标语境中的话语目的和效果,比较不同译文的话语功效,从而对现有译文做出恰如其分的评价并提出可能的努力方向。

## 三、以面向西方受众的典籍翻译实践形塑正面的中国"修辞国格"

随着后疫情时代的真正开启及人工智能领域新技术的突飞猛进,当前中国和以美国为代表的西方在科技、经济及诸多关键且敏感的领域处于既合作又竞争的微妙关系中,部分领域不仅有对抗甚至还有冲突风险,但是这不是,也不应该是以中美关系为代表的中西关系的基本局面。中外关系无论是合作还是竞争,彼此的文化交流都不应间断。"文化"是中外交流最为坚实的共同基础,在百年未有之大变局正在发生的当下,认识到这一点尤为重要。为了推

---

① 在具体的文化翻译中,对这些语料的选择要注意比例、推送时机以及译者对这些有争议的价值与行为的反思与批评。

② 所选译文虽然多数为名家名作,但是学术观点在本质上只是一种修辞意见;正所谓"智者千虑必有一失",即便是思维最缜密的译者也难免有疏忽或偏离的地方,这为修辞批评提供了可能性。

进中国文化与西方文化的交流与融合,翻译自然是不可或缺的。作为语言文化交流与沟通的桥梁与纽带,翻译的作用是怎么强调都不为过的。挖掘中国传统文化精华选本中与当下主流价值合拍的内容,有助于构筑正面的"修辞国格",获得西方受众对中国国家形象作为一个整体的认可与赞赏。本书意在通过对西方受众的阅读习惯与预期的考察与分析、对可以采用的修辞话语工具的具体展示和对现有译本得失的比较研究,为中国文化尤其是中国传统文化典籍对外翻译与传播贡献一个基于受众的西方修辞话语分析视角。基于西方修辞视角的文化翻译研究有助于通过对受众(目标读者)的顺应与适当"施压",[①]一方面促进中国优秀传统文化获得最广泛受众的了解与喜爱,另一方面促进中国话语以独特的主体性或修辞人格参与国际对话与论辩。恰当的中国文化选本及其富有修辞受众意识的、以效果为导向的翻译的价值显而易见:一是有助于构建中国文化特有的"人格魅力",重构中国话语体系,让中国自信地走向世界。二是有助于改变西方对中国的固有认识[②],让世界乐于认识中国。三是有助于中国文化参与国际对话与论辩。通过翻译中国文化来间接表达中国立场,是一种不辩之辩,既不会挑起争端,产生国际关系裂痕,又能够捍卫中国价值,有利于维护中国形象与国家核心利益。四是有助于促进世界文化的多样性。中国"和而不同"的文化哲学本身就是文化多样性的鲜活例子。中国文化走向世界,让世界文化花园增添新品种,既是世界给中国的机会,也是中国给世界的机会。中国文化为世界文化注入活力,而身处世界文化之海的中国文化必然可以从中获得发展与创新的机会。

---

① 即适度改变乃至挑战其阅读习惯与预期。
② 比如中国没有真正的哲学、中国人缺乏理性思维、中国古代没有系统的修辞论辩理论等偏见。

# 第一章 《论语》英译比较与评析

一、子曰："学而时习之，不亦说乎？有朋自远方来，不亦乐乎？人不知，而不愠，不亦君子乎？"

——《论语·学而》①

The Master said, "Is it not pleasant to learn with a constant perseverance and application? Is it not delightful to have friends coming from distant quarters? Is he not a man of complete virtue, who feels no discomposure though men may take no note of him?"

(理雅各 译)②

Confucius remarked, "It is indeed a pleasure to acquire knowledge and, as you go on acquiring, to put into practice what you have acquired. A greater pleasure still it is when friends of congenial minds come from afar to seek you because of your attainments. But he is truly a wise and good man who feels no discomposure even when he is not noticed of men."

(辜鸿铭 译)

The Master said, "Is it not a pleasure, having learned something, to try it out at due intervals? Is it not a joy to have friends come from afar? Is it not gentlemanly not to take offence when others fail to appreciate your abilities?"

(刘殿爵 译)

**子曰**

关于《论语》中反复出现的"子曰"（一般默认为孔子的言论），理雅各（James Legge）使用 master（大师）进行翻译，有助于体现孔子在中国文化中

---

① 若无特别说明，本章所涉及的《论语》引文均出自《论语译注》，为节约篇幅，不一一标注，特此说明。出处详见杨伯峻.论语译注.北京：中华书局，2012.

② 若无特别说明，全书主体部分（第二章至第九章）所有英译引文出处均已列在各个单元之后"本章参考的英译本"一栏，为节约篇幅，不一一标注。

的地位,也使引用其思想学说的后学感到安心。但是在不同的文化中,甚至在中国文化内部,大师(master)级的人物并不少见,因此 master 的识别度并不高,无法成为一个独特的文化符号,为了避免混淆,往往需要加注说明。辜鸿铭使用孔子在英语世界的通用英文名称 Confucius,有助于读者便捷地把握相关语境涉及的主要人物(孔子),能够更多地去关注孔子的话语而不是将注意力耗费在识别发言人的身份上。不足之处就是无法传达话语记录者对孔子的敬意,在某些特定语境中,甚至会让西方读者误以为弟子直呼老师之名乃中国文化传统的话语规范。假如是一整本探讨《论语》的英文书,不妨如理雅各这样使用 the master 以便完整呈现孔子的修辞人格;如果是超越特定语境的文本,则退而求其次,在加以必要的说明的情况下,以使用 Confucius 为宜。

### 学而时习之,不亦说乎

在这个修辞性疑问中蕴含一个推理,也就是"学"能够致用(习),因此能够给人带来快乐。翻译时如果能把这个快乐的理由呈现出来,对译文受众会更有说服力。理雅各译文使用 constant perseverance(持之以恒)and application 翻译"时习之",尤其是使用 perseverance(不屈不挠,坚持不懈)这个隐含"坚忍"意义的辞屏,难免令读者疑窦丛生:需要坚持不懈地面对各种困难并且要不断和惰性做斗争的学习何乐之有?刘殿爵使用 to try it out 就明确表达了将所学付诸实践(学以致用的乐趣)这一层意思。但是使用 at due intervals 显得比较刻意,不够自然。何时将所学付诸实践更多的是一种机缘巧合,并非人为安排。詹宁斯(William Jennings)将"时"翻译成 opportunely(适时地),[①]符合实际情境。

### 有朋自远方来

辜鸿铭不仅为"朋"增补 of congenial minds(志同道合的)这个定语,还进一步说明"朋"所为何来:your attainments(你的造诣)。两处增补,前者无伤大雅,因为"道不同不相为谋";后者则有蛇足之嫌,毕竟朋友可能因为仰慕你的才华、成就、品德或其他优点而造访,不加限定反而给解读留有余地。

### 人不知,而不愠

韦利(Arthur Waley)将"人不知"译作 even though one's merits are un-

---

[①] 本书主体内容各章节在讨论具体段落、句子乃至词语翻译时,为了丰富视角、挖掘英语语言潜能、探索翻译的可能性,不时引用一些可以相互佐证、互相发明的各家翻译只言片语。因篇幅所限,无法引用全文,各引文片段出处均已在引文当页或本章末尾加以说明。

recognized(即便自己的优点没有被人赏识),李克曼(Simon Leys)将其译作 when one's merits are ignored(自己的优点被人无视),二者均增补了"人不知"的具体对象,也让译文逻辑更加严密。刘殿爵将"知"的对象翻译为 abilities(才能),似乎未能将品德这一维度考虑在内,使用 merits 恰好能够涵盖才与德两个方面。愠,根据刘毓庆解读,主要是"怨"而非"怒"①。理雅各翻译中使用的 discomposure(implies some degree of loss of self-control or self-confidence especially through emotional stress)主要是一种指向自身感受的"心乱,不安",不如刘殿爵的 take offence(见怪)。

### 不亦君子乎

君子固然是有较高道德修养之人,却并非道德上毫无瑕疵之完人,理雅各将其翻译为 a man of complete virtue(具有完善道德之人)未免言过其实。辜鸿铭用 a wise and good man(明智且良善之人)虽然欠简约,但至少将君子的才与德两方面都立体地呈现出来了。庞德(Ezra Pound)将"不亦君子乎"翻译为 indicative of high breed(是良好教养的表现),描绘了君子的品质,也巧妙回避了颇具争议的君子这个概念的翻译②。李克曼使用 gentleman 翻译君子,并对其概念演变进行了系统归纳:"在孔子之前,君子这个词仅仅表示一种社会地位。剥离君子这个概念的社会性定义,更新并注入纯粹伦理的内容,是儒家思想的一个主要创新。这一概念的(修辞)更新影响巨大,意义深远,因为它最终对贵族封建秩序根本结构(的合法性)提出了质疑。世袭精英的陈旧概念为重新界定过的新精英概念所取代。精英身份不再是由出身或财富决定,而是纯粹由美德、教养、天资、能力和功绩决定。这样的转变显然并非一蹴而就,纵观《论语》,不难发现这个概念在各个阶段的嬗变:在极少数地方,君子仍然以其最初的狭义社会意义被使用;多数场合则是模棱两可地涵摄社会等级和道德品质两个方面。儒家这一独创性的观点在许多聚焦于提升君子道德水平的论述中体现得淋漓尽致:从伦理角度来看,平民可以通过道德修为的提升

---

① 刘毓庆.论语绎解.北京:商务印书馆,2017:1.
② 在《论语》英译其余部分庞德主要使用 gentleman 翻译"君子"。

# 第一章 《论语》英译比较与评析

成为君子,而贵族则会因为道德堕落而失去获得这种头衔的资格。"①

## 二、子曰:"巧言令色,鲜矣仁!"
——《论语·学而》

Confucius remarked, "With plausible speech and fine manners will seldom be found moral character." （辜鸿铭 译）

The Master said, "It is rare, indeed, for a man with cunning words and an ingratiating face to be benevolent." （刘殿爵 译）

**巧言令色**

刘毓庆对这一节的解读如下:

花言巧语而又媚态可掬的人,很少有真心向善的。因为"巧言"的关键在顺人之意以为说辞,"令色"的关键在承人之好以温顺其态,都是在以媚人、讨好人的方式,达到个人的目的,而不是要与人为善。② 我们认为"巧言"主要涉及话语的"理"(内容)方面,"令色"主要是说话人说话时的样态与风格。

辜鸿铭用 plausible(superficially pleasing or persuasive)形容那些听起来令人愉悦且容易接受、似是而非的话语,相当形象。刘殿爵用 cunning (showing or made with ingenuity; artfully subtle or shrewd)words 这一辞屏

---

① 李克曼关于君子的论述原文如下:"gentleman: before Confucius, the word junzi (gentleman) merely indicated social status. A major originality of Confucian thought is to have progressively divested this notion of its social definition and to have endowed it with a new, purely ethical content. This transformation had huge and radical implications, as it was eventually to call into question the fundamental structure of the aristocratic-feudal order. For the old concept of an hereditary elite it substituted the notion of an elite based not upon birth or wealth, but purely determined by virtue, culture, talent, competence, and merit. Naturally such a transformation did not take place all at once; throughout the Analects, one can identify various stages of the concept: in a very few places, junzi is still used in its original, narrowly social meaning; more often, it is found in an ambiguous sense which confuses social rank and moral quality. The originality of the Confucian view is fully displayed in the many occurrences where it is the moral dimension of junzi which is exclusively developed: on ethical grounds, a commoner can achieve the quality of 'gentleman' whereas an aristocrat can lose his qualification for such a title.". 参见 The Analects of Confucius. Simon Leys, trans. New York: W.W. Norton Company, 1997: 105-106.

② 刘毓庆. 论语绎解. 北京: 商务印书馆, 2017: 7.

翻译巧言,重在刻画说话人不真诚、机巧滑头的修辞人格,与辜译侧重话语内容略有不同,但是二者在表达对这类伪善行为的谴责方面,修辞效果不相上下。

辜译用 fine manners 翻译"令色"则不是那么妥当,因为 fine(marked by elaborate rhetoric or florid style)主要意思是"过度修辞的",并没有传递出说话人刻意迎合、顺应听话人这一意思。林语堂曾经使用 an ingratiating appearance(谄媚的样子)将"承人之好以温顺其态"刻画出来。刘译调整为 an ingratiating face,将读者注意力集中在说话人的面部表情上,与"色"固然在字面上更加对应,但考虑到肢体语言也能够传达独特的符号意义,语义范围更广的 appearance 似乎更可取。

**鲜矣仁**

辜鸿铭避开对抽象的"仁"的描绘,用贴近日常经验的 moral character(道德品质)加以翻译,使读者能够轻松把握原文意思。刘殿爵用 benevolent(善心的),与原文基本对等,也是英语世界对"仁"的主流翻译。就内容而言,二者翻译大体相当;就结构而言,辜译使用倒装句成功传达了原文结构。

### 三、曾子曰:"慎终,追远,民德归厚矣。"

——《论语·学而》

The philosopher Tsang said, "Let there be a careful attention to perform the funeral rites to parents, and let them be followed when long gone with the ceremonies of sacrifice; then the virtue of the people will resume its proper excellence."
(理雅各 译)

A disciple of Confucius remarked, "By cultivating respect for the dead, and carrying the memory back to the distant past, the moral feeling of the people will waken and grow in depth."
(辜鸿铭 译)

Zeng Zi said, "By carefully conducting funeral services for the recent dead and memorial rites for the long departed, the virtue of the masses will return to eminence."
(丘文明等 译)

Master Zeng said: "When the dead are honored and the memory of remote ancestors is kept alive, a people's virtue is at its fullest."
(李克曼 译)

**曾子**

曾子被理雅各译为 The philosopher Tsang(哲学家曾氏),被辜鸿铭译为

a disciple of Confucius(孔子的一个弟子),被詹宁斯译为 The Scholar Tsang(学者曾氏),被李克曼、华兹生(Burton Watson)译为 Master Zeng(曾大师)。与其说是翻译,不如说是作为修辞者的翻译家们对曾子学术身份与地位认知的一种投射。这些关于曾子的身份定位是否符合客观情况,在学术界尚存争议。比如我国的西方修辞学学者刘亚猛就认为先秦诸子主要的学术身份应该是修辞者。① 有鉴于"子"是对一个人的尊称,又为了与孔子相区别,在《论语》这个特定语境中不妨把曾子翻译为 Master Zeng;如果需要,还可以将辜鸿铭的译文②作为注解以方便对中国文化比较陌生的读者识别曾子的身份。

*慎终,追远*

以上各版本的译文中,理雅各的译文将慎终追远的对象理解为同一个人,其译文相当于"慎终而追(其)远"。其余译文大体上将慎终追远的对象视为不同的两批人,一批是刚刚去世的父母,另外一批则是作古已久的先人,译文相当于"慎终且追远"。持"慎终而追(其)远"观的支持者在诠释史上就有宋代著名的邢昺。他对"追远"是这样解读的:"远,谓亲终既葬,日月已远也。孝子感时念亲,追而祭之,尽其敬也。"③理雅各的翻译或许是受其启发,固然不无道理,然而,考虑到"慎终且追远"这样的主流解读能够涵盖更广的范围,我们倾向于采纳这一与理氏不同的解读。辜鸿铭对"慎终"的翻译并未提到葬礼,只是说"培养对逝者的敬意",对"追远"的翻译也是泛泛而论,只是说"追忆遥远的过去"。因此还有待于进一步细化。丘文明等的译文用 the recent dead(新近离世的)与 the long departed(作古已久的)形成强烈对比,明白无误地告诉读者这不是同一批人。李克曼关于"慎终,追远"的译文最为简约,虽然只提到给逝者以哀荣以及对祖先的记忆不可遗忘,但"慎终,追远"显然已是译文题中应有之义了。

*民德归厚矣*

上列译文中除辜译将"德"译为 moral feeling(道德感)外,其余三位译者均译为 virtue。关于"德"字的翻译,韦利有以下评论:"这个词与拉丁语 virtus 非常接近。正如 virtus 那样,它的意思是指特定的品质或潜藏在任何事物中的 virtue。在早期汉语中它从来没有(除非出现特定例外语境)表示(与恶习

---

① 参见 Liu Yameng. Three Issues in the Argumentative Conception of Early Chinese Discourse. *Philosophy East and West*,1996(46):33-58.
② 除了个别例外,辜鸿铭在大部分情况下习惯模糊地用 a disciple of Confucius 替代式翻译大部分有名有姓的孔子门徒。
③ 转引自高尚榘.论语歧解辑录.北京:中华书局,2011:21.

相对的)'美德'的含义,而是如 in virtue of(凭借)或 the virtue of this drug(这种药物的优点)这些英文表达方式中表示'凭借''优点'的意思。在个人身上,它是一种与我们所谓的品德非常相似的力量,并且经常与力(物理力量)形成对比。人们经常把它翻译成'美德',这只会误导读者。即使我们预先提醒过读者,他们也一定会从通常意义上而非与拉丁语 virtus 对应的相对罕用的词义角度解读这个词(将其当作与恶习相对的'美德')。有鉴于此,我通常用 moral force(道德力量)一词来翻译'德',特别是当它与力(物理力量)相对照时。然而,我们不能把马的德说成是它的'道德力量'。在这里,character(品格)是唯一可能的对等表达。如果是用来形容人,那么 prestige(声望)一词则比较接近于'德'的含义。"①

韦利对"德"的理解无疑是深刻的,但是他将"德"翻译为 moral force(道德力量)则比较勉强:"德"的确是一种(象征)力量,但这并不意味着要在其英语译文中专门凸显这一点。理雅各与丘文明等的译文将"归"理解为恢复到原来(良善)的状态,李克曼的译文使用 is at its fullest(处于最佳状态),均失之偏颇。从修辞角度而言,本节讨论的是丧礼和祭祀这类典型的仪典修辞行为的社会教化功能。谈论修辞就难免要探究具体修辞行为所产生的社会文化效果(后果)。理译与丘译都只是提到教化对道德水平的"复位"功能,并未提到民众在道德水平上的实质性提高;李译直接使用静态的 be 动词,也未能凸显仪典修辞行为所带来的变化。只有辜译立体呈现了民众的道德感被丧礼和祭祀这样的(仪典)修辞行为唤醒,民风趋于敦厚这一理想的修辞结果。森舸澜就本节话语的修辞语境进行重构,推测对话场景为宫廷之中,受众为君主或王

---

① 韦利原文为:"This word corresponds closely to the Latin virtus. It means, just as virtus often does, the specific quality or 'virtue' latent in anything. It never (except by some accident of context) has in early Chinese the meaning of virtue as opposed to vice, but rather the meaning of 'virtue'; in such expressions as 'in virtue of' or 'the virtue of this drug'. In individuals it is a force or power closely akin to what we call character and frequently contrasted with li, 'physical force'. To translate it by 'virtue', as has often been done, can only end by misleading the reader, who even if forewarned will be certain to interpret the word in its ordinary sense (virtue as opposed to vice) and not in the much rarer sense corresponding to the Latin virtus. For this reason I have generally rendered te by the term 'moral force', particularly where it is contrasted with li, 'physical force'. We cannot, however, speak of a horse's te as its 'moral force'. Here 'character' is the only possible equivalent; and in the case of human beings the term 'prestige' often comes close to what is meant by te." 参见 The Analects of Confucius. Arthur Waley, trans. London: Taylor and Francis Group, 1938:33.

储,主旨是"欲治其国,君主必须先正其身"①。

四、子曰:"父在,观其志;父没,观其行;三年无改于父之道,可谓孝矣。"

——《论语·学而》

The Master said, "While a man's father is alive, look at the bent of his will; when his father is dead, look at his conduct. If for three years he does not alter from the way of his father, he may be called filial."　　(理雅各 译)

Confucius remarked, "When a man's father is living the son should have regard to what his father would have him do; when the father is dead, to what his father has done. A son who for three years after his father's death does not in his own life change his father's principles, may be said to be a good son."
(辜鸿铭 译)

The Master said, While a man's father is alive, you can only see his intentions; it is when his father dies that you discover whether or not he is capable of carrying them out. If for the whole three years of mourning he manages to carry on the household exactly as in his father's day, then he is a good son indeed.
(韦利 译)

理雅各的译文从传统语言学的角度而言基本传达了原文的意义,但是从以受众为核心关注点的西方修辞学角度而言,话语效果并不是那么理想。对中国文化不太熟悉的英语读者难免会感到困惑:当父亲在世的时候,他人为什么只能通过考察儿子的理想而不能同时观察具体行为以评判儿子的操守?韦利的译文无意中②对此稍微做了解释(虽然解释的方向略有偏颇):当一个人的父

---

① 原文为:"The target audience for this saying seems to be rulers or potential rulers, the message being that the key to ordering the state is paying attention to one's own behavior."。参见 Confucius Analects: With Selections from Traditional Commentaries. Edward Slingerland, trans. Indianapolis: Hackett Publishing Company, 2003:4.

② 韦利的译文生产是在辜鸿铭的文本生产之后,为了讨论方便,我们这里打乱时间顺序,先讨论后出的韦利译本。假如不考虑文本生产的具体时空限制,将三位译者的译文并置,用彼此的观点互相校正、补充,读起来就犹如一场富有成果的学术对话。与辜鸿铭的文本一样,韦利的文本的原初修辞目的是翻译,并非为了解释《论语》内容而产生的注解类副文本,只是从修辞效果看来,倒更像是在替读者解说孔子话语隐含的内在逻辑。

亲活着的时候,外人只能看到他的理想,至于他有没有能力真正实现自己的志向,只有当他的父亲去世的时候才能发现。之所以说韦利的译文解释的方向有失偏颇,是因为"观其志"是观察儿子对父亲心意的遵从程度,"观其行"是观察他是否能够坚持父道。辜鸿铭的译文客观上①在解答读者可能存在的前述困惑时倒是一语中的:父亲在世时做儿子的不能擅自做主,而应该遵从父亲的安排。因此不难理解为什么父亲尚在时他人无法通过观察具体行为以评判做儿子的是否真的孝顺。即便如此,不了解中国"孝"文化的英语读者依然可能会对这个中国儒家核心价值观存疑,如果不对"孝"的观念进行解说,他们难免会对中国文化形成一种偏见。其修辞后果显而易见:一是影响中国文化的推广,即便推广了也难免产生反面作用;二是影响中国修辞国格建构,进而影响中国政治、经贸等各领域的对外交流与发展。韦利专门就"孝"在中国文化中的观念演变与实践做了研究,认为"孝"经由了事"死"(祖先、亡父母)到拓展为兼及事"生"的过程,一度成为百德之首②。他特别提到"孝"在中国话语尤其是先秦话语内部引发的争议:孔子的追随者与墨子的追随者正是在关于"孝"的理解与实践方面产生分歧,墨家学说主张应该无差别地关爱或将关怀延及全人类(也就是兼爱),而不是在特定程度上只保留给父母或亲戚(如人际交往中侧重孝亲敬长这类有等差的爱)。③ 这些说明对澄清目标读者的误会不无裨益。

---

① 辜鸿铭的文本生产的原初修辞目的是奔着翻译而去,而非给读者答疑解惑,只是因为采用了"为人子者,父在则应观其父之志而承顺之,父没则应观其父之行而继述之"这样的解读,译文于是改变了原文的描述修辞功能(原文只是在讲述一种考察儿子是否"孝"的方法),成为一个不折不扣的要求儿子承守父道的劝说型修辞文本。

② 中国民间就有"百善孝为先"的说法。

③ 韦利原文为:"This word seems originally to have meant piety towards the spirits of ancestors or dead parents. In the *Analects* it still frequently has this meaning; but it is also applied to filial conduct towards living parents, and this is its usual meaning in current Chinese. ... But it seems clear that during the fourth century B.C. a place of extreme importance had already been allotted by the Confucians to hsiao in its extended sense of piety towards living parents. For it was with reference to this virtue that the followers of Confucius came into conflict with those of Mo Tzu, who taught that affection and solicitude ought to be equally extended to all mankind and not reserved in a special degree for parents or relations. Towards the end of the third century B.C. hsiao became, at any rate in certain Confucian schools, the summit of all virtues, and in the *Canon of Filial Piety* which may have existed in some form in the third century, but did not, I think, reach its present form till at least a century later, hsiao is surrounded by the mysterious halo that attends the term jen in the *Analects*."。参见 The Analects of Confucius. Arthur Waley, trans. London: Taylor and Francis Group, 1938:38.

五、子曰:"不患人之不己知,患不知人也。"

——《论语·学而》

The Master said, "I will not be afflicted at men's not knowing me; I will be afflicted that I do not know men." (理雅各 译)

Confucius remarked, "One should not be concerned not to be understood of men; one should be concerned not to understand men." (辜鸿铭 译)

The Master said: "Don't worry if people don't recognize your merits; worry that you may not recognize theirs." (李克曼 译)

从话语的修辞功能而言,这一节主要是一种劝导修辞,而非泛泛而论某种社会现象。孔子意在提醒谈话对象注重提升自我能力与修养,至于个人的能力与品德是否为人所赏识则不应刻意去追求。理雅各译文使用 I will not(我不会如何),读起来似乎是孔子在向弟子表明自己的心迹,未能呈现出原文本的劝诱功能。辜鸿铭使用 One should not(人不应该如何),比较切合预期话语功能。李克曼使用 Don't worry if(用不着担心)言简意赅地翻译出了这个意思。就"患"的翻译而言,理译望文生义,使用与疾病密切相关的辞屏 afflicted [grievously affected or troubled(as by a disease)],过犹不及。辜译使用 be concerned(关注,关切)十分准确。在"知"的翻译上,理与辜译均未点明"知"的具体内容,不如李译一目了然。

六、子曰:"吾十有五而志于学,三十而立,四十而不惑,五十而知天命,六十而耳顺,七十而从心所欲,不逾矩。"

——《论语·为政》

The Master said, "At fifteen, I had my mind bent on learning. At thirty, I stood firm. At forty, I had no doubts. At fifty, I knew the decrees of Heaven. At sixty, my ear was an obedient organ for the reception of truth. At seventy, I could follow what my heart desired, without transgressing what was right."(理雅各 译)

Confucius remarked, "At fifteen I had made up my mind to give myself up to serious studies. At thirty I had formed my opinions and judgment. At forty I had no more doubts. At fifty I understood the truth in religion. At sixty I could understand whatever I heard without exertion. At seventy I could follow whatever my heart desired without transgressing the law." (辜鸿铭 译)

The Master said, At fifteen I set my heart upon learning. At thirty, I had planted my feet firm upon the ground. At forty, I no longer suffered from perplexities. At fifty, I knew what were the biddings of Heaven. At sixty, I heard them with docile ear. At seventy, I could follow the dictates of my own heart; for what I desired no longer overstepped the boundaries of right.　　　　　　（韦利 译）

Confucius said, "At fifteen I began to be seriously interested in study. At thirty I had formed my character. At forty I had no more perplexities. At fifty, I knew the will of Heaven. At sixty nothing that I heard disturbed me. At seventy, I could let my thought wander without trespassing the moral law."　　（林语堂 译）

### 十有五而志于学

理雅各译为 bent on learning(to be very determined to do something)，以描绘原文"立志学习"的形象，比这里所列其余各家文字更简约，形象更立体。

### 三十而立

理雅各与韦利的翻译(意思是站稳脚跟)都有些望文生义，辜译(意思是形成自己的观点和判断力)与林译(意思是人格基本成型)就其观点本身固然言之成理，与原文却相去甚远。丘文明等以模糊译模糊，不把这一阶段的成就具体化，宽泛地翻译为 I became established(我已有所建树)，更符合原文精神。倪培民的注解(倪将"而立"翻译为"Taking a stand")从侧面也证明了丘译的合理性："'Taking a stand' has been variously taken to refer to having mastered the Five Classics, or having learned in general, or having mastered ritual propriety so that one has a basis to establish oneself, or having obtained a certain social and cultural status."①。(关于"而立"，有学者认为是指掌握五经，有认为指学有所成，有认为指掌握礼因而可以自立，也有认为指获得某种社会文化地位。)

### 四十而不惑

理雅各与辜鸿铭的翻译虽然只有一字之差(no 与 no more)，修辞效果却迥然有别。理译只是生硬地宣称"我没有疑惑"，辜译则通过"我不再有疑惑了"传达出一种因认知上的进步而喜悦的心情。韦利的译文则更加高明：I no longer suffered from perplexities，通过使用 suffered from(遭遇某种不幸的情形)以及 perplexities(困惑)这两个辞屏，使译文话语成功构筑出一种摆脱困扰、

---

① Ni Peimin. Understanding the Analects of Confucius: A New Translation of *Lunyu* with Annotations. New York: State University of New York, 2017:97.

如释重负的人物形象。倪培民对"不惑"的注解对于增进英语读者理解不无裨益:"Commentators generally take 'having no perplexities' to be mastery of the art of quan(权), or using discretion."①[评论家们大都把"不惑"理解为掌握了权道(变通之道)。]。

**五十而知天命**

理雅各和韦利、林语堂均使用 knew(知道)翻译"知",不如安乐哲等所用的 realized(开始认识到)更能体现个体认知方面产生的变化。除了辜鸿铭把"天命"误译为宗教中的真理外,大部分译者都是把"天"翻译为 Heaven,把"命"翻译为(个人无法加以改变的)天意。安乐哲等对使用 Heaven 这个辞屏翻译"天"持反对意见,认为它会误导不熟悉中国文化的英语读者用他们一向熟悉的那一套基督教神学观念体系来解读中国文化有关"天"的话语。受客观条件所限,他们一时也没能想到更好的译文,只好使用音译(tian)附加汉字原文以及添加专题解读的方式给读者提供尽量多的信息。安氏等人的顾虑固然不无道理,但是考虑到这种陌生化翻译策略可能潜在地使目标读者产生疏离感,带来负面修辞效果,我们建议保留 Heaven 作为"天"的错位对应译文,并在必要的地方给目标读者尽可能多的提示。安氏等人将"命"译为 propensities(倾向),令人耳目一新。这一译文淡化了其他译文往往带有的神秘主义色彩,凸显了"修辞情境"意味,不仅显得客观,而且容许个体与之进行修辞互动以改变自己的现状。倪培民对天命的注解与安氏的翻译遥相呼应:大多数论者认为知天命就是知道天召。天召有别于所谓的命运,更不是先定的命运。知天命并不是简单地放弃影响世界的努力,一味被动地接受,而是代表主动的选择、渴望承担责任并付诸行动以改变世界的一种使命感。②

---

① Ni Peimin. Understanding the Analects of Confucius: A New Translation of *Lunyu* with Annotations. New York: State University of New York, 2017:97.

② 倪培民注解原文:"Most commentators believe that in this case knowing tianming means knowing heaven's call, or his vocation, which is different from knowing destiny, much less a predetermined fate. Contrary to simply giving up making effort to affect the world, knowing tianming means to aspire to carry on a mission to transform the world. It is not only an objective realization but also a subjective acknowledgment or choice of what is good for human beings and what one should do—a sense of mission, which entails a subjective commitment, or the action of committing. Yet early commentators, such as Huang Kan and those he quotes, take tianming to be destiny determined by heaven and associate it with the fact that a person at the age of fifty is declining and hence able to see how far one is able to reach, that is, there is not much future anymore." 参见 Ni Peimin. Understanding the Analects of Confucius: A New Translation of *Lunyu* with Annotations. New York: State University of New York, 2017:97.

六十而耳顺

理雅各和韦利都强调耳朵"听得进"真理或天的吩咐；辜鸿铭重在表达毫不费劲"听得懂"的理解力；林语堂首先承认"耳顺"这两个字既给译者造成翻译压力也给译者不少发挥的空间，因此他的翻译也不过是一种权宜之译①。林译字面意思是"无论听到什么都不觉得逆耳"，也就是把"耳顺"倒过来理解为"顺耳"进行翻译，体现的是听话人孔子在该阶段的修养境界，从修辞人格角度而言是比较合理的译文。倪培民也承认"耳顺"令人困惑。他指出"耳顺"有两解②，其中一种理解是"一个人到了人生这一阶段，不会因为听到不顺耳的话就生气，也更加愿意去听取别人的（建设性的）批评意见"。这一解读与林语堂的翻译一脉相承，也更加全面。

七十而从心所欲，不逾矩

以上几个"从心所欲"的翻译大同小异，倒是后来的亨顿（David Hinton）因为把"从"误解为"随意"的"随"，把这句话译成了：And at seventy I followed the mind's passing fancies（随心所欲）。一字之差，谬以千里，翻译可不慎乎？

"矩"，理雅各与韦利迂回翻译成 right，即大部分人认为善的且道德上可取的那些标准。辜鸿铭译为"法"，比较偏狭。林语堂翻译成 the moral law（道德法则），符合这一特定的修辞情境。为了让读者理解孔子为何能够做到这一点，森舸澜译文引用了梁朝皇侃的解读："年至七十，习与性成，犹蓬生麻中，不扶自直，故虽复放纵心意，而不越于法度也。"③这比不加解释而直接翻

---

① 林语堂对这一翻译进行说明的原文："Here is an example of the great responsibility and room for conjecture on the part of a translator of ancient texts. The original text merely consists of two words 'ears accord'."参见林语堂.孔子的智慧.北京：外语教学与研究出版社，2009：125.

② 原文为："'Having attuned ears' is a puzzling statement. There are two main interpretations of shun: One is to take it to mean that at this stage, one would no longer be irritated by what one hears and would be more ready to hear what is good in others' words, and the other is that at this stage, one finds the ear easy to use—sensitive enough to hear what others are saying, even behind their words."参见 Ni Peimin. Understanding the Analects of Confucius: A New Translation of Lunyu with Annotations. New York: State University of New York, 2017：98.

③ 森舸澜的解读原文：As Huang Kan explains, "By age seventy, Confucius reached a point where training and inborn nature were perfectly meshed, 'like a raspberry vine growing among hemp, naturally standing upright without the need for support.' Therefore he could then give free rein to his heart's intentions without overstepping the exemplary standards."参见 Confucius Analects: With Selections from Traditional Commentaries. Edward Slingerland, trans. Indianapolis: Hackett Publishing Company, 2003：9.

译(未免让人觉得孔子形象太过玄乎)更有利于译文中孔子修辞人格的建构并促进受众对译文的认同。倪培民对孔子自传最后阶段的陈述有如下评论:"似乎象征着儒家修为的最高目标——培育收放自如的自由状态。"① 这一评论可谓画龙点睛之笔,既解释了语义,也提炼并升华了这一节的主旨精神。

倪培民译文注解中对这一节评论如下:"This very condensed autobiography of Confucius' spiritual journey is so influential in Chinese culture that people would use the phrases as alternative ways of expressing a person's age."②。(本节关于孔子心路历程的浓缩自传在中国文化中影响深远,人们甚至引用孔子这里提到的人生不同阶段的状态或成就以指代具体的年龄。)

七、孟武伯问孝。子曰:"父母唯其疾之忧。"

——《论语·为政》

Mang Wu asked what filial piety was. The Master said, "Parents are anxious lest their children should be sick." （理雅各 译）

A son of the noble mentioned above put the same question to Confucius as his father did. Confucius answered, "Think how anxious your parents are when you are sick, and you will know your duty towards them." （辜鸿铭 译）

To a query of Mang Wu respecting filial piety, the Master replied, "Parents ought to bear but one trouble—that of their own sickness." （詹宁斯 译）

Lord Meng Wu asked about filial piety. The Master said, "The only time a dutiful son ever makes his parents worry is when he is sick." （李克曼 译）

Meng Wubo asked about filial conduct(xiao). The Master replied, "Give your mother and father nothing to worry about beyond your physical well-being."③

（安乐哲等 译）

---

① 原文:"The statement about the last stage is quoted more often than any other, as it seems to signify the highest aim of the Confucian cultivation—a state of freedom of cultivated spontaneity."。参见 Ni Peimin. Understanding the Analects of Confucius: A New Translation of Lunyu with Annotations. New York: State University of New York, 2017:98.

② Ni Peimin. Understanding the Analects of Confucius: A New Translation of Lunyu with Annotations. New York: State University of New York, 2017:98.

③ 此处原注为:"This passage is ambiguous; it can also mean 'Give your mother and father nothing to worry about beyond their own physical well-being'."。参见 The Analects of Confucius: A Philosophical Translation. Roger T. Ames, Henry Rosemont, Jr., trans. New York: the Ballantine Publishing Group, 1998:232.

父母唯其疾之忧

由于文法上的模糊性,汉语学界关于这个对话中"其"所指代的究竟是父母还是子女一直有争议,由此产生了"子忧父母"与"父母忧子"两种主要的解读分歧①。持前说者如王充、高诱②等认为"其"字是指代父母而言,意思是"父母最令子女担心的是(因为寿高而伴生的)疾病"。持后说者如马融③等认为"其"字是指代子女,意思是"父母最担心的是子女生病"。杨伯峻认为两说都可以,在进行语内翻译时采取了"父母忧子"说。④ 我们认为若撇开上下文与文化语境,孔子回答孟武伯的这句话从纯语言学角度而言,的确允许两解。但是如果基于这一对话发生的具体修辞情境,尤其是从修辞者与受众话语交流的意图出发,不难发现孟武伯想求教的是作为孝子应该要有哪些行为规范;基于话语合作原则(the cooperative principle),孔子的回答理应是对其行为进行指导。从话语功能角度来看,如果把孔子说的话理解成"父母最令子女担心的是年纪大了容易生病",这只是描述了一种几乎是人尽皆知且无力改变的状况。因为人类机体退行性病变往往非人力所能逆转,子女除在父母生病时悉心照料之外并没有更好的办法。西方修辞学关于活动(motion)与行动(action)的区分对这一解读也有一定的参照意义。所谓活动涉及的主要是人的意志无法加以改变的那些现象或进程(如新陈代谢等生理变化),而行动涉及的则主要是包括语言在内但不限于语言的象征手段(如话语的调适、态度的调整等)所能加以改变的局面或状态。父母机体退行性生理病变超越了人类话语所能有效改善⑤的范围,属于典型的"活动"范畴。换句话说,除非是为了劝导提问者孟武伯"听天由命"(有鉴于孔子积极进取的修辞人格,我们认为这种

---

① 另外一种非主流解读则是"父母忧己"说:父母年纪大了,孝顺的儿子就应该设法创造条件,让父母不用操心其他事务,唯一需要担心的是自身健康出问题(这种不可控因素)。詹宁斯的译文即是基于这一诠释进路。翻译成中文则是:"什么是孝?""父母只有自己生病这个事需要担心。"但是由于译文缺乏必要的逻辑衔接与交代,话语显得生硬,让读者感到莫名其妙。

② 王充《论衡·问孔篇》说:"武伯善忧父母,故曰,唯其疾之忧。"《淮南子·说林训》说:"忧父之疾者子,治之者医。"高诱《注》云:"父母唯其疾之忧,故曰忧之者子。"以上三个注解均引自杨伯峻. 论语译注. 北京:中华书局,2012:19.

③ 原文为:"言孝子不妄为非,唯疾病然后使父母忧。"转引自杨伯峻. 论语译注. 北京:中华书局,2012:19.

④ 杨伯峻的解释为:"孟武伯向孔子请教孝道。孔子道:'做爹娘的只是为孝子的疾病发愁。'"参见杨伯峻. 论语译注. 北京:中华书局,2012:19.

⑤ 通过修辞话语对精神类疾病的干预治疗不在此讨论之列。

可能性很小),这样的答复其实并未具备有效干预(并着力改善)现实的话语功能,无法为孟武伯的行动做出有意义的指引,因此这一解读的合理性存疑。

另外一种解读则强调父母对子女无微不至的关爱,这种解读隐含的推论即子女应该懂得感恩和自重自爱。其话语功能是告诫孝子不可糟践自己的躯体(以免生病或少生疾病),不应违法乱纪(以免于刑戮),以安父母之心。相对于前一种解读,这一理解至少是对孟武伯提问的劝勉式修辞回应,很可能会影响其关于"孝"的认知、对待父母的态度乃至对待父母的具体行为。这一理解既与孔子的话语体系高度兼容,从话语修辞目的①上也能自圆其说。英语翻译中,理雅各、辜鸿铭与李克曼的译文都是基于这一诠释进路,但是由于具体表达时各自的修辞素养与受众意识存在较大差异,其译文修辞效果也迥然有别。理雅各译文的优点是忠实,几乎把原文的所有文字信息都"拷贝"过去了,从纯文本角度而言,译者已经完成了文字翻译的任务,但是不熟悉中国文化的英语读者从这个译文中提取完关键信息②后或许头脑中只有两个孤立的话语构件,无法真正将两个句子有机联系起来。

换言之,这个表面上忠实的译文对目标读者产生的实际修辞效果很可能不尽如人意。其不足之处主要是以文本为导向(注重忠实)而非以受众为导向(顺应目标读者的阅读习惯与期待),未能帮助读者清除文化障碍并将话语部件以合乎逻辑的方式构筑起一个容易理解与接受的修辞语境。辜鸿铭的译文回译成中文是:想一想你生病的时候你的父母是何等焦虑,你就会知道你对父母负有什么样的责任(应该如何对待你的父母)。如果以世俗的忠实标准衡量,辜鸿铭的译文无疑有不少自由发挥的地方。但是当读者看到这么一个逻辑自洽、切近生活经验且几无文化隔阂的译文时,认同感几乎是油然而生的,因为人同此心、心同此理,这个译文描绘的是任何一个有理性、有情感的人都不可否认的普世经验。这种为受众进行语境重构的修辞性翻译所能起到的话语效果远超常见的那类追求忠实的语言学意义上的翻译,不仅能够有效传递原文信息,还兼带了解惑功能,让读者不仅知其然,而且知其所以然。由此也不难发现语言学意义上的翻译更多追求的是文本意义上的一致或忠实,而西方修辞学意义上的翻译更倾向于以受众为中心,主动调适文本以便利目标读者的理解与接受。

读者的确可以从李克曼的译文(一个尽职尽责的儿子唯一让父母担心的

---

① 是以劝勉为目的的话语修辞。
② 相当于这样一个对话:"什么是孝?""父母最担心孩子生病了。"

场合就是他生病的时候)中推出"一个好儿子除了自己生病这种(不能由自己把控的)事情,其他任何时候都不可以(胡作非为)让父母担心"。究竟有多少人在读完这个句子之后能够耐着性子沿着译者暗示的话语路标走到目的地践行译者预期的结论,全是未定之数。因此,这一译文很有可能是疏离受众而非拉近与受众的距离,无法让受众喜闻乐见。

后出的安乐哲译文颇具修辞意识:有别于大部分译者只是翻译出什么是孝,安乐哲译文使用了 asked about filial conduct(Xiao)(问什么是孝的行为),回答则针对性地建议说"除了你自身健康出问题(这种不可控因素),别让父母(为你自己原本应该负责的行为)担心"。这里安乐哲的解读依据显然是"父母忧子"说。得益于译者对话语的调整,安乐哲提供的基于非主流的"父母忧己"说的翻译在逻辑上也能够自洽:"除了自身健康出问题(这种不可控因素)以外,别让父母(为你自己原本应该负责的行为)担心"。即便安乐哲译文颇有可观之处,如果与辜鸿铭的译文对比,差别也还是比较明显的。辜鸿铭是回答提问者尽孝应该做什么(虽然语焉不详,至少给了个大方向),而安乐哲则是告诫提问者不要做什么(话题固然相关,但显得比较迂曲)。

**八、子游问孝。子曰:"今之孝者,是谓能养。至于犬马,皆能有养;不敬,何以别乎?"**

——《论语·为政》

Ziyou asked about filial devotion. The Master said, Nowadays it's taken to mean just seeing that one's parents get enough to eat. But we do that much for dogs or horses as well. If there is no reverence, how is it any different?

(华兹生 译)

Tzu-yu asked about the treatment of parents. The Master said, "Filial sons" nowadays are people who see to it that their parents get enough to eat. But even dogs and horses are cared for to that extent. If there is no feeling of respect, wherein lies the difference?

(韦利 译)

Tzu-yu asked about being filial. The Master said, "Nowadays for a man to be filial means no more than that he is able to provide his parents with food. Even hounds and horses are, in some way, provided with food. If a man shows no reverence, where is the difference?"

(刘殿爵 译)

When Zi You asked about filial duty, the Master said, "Filial sons of today only take care their parents are well fed. But even dogs and horses are well fed now. What is the difference if their parents are fed without reverence?"

(许渊冲译)

### 问孝

这一节的修辞目的在于强调对父母要养而能敬,而不是只要能够养活爹娘就算是在尽孝了。问孝,吴国珍译为 asked how to show filial piety(问怎样才能表现出孝心),凸显了孝具有"行动"的典型特征。只是 show 这一辞屏或许会引导读者往"秀"或"做出某种样子"(而内心实际并不是这么想的)这样的角度去理解。

### 今之孝者,是谓能养

华兹生译文大意:如今人们把孝理解为只需要管父母吃饱饭,潜台词就是不用考虑父母可能存在的其他的需求。但是从修辞角度而言,需要受众自行推理并补足内容,因此弱化了批判的力度。

韦利的翻译特意给"孝子"加了引号,含蓄地表达了对这一种行为的不认可态度,是一种典型的修辞翻译。反讽式地凸显这一所谓孝子的称谓,将读者的注意力吸引过来,有助于在现实中对这种行为进行反思、批判与纠偏。

刘殿爵的翻译使用 no more than(不过是)婉转表达了对这种行为的否定态度。

以上三位译者都是用主动语态翻译如何对待父母,许渊冲的译文则另辟蹊径,使用被动态(其译文连用了三个表示被投喂的 fed)明确地表达出了父母那种只能被动接受子女的安排(吃什么、怎么吃)的无助的状态。许译很形象、有画面感,读者仿佛可以看到一个儿子拿着勺子在给年迈的父母喂食。只是不是那种充满爱心的温馨场面,而是不带情感、没有温度的投食。其译文容易引发读者共情,对他人这种"养而不敬"的行为产生愤慨之情,也提醒自己反思对待父母的方式。这样的译文具有明显的修辞效果,影响人的思想、形塑人的价值观。

### 至于犬马,皆能有养

除了刘殿爵,以上大部分译者都使用 dog 翻译"犬"。由于犬在东西方文化中的不同情感意涵[①],dog 这个译文很难给目标读者传递那种源语文化读者

---

① 古代东方文化中的犬主要是用来看家护院,地位比较卑微,由于风俗缘故,个别情况下甚至可能把它当作食物;西方文化中的犬虽然也不乏实用功能,但在一般民众看来,dog 主要是宠物,在很多家庭中和普通家庭成员地位并无二致,也享有生荣死哀的待遇。

所能够感受到的微不足道的意思,读者有可能因为对狗的好感而对这个极端示例产生怀疑。因为在他们看来,狗是人类最忠实的朋友,能够与人在精神上互相取暖。狗不仅常常从主人那里得到自己喜爱的食物,获得人们的关爱,也时时给人以安慰与寄托。基于这样的文化心理,用even(甚至)形容连狗都能得到这样的待遇在逻辑上就变得可疑。刘殿爵使用hound(猎犬)与役畜马并列,将读者的注意力引到这些动物服务人类的功能上,消解了文化上可能产生的不兼容性。从语言修辞格角度而言,hound 和 horse 的头韵修辞也给读者带来审美愉悦,从而更容易让译文被读者接受。

九、子曰:"温故而知新,可以为师矣。"

——《论语·为政》

The Master said, "If a man keeps cherishing his old knowledge, so as continually to be acquiring new, he may be a teacher of others." （理雅各 译）

The Master said, "He who by reanimating[①] the Old can gain knowledge of the New is fit to be a teacher." （韦利 译）

The Master said, "A man is worthy of being a teacher who gets to know what is new by keeping fresh in his mind what he is already familiar with." （刘殿爵 译）

此处谈的是为师之难,涉及创新型教师素养的这个话题。牛泽群认为孔子的语旨在标鉴才力,而非教、学方法[②],符合实际。朱熹的解读[③]很全面,强调对知识的创新性反思与应用是合格教师的标准。理雅各的译文相当于为了"知新"而"温故",译文所呈现的与其说是一种素养,倒不如说是一种方法,与后面的"可以为师"在逻辑上关联并不强。韦利的译文用 reanimating(to give new life or energy to something)这个表示激活或复活的辞屏引导读者朝着

---

① 此处原注为:"Literally, 'warming up'. The business of the teacher is to give fresh life to the Scriptures by reinterpreting them so that they apply to the problems of modern life. All scriptures(Homer, the Koran, our own Bible)have been used in this way."。参见 The Analects of Confucius. Arthur Waley, trans. London: Taylor and Francis Group, 1938: 90.

② 牛泽群.论语札记.北京:北京燕山出版社,2003:33.

③ 原注为:"言学能时习旧闻,而每有新得,则所学在我,而其应不穷,故可以为人师。"大意是:时常回顾已有的知识(道理等)并结合自身处境不断生发新的感知和体会,让自身素养不断提升,能更好地去面对或应对变化着的现实世界,因此可以当别人的老师。朱熹注解参见朱熹. 四书章句集注.北京:中华书局,1983:357.

创新的方向联想。韦利的注解提到教师的主要任务就是让经典常读常新,通过全新的诠释解决当下的实际问题,但是他使用 the Scriptures(经文)翻译"故"显得比较狭隘。刘殿爵译文没有直译"温故",只是说要给旧知识保鲜,修辞效果十分明显。因为要让旧知识保鲜,必然要注入新的元素,思考与学习也就成为题中应有之义了。无论是 is fit 还是 is worthy of 都成功表达了"具备资质、能够胜任"这个意思。

十、子曰:"君子不器。"

——《论语·为政》

Confucius remarked, "A wise man will not make himself into a mere machine fit only to do one kind of work." （辜鸿铭 译）

Confucius said, "The gentleman should not be like an instrument."①

（丁往道 译）

此节文字虽少,修辞意涵却颇为丰富。其中"不"字并非一般意义上关于是与否的判断,而是意在劝导听众不要朝着错误的方向去努力,不"系守一业"②(一心成为仅具某种专门用途的工具人)。

辜鸿铭译文大意:一个明智之人不会让自己成为只能完成一个具体任务的机器。虽然译文主要的话语功能是描述而非劝导,但是由于使用了"明智之人"这样带有价值判断的词,译文在某种程度上还是传递出了劝导的修辞意图。丁往道译文则使用 should not(不应该)明确提示读者此处话语的修辞功能为劝阻。

### 君子

有别于大部分译者将君子翻译成 gentleman(绅士),辜译使用 wise man (智者)来翻译君子,丘文明等使用 noble person(高贵之人)进行翻译,两个解读与当下语境均比较契合。君子通常是明达之士,在特定语境下,君子也有可

---

① 此处原注为:"A thing that has only one specific use. Confucius probably means that the gentleman should be able to tackle crucial problems mankind faces instead of acquiring one specific skill and working like an instrument."参见论语(节选)(汉英对照).丁往道,选译.北京:中国对外翻译出版有限公司,2012:111.

② 皇侃的解读非常周全:"此章明君子之人不系守一业也。器者,给用之物也,犹如舟可泛于海不可登山,车可陆行不可济海。君子当才业周普,不得如器之守一也。"参见皇侃.论语集解义疏(卷一).台北:台湾艺文印书馆,1966:25.

能是官员(official)。

## 器

辛鸿铭译文明显的不足之处是出现了时代错乱,使用具有典型近现代意味的 machine(机器)翻译"器",这样的辞屏容易使读者对孔子所处的社会生活条件产生错误认知。孔子的时代即便有机器也是非常少的,更大的可能是工具或器具(implement)。韦利就是用 implement 翻译这个"器"并使用 a specialist(专门家)做同义解释,认为君子只需要培养通识,注重道德修养,无需成为专门家。①

李克曼用"pot"(罐子)翻译"器",未必妥当,但是他关于官员为何需要"不器"的解说②对于不了解中国古代文化与封建时代官员基本素养要求的读者来说具有"文化科普"意义:儒家人文主义的普遍培养目标对我们今天应该有特别的意义,因为我们的现代大学似乎越来越关注培训"专门的野蛮人"。两千年来高效管理中国的科举制度体现了儒家的理想:官员是通过考试制度选拔出来的,主要是测试他们关于儒经的知识和文学才能。有了这样的知识储备,一个知县被期望能单枪匹马地管理一个人口众多的大地方的所有事务,同时履行行政长官、法官、工程师、经济学家、警察、农学家、建筑师、军事指挥官等职能(更不用说在闲暇时间,他还应该是一个合格的书法家、诗人、作家、画

---

① 韦利的解释原文为:"i.e. a specialist, a tool used for a special purpose. He need only have general, moral qualifications."。参见 The Analects of Confucius. Arthur Waley, trans. London: Taylor and Francis Group, 1938:90.

② 原文为:"One might also translate 'a utensil' or 'a tool'—the idea is the same: the capacity of a gentleman is not limited as is that of a container; his abilities are not circumscribed to one narrow and specific function, like a tool which is designed for only one particular purpose. The universal aim of Confucian humanism should have particular relevance for us today, as our modern universities seem increasingly concerned with the mere training of 'specialized brutes.' The civil service which was to run China with great efficiency for two thousand years embodied the Confucian ideal: officials were selected through an examination system that essentially tested their knowledge of the Classics and their literary talent. With such an intellectual equipment, a local prefect was expected to dispatch singlehandedly all the affairs of a large territory with a vast population, performing simultaneously the functions of administrator, judge, engineer, economist, police officer, agronomist, architect, military commander, etc. (not to mention that in his leisure time he was also supposed to be a competent calligrapher, poet, writer, painter, musician, and aesthete).". 参见 The Analects of Confucius. Simon Leys, trans. New York: W.W. Norton Company,1997:115-116.

家、音乐家和美学家)。

与刘殿爵一样,安乐哲等人及倪培民的译文均使用 vessels(容器)翻译"器"并附有详尽程度不一的解读,对于读者深入了解为什么君子要不"器"很有帮助。安乐哲认为孔子注重对教育与培训进行区分,培养个人修养主要是培育人格,而不是获得具体技能(因此"君子不器")。① 倪培民对"君子不器"进行了澄清,它不是反对君子成为有用之人,而是反对君子仅成为单一"工具"。这一教义与如今我们通识教育的关联性是显而易见的。这样的教育目的不是职业培训,而是培养"成人"——帮助人们成长为受过良好教育的人。②

十一、子曰:"学而不思则罔,思而不学则殆。"

——《论语·为政》

Confucius said, "It throws one into bewilderment to read without thinking whereas it places one in jeopardy to think without reading." （赖波等 译）

The Master said, "Learning without due reflection leads to perplexity; reflection without learning leads to perilous circumstances."③ （安乐哲等 译）

The Master said, "Learning without reflection will end up in confusion; reflection without learning will end up in peril." （林戊荪 译）

---

① 原文为:"Confucius is keen to maintain a distinction between education and training. Personal cultivation is a matter of developing character, not acquiring specific skills."。参见 The Analects of Confucius: A Philosophical Translation. Roger T. Ames, Henry Rosemont, Jr, trans. New York: the Ballantine Publishing Group, 1998:233.

② 原文为:"This saying is not against being useful(cf. 13.25)but rather against being a mere instrument. The relevance of this teaching to what is called 'liberal education' today is obvious. Such an education is not for job training(making the person a mere vessel that fits only particular functions)but for person-making—helping people to grow as well-educated human beings (cf. 1.15)."。参见 Ni Peimin. Understanding the Analects of Confucius: A New Translation of *Lunyu* with Annotations. New York: State University of New York, 2017:104.

③ 此处原注为:"The medieval philosopher, Chengzi, comments on this passage: 'Learn broadly, ask searchingly, reflect carefully, distinguish clearly, and act earnestly. To be lacking in one of these is to fail to learn.'"。参见 The Analects of Confucius: A Philosophical Translation. Roger T. Ames, Henry Rosemont, Jr., trans. New York: the Ballantine Publishing Group, 1998:233.

刘毓庆认为"罔"是"不能辨明是非，感到无所适从"①，朱熹认为"殆"是"不习其事，故危而不安"②。结合二者的解读，本节大意是"一味学习，却不思考，就会困惑；只是空想，却不学习，（在实际遇到挑战或困难时）就会处于险境"。赖波等的译文总体表达了不思或不学③会招致的后果。安乐哲等及林戊荪对"学"与"思"的翻译都是原文的确切反映。安乐哲等把"罔"翻译为"困惑"，林戊荪则翻译为"混乱"，不相上下。对于"则"的翻译，安乐哲的处理办法中规中矩，林戊荪的 end up 则是一个提示不利结果的辞屏，从修辞角度而言对受众心理的引导更成功。"殆"的翻译林戊荪只是泛泛而论提到"危险"的意思，安乐哲译文用"陷于危险的情境中"则更具体形象。考虑到读者可能对"学"和"思"的密切关系不甚了了，作为译者的安乐哲主动替原作者扛起学术举证责任，引用《中庸》观点④证明"学"和"思"二者缺一不可。

十二、子曰："攻乎异端，斯害也已。"

——《论语·为政》

The Master said, "The study of strange doctrines is injurious indeed!"

（理雅各 译）

The Master said, "To become accomplished in some heterodox doctrine will bring nothing but harm."⑤

（安乐哲等 译）

---

① 刘毓庆.论语绎解.北京：商务印书馆，2017：33.
② 朱熹.四书章句集注.北京：中华书局，1983：57.
③ 赖波等把"学"翻译为"阅读"，缩小了学习的范围，比较偏狭。
④ 《礼记·中庸》中提到曾子原文为："博学之，审问之，慎思之，明辨之，笃行之。有弗学，学之弗能，弗措也。"原文参见黄侃.黄侃手批白文十三经.上海古籍出版社，2008：201.
⑤ Here we follow the Dingzhou text which has "to be accomplished in, to specialize in(gong 功)" rather than "to attack(gong 攻)" as found in the received editions. Because the character gong "to attack" appears three other times in the *Analects* and in each case means "to attack", Yang Bojun, ignoring the fact that gong here is followed by the prepositional particle "in hu(乎)", rejects the commentaries that would read this as "to pursue study in". He reads this passage as "If one attacks heterodox doctrines, it will put an end to their harm". The Dingzhou text seems to resolve this debate.参见 The Analects of Confucius: A Philosophical Translation. Roger T. Ames, Henry Rosemont, Jr, trans. New York: the Ballantine Publishing Group, 1998: 233.

针对这一节,学界围绕"攻"的解读一直存在争议。杨伯峻认为这句话表面上看起来虽然允许有两解,①但他基于对《论语》中"攻"字实际使用的互文本语境的考察,得出本节"攻"字不应该作"治学"的"治"解,应该作"攻击"解。从修辞受众角度而言,即便译者能够不折不扣地把这一理解传递给(不了解这一诠释争议的)英语读者,他们也难免会心生疑惑:为什么不正确的议论一经批判就会销声匿迹？英语世界的读者大多经过西方修辞传统的熏陶,对于修辞论辩这一日常话语交流模式都比较熟悉。对于任何的批评话语他们都期待着一个你来我往的批评与反批评(辩护或反击)的论辩互动。他们很难想象一个被界定为"不正确"的议论的持论者一听到对手的批评就自动放下话语的武器,落荒而逃。在西方的话语交流中,"屡败屡战"是常态,"不战而败"则十分罕见。长期浸淫于西方修辞话语互动传统的读者多数早已内化了这样一个观点:不能用拳头捍卫自己的利益(体力上弱于同龄人)是令人羞耻的,而不能用舌头捍卫自己的立场或权利同样是令人尴尬的。虽然强逞口舌之能无论在东西方文化中都是被人唾弃的,但是正如伊索克拉底所言,良好的表达能力是具有正常头脑的最准确标志。② 有鉴于在论辩中不战而败会让旁观者或裁判对话语缴械者的智力产生怀疑,为了避免自己的话语修辞人格受创,理性的话语修辞者都会步步为营,据理力争。即便在话语对抗中处于下风,也会且战且退,而非完全放弃抵抗。如果从受众角度来讨论,这一节的翻译似乎要给他们提供其他的(在逻辑与文化习惯上更容易接受的)解读。另一种解读就是反对从事"有悖于以传统道德为核心的价值体系的学术研究"③。对于普通英语读者而言,这种解读在逻辑上是自洽的,因而更容易被接受。

安乐哲等借助考古发掘的版本将"攻乎异端"的"攻"修改为"功"加以诠释并翻译为 to become accomplished in(致力于),相当于从文本层面肯定了第

---

① 杨伯峻认为两种解读分别是:(1)孔子说:"从事于不正确的学术研究,这是祸害哩。"(2)孔子说:"批判那些不正确的议论,祸害就可以消灭了。"对于第一种解读,杨伯峻认为"一般的讲法是如此的,虽能文从字顺,但和《论语》词法和句法都不合",因而实际是主张第二种解读,也就是"attack erroneous doctrines(or, if you like:'smash heresies')and you will put an end to all harms"。参见杨伯峻. 论语译注. 北京:中华书局,2012:24-25.

② 转引自刘亚猛. 西方修辞学史. 北京:外语教学与研究出版社,2008:44.

③ 杨伯峻翻译所提到的"不正确"的学术研究未必是我们现代意义上的政治上的不正确(political incorrectness),更多是关于价值观教育的问题。参见刘毓庆. 论语绎解. 北京:商务印书馆,2017:33.

二种解读①。此外,我们认为不妨从说话人的修辞人格角度进一步加以讨论。基于我们对孔子的基本了解,他是一个谦谦君子。面对与自己不同的学说或者不正确的价值观,如果他就那么直截了当地宣布"把它拎出来批判一下就可以消灭了",听众难免会觉得他过于自信或强势,这明显与孔子一贯谦逊的修辞人格不一致。李克曼就认为将本节话语解读成"孔子断然宣布将'异端学说'一劳永逸消灭"会让人误读孔子。② 与此相反,另一种解读不仅合乎实际,而且充满画面感:老夫子(捶胸顿足地)说,从事不正确的研究,这是祸害哩。这样的解读与孔子的修辞人格高度兼容。

理雅各译文语气与原文如出一辙,只是使用 strange doctrines(奇怪的教义或学说)翻译"异端"还有些不妥,因为有些所谓奇怪的东西,只不过是因为我们对它们不熟悉(strange 有一个义项恰好就是"陌生的"),熟悉之后也就见怪不怪了。

安乐哲等使用 heterodox doctrine(非正统学说)来翻译"异端",虽然在字面上大致相当,但是在真实的文化历史语境中"异端"可能与此大相径庭。李克曼在其解读中提出在孔子的时代根本就没有所谓的儒教,所谓的异端邪说(heresy/heterodox doctrine)又从何谈起?因此他建议使用 erroneous doctrine(错误的学说)翻译,同时对(在语义上)将"攻"理解为攻击以及本句使用"乎"的必要性持保留意见。③

---

① The Analects of Confucius: A Philosophical Translation. Roger T. Ames, Henry Rosemont, Jr trans. New York: The Ballantine Publishing Group, 1998:233.

② In the other camp, Yang Bojun who is not encumbered with theological preconceptions and looks at the *Analects* from the dispassionate angle of a linguist, a grammarian, and a social historian, proposes a radically new interpretation for this passage: "attack erroneous doctrines (or if you like: 'smash heresies') and you will put an end to all harms." In this reading hai ("harm") is a noun subject of yi which functions no more as a final particle but as a verb "to stop". This daring interpretation could have disturbing implications for our understanding of Confucius's personality. 参见 The Analects of Confucius. Simon Leys, trans. New York: W. W. Norton Company, 1997:117.

③ yiduan literally means "the other end"; it came eventually to mean "heterodox doctrine", "heresy". If one considers that there was no Confucianism in the time of Confucius and therefore little possibility for heresy, an alternative interpretation can be suggested: "erroneous doctrine." This, however, leaves a grammatical problem unresolved: why is the direct object "doctrine" linked to the verb (gong) with a preposition (hu)? 参见 The Analects of Confucius. Simon Leys, trans. New York: W.W. Norton Company, 1997:117.

十三、子曰:"非其鬼而祭之,谄也。见义不为,无勇也。"

——《论语·为政》

The Master said, "For a man to sacrifice to a spirit which does not belong to him is flattery. To see what is right and not to do it is want of courage."

(理雅各 译)

The Master said, "To worship gods that are not yours, that is toadyism. Not to act when justice commands, that is cowardice."

(李克曼 译)

Confucius remarked, "To worship a spirit to whom one is not bound by a real feeling of duty or respect is idolatry①; to see what is right and to act against one's judgment shows a want of courage."

(辜鸿铭 译)

这一节主要讲违礼弃义的问题。根据刘毓庆的解读②,这里的"谄",讨好的对象其实是人而不是鬼。他还尝试重构本节话语的修辞情境:"这当是有一士大夫中人,人们觉得他温恭克让,像个君子。孔子则举其行事,指明了他违礼、弃义的本质。说明他是乡愿式的人物,不值得称道。"③通过这一违礼行为,本节话语反映了当事人负面的修辞人格,从而影响目标受众的价值判断,进而促使他们采取合乎道义的行动。

### 非其鬼而祭之

关于"祭鬼"的翻译,理雅各使用 sacrifice to a spirit 是准确的。spirit 虽然有灵魂(soul)④的义项,但是和 sacrifice(祭祀)搭配,也就只有鬼魂(ghost)⑤这个意思合适了。

李克曼用 gods(诸神)翻译"鬼",失之偏颇。詹宁斯用 departed spirits(离开躯体的灵魂)倒也明白无误地译出了"鬼"这一层意思。韦利使用 ancestors (祖先)也是十分得体的翻译。"非其鬼",理雅各与李克曼均翻译为"不属于你

---

① 意思是"servility".
② 刘毓庆提到助祭与谄这一违礼行为的关联:在西周,天子祭祖,诸侯助祭。可能到了春秋,大小贵族之间也出现了助祭的现象,即士大夫为了讨好权贵,去到权贵家庙助祭,或以为恭敬,而孔子则指出此种行为的本质是"谄"。参见刘毓庆.论语绎解.北京:商务印书馆,2017:41.
③ 刘毓庆.论语绎解.北京:商务印书馆,2017:41.
④ An immaterial force within a human being thought to give the body life, energy, and power.
⑤ The soul of a dead person thought of especially as appearing to living people.

（他）的鬼"，逻辑不通。辜鸿铭的译文虽然比较繁复迂曲①，但至少达意且有深度。詹宁斯的 not belonging to one's own family（不属于自家的）比较准确。

### 谄

大部分译文均使用了表达"巴结/奉承/讨好"意义的词汇。辜鸿铭虽然使用 servility（卑躬屈膝）作注，但他使用 idolatry（偶像崇拜），已经不是在翻译，而是在讨论另外一个话题了。

### 见义不为，无勇也

理雅各基本是直译，一目了然。李克曼译文有明显可感的修辞张力，使用拟人修辞格将抽象的"义"描绘成一个人，在召唤英勇的行动。辜鸿铭使用 act against one's judgment 形象地表达了实际采取的行动与内心真正的认知背道而驰的冲突状态，从而在貌似客观的描述中表达了评价，尤其是其中的 against，有如春秋笔法，能够引导读者关注到当事人可疑的修辞人格，从而起到话语预期的批判或劝诫的功能。

**十四、子贡欲去告朔之饩羊。子曰："赐也！尔爱其羊，我爱其礼。"**

——《论语·八佾》

Tsze-kung wished to do away with the offering of a sheep connected with the inauguration of the first day of each month.
The Master said, "Ts'ze, you love the sheep; I love the ceremony."

（理雅各 译）

Once, seeing that his disciple Tsz-kung was desirous that the ceremonial observance of offering a sheep at the new moon might be dispensed with, the Master said, "Ah! You grudge the loss of the sheep; I grudge the loss of the ceremony."

（詹宁斯 译）

A disciple wanted to dispense with the sheep offered in sacrifice in the religious ceremony held at the beginning of every month. "What you would save," said Confucius to him, "is the cost of the sheep; what I would save is the principle

---

① 译文意为"既非基于血缘纽带亦非发自内心的敬（却跑去祭祀别人家的祖先）"。

of the rite." (辜鸿铭 译)

### 欲去告朔之饩羊

大部分译者都是直接翻译子贡的行为,虽然文从字顺,但是缺乏必要的交代。亨顿在译文开头使用 As the ceremony had fallen into neglect(由于这一礼仪逐渐为人们所忽略)为读者做了语境方面的交代,为下文子贡的行为进行修辞铺垫。关于告朔之饩羊①,森舸澜的翻译 do away with the practice of sacrificing a lamb to announce the beginning of the month 增补了 practice②,凸显了它作为一种传统惯例的特征。辜鸿铭使用 the religious ceremony(宗教仪典),虽然也对其作为一种仪式做了说明,但是 religious(宗教)这个辞屏与"颁告朔"的实际政治修辞功能并不一致,与其说是宗教仪典,不如说是礼制(ritual ceremony)。

### 尔爱其羊,我爱其礼

理雅各使用 love(喜爱)翻译"爱",实际上由于这个"爱"是"舍不得"的意思,这个表面上完全对应的翻译反而弱化了译文的修辞效果。詹宁斯使用

---

① "告朔饩(xī)羊"是古代的一种制度。每年秋冬之交,周天子把第二年的历书颁给诸侯。这历书包括那年有无闰月,每月初一是哪一天,因之叫"颁告朔"。诸侯接受了这一历书,藏于祖庙。每逢初一,便杀一只活羊祭于庙,然后回到朝廷听政。这祭庙叫作"告朔",听政叫作"视朔",或者"听朔"。到子贡的时候,每月初一,鲁君不但不亲临祖庙,而且也不听政,只是杀一只活羊虚应故事罢了。所以,子贡认为不必留此形式,不如干脆连羊也不杀。孔子却认为尽管这是残存的形式,也比什么也不留好。详见杨伯峻.论语译注.北京:中华书局,2012:41.

② 森舸澜另对这一惯例做了介绍:"According to commentators, this lamb sacrifice had originally been part of a larger ritual in the state of Lu to mark the official beginning of the new month, and which was discontinued during the reign of Duke Wen. According to Huang Kan, although the larger ritual itself was no longer being practiced by the rulers of Lu, the practice of sacrificing the lamb was being kept alive by traditionally-minded government functionaries. Zigong does not see the point of continuing this vestigial, materially wasteful practice in the absence of its original ritual context. Insisting upon the continuance of this practice, however, is Confucius' way of mourning the loss of the original rite and keeping its memory alive, which in his view is worth the cost of an occasional lamb. The valuing of ritual propriety over pragmatic or financial considerations links this passage to 3.13, and the fact that Lu—as the inheritor of Zhou culture—still preserved at least the forms of the ancient rites links it to 3.9 and 3.14.". 参见 Confucius Analects: With Selections from Traditional Commentaries. Edward Slingerland, trans. Indianapolis: Hackett Publishing Company, 2003:24.

grudge(not want to spend time or money on someone or something, or not want to give something to someone)表达的吝惜之意符合第一个"爱",却不符合第二个"爱"(要保留)的意思。辜鸿铭译文中的 save(有"节省""挽救"之意)成功解决了詹宁斯的翻译思路遇到的尴尬,可谓一语双关,颇具修辞意味。与 cost(费用)搭配,意思是"节省费用";与 principle(原则)搭配,则是"维护"的意思。用同一个词(save)翻译两人各自的"舍不得",容易让读者将注意力放在不同的"舍不得"对象上,是一种典型的修辞比较,通过比较,两人的修辞人格高下立见。

十五、子曰:"不仁者不可以久处约,不可以长处乐。仁者安仁,知者利仁。"

——《论语·里仁》

Confucius remarked, "A man without moral character cannot long put up with adversity, nor can he long enjoy prosperity. Men of moral character find themselves at home in being moral; men of intelligence find it advantageous to be moral."

(辜鸿铭 译)

Confucius said, "One who is not a true man cannot long stand poverty, nor can he stand prosperity for long. A true man is happy and natural in living according to the principles of true manhood, but a wise man thinks it is advantageous to do so."

(林语堂 译)

The Master said, "Without Goodness a man Cannot for long endure adversity, Cannot for long enjoy prosperity. The Good Man rests content with Goodness; he that is merely wise pursues Goodness in the belief that it pays to do so."

(韦利 译)

The Master said, "Without Goodness, one cannot remain constant in adversity and cannot enjoy enduring happiness. Those who are Good feel at home in Goodness, whereas those who are clever follow Goodness because they feel that they will profit(li 利)from it."

(森舸澜 译)

读者凭借直觉即可认同"不仁者不可以久处约",但是对于"不仁者不可以长处乐"或许会有些许困惑。朱熹以"久乐必淫"[①]回应了这个质疑。关于"安

---

① 原文为:"不仁之人,失其本心,久约必滥,久乐必淫。"参见朱熹. 四书章句集注. 北京:中华书局,1983:69.

仁",杨伯峻不仅从正面解说:"(有仁德的人)实行仁德便心安",还从反面补充说"不实行仁德心便不安";关于"知者利仁",他不仅对字面进行翻译(聪明人利用仁),还考虑到读者可能的困惑,说明"知者利仁"是因为"他认识到仁德对他长远而巨大的利益,他便实行仁德"①。

**不仁者不可以久处约,不可以长处乐**

辜鸿铭使用 put up with(忍受)与 enjoy(享受)对同一个"处"字在特定语境中的不同意义进行呈现,同时使用押尾韵的 adversity(逆境)与 prosperity(顺境)形成强烈对照,不仅忠实传达了原文语言的意义,还提升了文字表达形式。译文在形式与音韵方面的修辞之美既能促进受众对话语的接受,也因为朗朗上口而方便记忆与使用。林语堂使用 stand(to successfully accept or bear something that is unpleasant or difficult)表达"处"的"忍受"的意思是很准确的,但是用它搭配"乐"(也就是需要表达"享受"的意思)则在逻辑上不兼容,可以说是因形害义的翻译失误(即便如此,译者想一语双关地翻译出这个"处"的努力还是值得肯定的)。从纯语言修辞角度来看,林语堂使用同时押了头韵和尾韵的 poverty(贫困)与 prosperity(富裕),比辜译更有修辞张力。但是从表达的准确性而言,"约"不单纯是经济方面的拮据,还包括政治上不得志等各方面的困窘状态,并不是一个 poverty 所能够涵盖的。韦利使用 endure(to suffer something difficult, unpleasant, or painful)翻译"处",比林译 stand 略胜一筹,二者的差异主要在于 stand(emphasizes even more strongly the ability to bear without discomposure or flinching)更多强调耐受力,而 endure(implies continuing firm or resolute through trials and difficulties)更凸显"熬"这种持久性。森舸澜对这句话的解读比翻译精彩,他用孔安国的评论"久困则为非"/"久乐必骄佚"②预先回应了目标读者对"不可以久处约/长处乐"可能存在的困惑,是以受众为中心的修辞性翻译。

---

① 杨伯峻. 论语译注. 北京:中华书局,2012:48.
② 关于孔安国对这句话的评论,森舸澜译文为:"Regarding the first half of this saying, Kong Anguo comments, 'Some cannot remain constant in adversity because sustained adversity motivates them to do wrong, and cannot enjoy enduring happiness because they inevitably fall into arrogance and sloth.'"。参见 Confucius Analects: With Selections from Traditional Commentaries. Edward Slingerland, trans. Indianapolis: Hackett Publishing Company, 2003:29-30.

### 仁者安仁，知者利仁

为了体现"仁者"与"知者"①的价值差，辜鸿铭的译文使用了 men of moral character 和 men of intelligence，让读者对德与智孰优孰劣做出自己的判断；林语堂使用 true(真)与 wise(智)，区分不是那么清晰；韦利使用 merely 明确了智不如德；森舸澜用 good(善)与 clever(巧)，效果与辜译类似。

辜鸿铭的译文用 find themselves at home(舒适)翻译"安"已然成为其他译者的范本，问世以来一直被模仿，至今尚未被超越。即便是一向被视为准确权威的刘殿爵译文也只是微调了一个字(feels at home)。但是用 advantageous(有好处)翻译"利"虽然达意，却未能凸显利仁的知者(智者)功利的特征。韦利的 in the belief that it pays to do so(觉得合算)以及森舸澜用的 profit from(从中获利)更能体现"知者"出于功利的考虑而行仁这一点。森舸澜的注解②对安仁与利仁的区分最为清晰：安仁者行仁是自发自觉的，利仁者(知者)行仁是受外在利益驱动的。由于行仁未必总会得到回报，行仁是否求回报便成为二者的分界线。其译文甚至寻求在更大的语境中解读"仁者"与

---

① 刘毓庆认为"仁者"修养达到了一种境界，仁德之行对于他们就像身安于衣、腹安于食一样，行之自然，处之泰然，若缺了便有不安。"利仁者"，也就是"智者"，明晓利害得失，预知未来变化，知仁义礼让虽会让出眼前利益，但可以取信于众，最终获得大利，他们是以仁为工具而弋猎高远之利的。参见刘毓庆. 论语绎解. 北京：商务印书馆，2017：62.

② 原注为："The second half is an explanation of the first: those who are truly Good are spontaneously and unselfconsciously Good—they 'feel at home' in virtue, having internalized it to the point that externalities no longer matter. Both Confucius(7.16,7.19) and Yan Hui(6.7,6.11) illustrate this quality. Those who are merely clever are motivated by the external benefits of being virtuous, and therefore follow Goodness in a more self-consciously goal-oriented manner. The problem with this is that virtue does not always pay(4.5), so when the going gets rough these people lack the genuine inner commitment to remain upon the Way. Alternately, when virtue does end up paying off with social acclaim, wealth, and official position, these clever people—having attained their external end and lacking any commitment to the Way as an end in itself—fall into immoral arrogance and idleness. A more elaborate version of this passage in the *Record of Ritual* adds a third level of self-consciousness and effort: 'Those who are Good are at ease in Goodness, those who are clever follow Goodness because they know that they will profit from it, and those who are afraid of punishment force themselves to follow Goodness.' See also 6.20, 'One who knows it is not the equal of one who loves it, and one who loves it is not the equal of one who takes joy in it.'". 参见 Confucius Analects: With Selections from Traditional Commentaries. Edward Slingerland, trans. Indianapolis: Hackett Publishing Company, 2003: 29-30.

"知者"的价值差:仁者安仁,知者利仁,畏罪者强仁。① 这些关于不同境界的行仁者的背景介绍无疑会增进读者对本节的"同情之理解",更有利于传播中国文化,给世界伦理体系贡献充满哲学洞见的中国价值观。

十六、子曰:"富与贵,是人之所欲也;不以其道得之,不处也。贫与贱,是人之所恶也;不以其道得之,不去也。君子去仁,恶乎成名?君子无终食之间违仁,造次必于是,颠沛必于是。"

——《论语·里仁》

Confucius remarked, "Riches and honours are objects of men's desire; but if I cannot have them without leaving the path of duty, I would not have them. Poverty and a low position in life are objects of men's dislike; but if I cannot leave them without departing from the path of duty, I would not leave them. A wise man who leaves his moral character is no longer entitled to the name of a wise man. A wise man never for one single moment in his life loses sight of a moral life; in moments of haste and hurry, as in moments of danger and peril, he always clings to it."

(辜鸿铭 译)

The Master said, "Riches and rank are what every man craves; yet if the only way to obtain them goes against his principles, he should desist from such a pursuit. Poverty and obscurity are what every man hates; yet if the only escape from them goes against his principles, he should accept his lot. If a gentleman forsakes humanity, how can he make a name for himself? Never for a moment does a gentleman part from humanity; he clings to it through trials, he clings to it through tribulations."

(李克曼 译)

与更早的理雅各一样,辜鸿铭也赞成用 riches and honors(财富与荣誉)翻译"富与贵"②,不足之处是荣誉未必与地位相关;李克曼则使用 riches and

---

① 所谓"更大的语境"指的是《礼记·中庸》中提到的"仁者安仁,知者利仁,畏罪者强仁"。孔子认为仁的实行有三种情况:一是自觉、安心地行仁,二是受利益驱动而行仁,三是勉勉强强而行仁。三者虽然都能达到仁的效果,但出发点不同。真正的仁人,不论在什么情况下都安于行仁;自以为是的人,看到有利可图才去行仁;害怕犯罪受罚的人,是迫不得已而勉强行仁。原文参见黄侃.黄侃手批白文十三经.上海古籍出版,2008:206.

② 杨伯峻把"富与贵"翻译为"发大财,做大官"。参见杨伯峻.论语译注.北京:中华书局,2012:49.

rank(财富与官阶)①改进了这一不足,并通过头韵修辞给读者留下深刻印象。撇开修辞美学的考虑,就理解的准确性而言,森舸澜使用 wealth and social eminence 可谓后来居上,尤其是 social eminence(显要的社会地位)比前面的译文更有涵盖能力,能够涵摄"贵"的多种可能性,比如因为位高而贵、因为德高而贵、因为才华而贵等。"欲",辜译用的 desire(希望得到)已经十分准确了,李译用 crave(渴望),更加生动。"不以其道",辜译用 leaving the path of duty(背离职责之路),具体所指比较模糊,李译用 goes against his principles (违背原则),能让读者一目了然。"贫与贱",辜译用 poverty and a low position 已经达意,但是不及使用尾韵修辞的李译②优美。"恶"的翻译,辜译的 dislike(不喜欢)不及李译 hate(憎恶)情感强烈。本节的"君子"主要是指有高尚情操者,辜译使用 a wise man(明智之人),与李译 gentleman(绅士)均有偏颇,后来的译者亨顿所用 the noble-minded 倒是颇有君子之风。"无终食之间违仁",两译均不提具体"一顿饭的工夫",而是调整为"片刻"(a moment)。"造次必于是,颠沛必于是",辜译达意但烦琐,李译漏译或误译"造次"③,但是再次灵活使用了头韵修辞手段,不忠实却优美。

十七、子曰:"我未见好仁者,恶不仁者。好仁者,无以尚之;恶不仁者,其为仁矣,不使不仁者加乎其身。有能一日用其力于仁矣乎?我未见力不足者。盖有之矣,我未之见也。"

——《论语·里仁》

The Master said, "I have not seen a person who loved virtue, or one who hated what was not virtuous. He who loved virtue, would esteem nothing above it. He who hated what is not virtuous, would practice virtue in such a way that he would not allow anything that is not virtuous to approach his person. Is any one able for one day to apply his strength to virtue? I have not seen the case in which his strength would be insufficient. Should there possibly be any such case, I have not seen it."

(理雅各 译)

---

① 比李克曼早的韦利曾经使用了 rank 翻译"贵"。
② 比李克曼早的韦利曾经使用了 poverty and obscurity 翻译"贫与贱"。
③ 杨朝明对"造次必于是,颠沛必于是"的解读是:"仓促匆忙时有仁德在,颠沛流离时也有仁德在。"详见杨朝明.论语诠解.扬州:广陵书社,2008:30.

Confucius remarked, "I do not now see a man who really loves a moral life; or one who really hates an immoral life. One who really loves a moral life would esteem nothing above it. One who really hates an immoral life would be a moral man who would not allow anything the least immoral in his life. Nevertheless, if a man were really to exert himself for one single day to live a moral life, I do not believe he will find that he has not the strength to do it. At least I have never heard of such a case."

(辜鸿铭 译)

The Master said, "I for my part[①] have never yet seen one who really cared for Goodness, nor one who really abhorred wickedness. One who really cared for Goodness would never let any other consideration come first. One who abhorred wickedness would be so constantly doing Good that wickedness would never have a chance to get at him. Has anyone ever managed to do Good with his whole might even as long as the space of a single day? I think not. Yet I for my part have never seen anyone give up such an attempt because he had not the strength to go on. It may well have happened, but I for my part have never seen it[②]."

(韦利 译)

### 我未见好仁者,恶不仁者

刘毓庆将这句话翻译为"我没有见过喜好仁的人和厌恶不仁的人",并指出包括这句话在内,本节"字面的意思不难懂,但道理难通"。为了让本句及本节其他地方说得通,他重新定义这个"者",认为它指的是各国的君主与权贵[③]。虽然这不是主流解读,但是富于解释力。遵循普罗泰戈拉提出的对言原则[④],我们在此予以保留以便利学界讨论。理雅各对这句话进行了字面翻译,却没有扛起举证责任,说明为什么孔子会说无论是"好仁者"还是"恶不仁者"他一个都没有见着。辜鸿铭在译文中增补一个 really(真正地),与理雅各仅一字之差,意境却迥然有别。由于少了一个 really,理译很难说服读者接受

---

① 此处原注为:"Wo as a nominative is more emphatic than Wu."。参见 Arthur Waley. The Analects of Confucius. London & New York: Taylor and Francis Group, 1938:103.

② "It is the will not the way that is wanting."。参见 The Analects of Confucius. Arthur Waley, trans. London: Taylor and Francis Group, 1938:103.

③ 刘毓庆认为天下没有一个"好仁者"打击一大片,这不符合孔子的思想。孔子这里指的不是一般社会上的人,而是当时各国的君主与权贵。在礼崩乐坏之际,这些人无一人用力于国计民生,用力于礼乐文明及世道人心的修复,故孔子才发出了此番感叹。参见刘毓庆.论语绎解.北京:商务印书馆,2017:65.

④ 即"针对任何一个争议都可以提出完全相反的两个论点"。

其话语逻辑,因为读者会觉得从自己身边找出一个好仁者并非什么难事。而辜译回译过来就是"我没有见过真正喜好仁的人和厌恶不仁的人",文从字顺,逻辑自洽,自然容易为读者所接受。

### 好仁者,无以尚之

关于这个"之"究竟指"人"(好仁者)还是"仁",学界有不同理解。朱熹认为"好仁者真知仁之可好,故天下之物无以加之"①,言之成理,逻辑自洽。以上译者基本按"仁"这一理解进行翻译,但是刘殿爵等学者在翻译实践中将其理解为"人",做出了不同的翻译。刘殿爵译文"A man who finds benevolence attractive cannot be surpassed."(无人能够超越好仁的人。),在逻辑上的确存在这种可能,虽非主流解读,但至少提供了一种新的视角。

### 恶不仁者,其为仁矣,不使不仁者加乎其身

三位译者都是把"为仁"理解为"行仁",把"不使"及以下内容理解为恶不仁者在为仁方面的具体表现。理雅各与辜鸿铭都是把"不使"翻译为 not allow(不允许),强调主观方面注意不让这样的事情发生;韦利是用 never have a chance to get at him[(不仁)无法乘虚而入]翻译,更多强调客观结果不会发生。理与辜译文更注重主观努力,对于建构"恶不仁者"的修辞人格更有利。刘殿爵将"为仁"理解为"之所以算得上是仁",把"不使"及以下内容理解为这一判定的依据。其译文"A man who finds unbenevolence② repulsive can, perhaps, be counted as benevolent, for he could not allow what is not benevolent to contaminate his person."相当于调整表达顺序为"恶不仁者,(因其)不使不仁者加乎其身,(故)其为仁矣"。这一非主流解读言之成理,聊

---

① 朱熹.四书章句集注.北京:中华书局,1983:70.

② 此处原注为"The word 'unbenevolence' has been coined because the original word has a positive meaning lacking in 'non-benevolence'."。(考虑到"non-benevolence"会让读者误以为带有否定意义,为了传达出"不仁"在本节上下文中所具有的正面意义,特意新造了一个"unbenevolence",以便弥补这一缺憾。)参见 D.C.Lau. The Analects Sayings of Confucius. New York: Penguin Books, 1979:72.刘殿爵非常警惕辞屏对译者可能的误导,因此其译文不惜通过生造词汇以表达自己的理解,这一学术努力无疑是令人钦佩的。遗憾的是,在其评论中有一个(可能是笔误)positive(积极的/正面的),使得整个评论在逻辑上未能自洽,读者不免困惑:"不仁"为何具正面意义?假如将这个 positive 修改为 negative,则整个评论变得文从字顺:"The word 'unbenevolence' has been coined because the original word has a negative meaning lacking in 'non-benevolence'."。(考虑到"non-benevolence"不足以传递原文带有的否定意义,为了传达出"不仁"在本节上下文中所具有的负面意义,特意新造了一个"unbenevolence",以便弥补这一缺憾。)

备一说。吴国珍译文"They practice benevolence merely in order to avoid being affected by wickedness."则将"不使不仁者加乎其身"理解为行仁的目的，也能够自圆其说。

**有能一日用其力于仁矣乎？我未见力不足者。盖有之矣，我未之见也**

理雅各在翻译这个问句时都没有直接回答"能不能"，而是和原文一样转而讨论"愿不愿"这个问题，从而成功传达了原文"非力不足者"的负面修辞人格信息并巧妙地寓褒贬于无形之中（批评其"非不能也，是不为也"）。译文建构出的说话人孔子温婉的修辞人格与中国文化中孔子的固有形象一致，对传播中华文化有促进作用。辜鸿铭将疑问句改为陈述句，开门见山地亮出自己的观点，爱憎分明，毫不含糊。就语言翻译而言，并无不妥；就修辞角度而言，译文话语所建构出的锋芒毕露的修辞人格与说话人孔子温良恭俭让的形象并不一致，容易造成英语读者对中国文化产生误解。韦利的译文在翻译这个问句时直接回答"我认为不能"，表面上看没有太大的问题，细看不难发现话语逻辑无法自洽。后出的李克曼译本①相比韦利的译文在这一点的误读上更明显。虽然钱穆也认为这句话有两种可能的解读②（其中一种便是韦利与李克曼的译文这样的理解），但他也顾虑所谓天下没有一个好仁者的说法"辞气似过峻"，也就是认为这一解读言过其实了。因为从逻辑角度而言，真正的好仁者固然不多见，要说一个都没有却是站不住脚的。

**十八、子曰："君子喻于义，小人喻于利。"**

——《论语·里仁》

The Master said, "The mind of the superior man is conversant with righteousness; the mind of the mean man is conversant with gain." （理雅各 译）

Confucius remarked, "A wise man sees what is right in a question; a fool,

---

① 译文为："Has anyone ever devoted all his strength to goodness just for one day? No one ever has, and yet it is not for want of strength—there may be people who do not have even the small amount of strength it takes, but I have never seen any."。参见 The Analects of Confucius. Simon Leys, trans. New York: W.W. Norton Company, 1997:16.

② 此两解为"或有用力而力不足者""或有肯一日用力于仁者，惜己未之见也"。"两解均可通。然谓未见有肯一日用力于仁者，辞气似过峻，今从前解。"参见钱穆.论语新解.北京：生活·读书·新知三联书店，2012:82.

what is advantageous to himself."① （辜鸿铭 译）

The Master said, "A gentleman considers what is just; a small man considers what is expedient." （李克曼 译）

### 君子/小人

关于"君子"的翻译，森舸澜与林戊荪分别使用 the gentleman（绅士）与 the man of honor（正人君子）。gentleman 主要是指有修养/教养之人，honor 主要是指具有强烈的道德行为意识之人（相当于 integrity）。森舸澜在注解中②明确指出《论语》中的君子与小人之别主要在于道德水平高下，考虑到彬彬有礼、温文尔雅之人未必就会是有德之人，林戊荪译文明显更胜一筹。关于"小人"，二者都用 the petty man（相当于 small-minded man）加以翻译，字面意思是"小器之人"，主要是指格局狭隘之人，与"道德低下者"还有一定距离。

### 喻

理雅各译文中，conversant 虽然曾有过 concerned/occupied（关注）这样的义项，如今已经过时（archaic）了。使用这样的义项，除非译者另有说明，否则读者很难领会到这一层意思；即便已经说明这一义项，读者未必有这一知识储备，结果可能会疏离读者，无法达到令读者喜闻乐见的修辞目的。conversant 现在主要是"熟悉"(to be familiar with, and have knowledge or experience of the facts or rules of something)的意思。"熟悉某项事务"是客观上就具备的能力、状态，用这样的词语翻译不能体现君子/小人主动选择义/利的行为，不

---

① 注解为："Sir Chaloner Alabaster translates thus：'The gentleman regards what is right; the cad regards what will pay.'"。需要说明的是，中华书局的《〈论语〉（中英双语评述本)》并未收录这一注解，该注引自《辜鸿铭文集》。参见《辜鸿铭文集》. 黄兴涛，著译. 海口：海南出版社，2000：371.

② 注解为："Some commentators argue that the distinction between the gentleman and the petty person (xiaoren) should be understood in terms of social class, because xiaoren is often used in Han texts to indicate simply the 'common people.' It is clear, though, that Confucius felt anyone from any social class could potentially become a gentleman (6.6, 7.7) and that social status did not necessarily correspond to actual moral worth. It is apparent that—in the *Analects* at least—the gentleman/xiaoren distinction refers to moral character rather than social status."。参见 Confucius Analects：With Selections from Traditional Commentaries. Edward Slingerland, trans. Indianapolis：Hackett Publishing Company, 2003：35.

利于君子/小人的修辞形象建构与价值判断的传递。辜鸿铭用"看到"，暗含"什么样的人就会看到什么样的东西"这样的判断，婉转描绘了君子或小人的修辞形象，但是褒贬的修辞效果淡化了许多。倒是他的注解提供的阿查立(Chaloner Alabaster)的译文使用 regard(to consider or think about something in a particular way, or to look carefully at someone or something)体现了"考虑"这个主观状态，能够反映君子和小人不同的道德风貌。李克曼译文更是直接使用了 consider 致敬辜鸿铭与阿查立。森舸澜在注解中提到"The gentleman is motivated by the inner goods of Confucian practice rather than the promise of external goods."（绅士行为的动机是儒家实践的内在的善，而不是外部利益的承诺/好处），也较好地传达了二者的差异。

利

理雅各使用 gain(profit or advantage)，意思是"增益或好处"，涵盖了"利"的大部分义项。阿查立的译文 pay(to give a profit or advantage to someone or something)意义与 gain 相同，却因为使用了动词而更有修辞张力。李克曼把"利"翻译为 expedient(characterized by concern with what is opportune, especially: governed by self-interest)，也就是权宜便利的意思，虽然也很通顺，与原意（利益）却是有偏差的。

## 本章参考的英译本

辜鸿铭文集. 黄兴涛, 著译. 海口:海南出版社, 2000:371.
林语堂. 孔子的智慧. 北京:外语教学与研究出版社, 2009.
《论语》《大学》《中庸》. 理雅各, 译释. 上海:上海三联书店, 2014.
论语(节选)(汉英对照). 丁往道, 译. 北京:中国对外翻译出版有限公司, 2012.
论语(文白、汉英对照). 蔡希勤, 中译. 赖波, 夏玉和, 英译. 北京:华语教学出版社, 1994.
论语(中英双语评述本). 辜鸿铭, 英译. 王京涛, 述评. 北京:中华书局, 2017.
《论语》最新英文全译全注本. 吴国珍, 今译、英译、英注. 2版. 福州:福建教育出版社, 2015.
丘文明, 丘文星, 丘文郊, 等. 论语英译今译. 北京:世界知识出版社, 1995.

论语:许渊冲,译.北京:五洲传播出版社,2011.

Analects Confucius. David Hinton, trans. Berkeley:Publishers Group West, 2014.

Confucius Analects:With Selections from Traditional Commentaries. Edward Slingerland, trans. Indianapolis:Hackett Publishing Company,2003.

Epiphanius Wilson, William Jennings. The Wisdom of Confucius. New York: The Colonial Press,1900.

Ezra Pound. Confucian Analects. London:Peter Owen Limited,1933.

Getting to Know Confucius: A New Translation of the Analects. Lin Wusun, trans. Beijing:Foreign Languages Press Co. Ltd,2011.

Ni Peimin. Understanding the Analects of Confucius:A New Translation of *Lunyu* with Annotations. New York:State University of New York, 2017.

Roger T. Ames, Henry Rosemont, Jr, trans. The Analects of Confucius:A Philosophical Translation. New York:The Ballantine Publishing Group, 1998.

The Analects of Confucius. Burton Watson, trans. New York:Columbia University Press,1925.

The Analects of Confucius. Arthur Waley, trans. London:Taylor and Francis Group,1938.

The Analects of Confucius. Simon Leys, trans. New York:W. W. Norton Company,1997.

The Analects Sayings of Confucius. D.C.Lau, trans. New York:Penguin Books,1979.

# 第二章 《孟子》英译比较与评析

一、孟子对曰:"王好战,请以战喻。填然鼓之,兵刃既接,弃甲曳兵而走。或百步而后止,或五十步而后止。以五十步笑百步,则何如?"曰:"不可。直不百步耳,是亦走也。"

——《孟子·梁惠王章句上·第三节》①

Mencius replied, "Your majesty is fond of war;—let me take an illustration from war—The soldiers move forward to the sound of the drums; and after their weapons have been crossed, on one side they throw away their coats of mail, trail their arms behind them, and run. Some run a hundred paces and stop; some run fifty paces and stop. What would you think if those who run fifty paces were to laugh at those who run a hundred paces?" The king said, "They should not do so. Though they did not run a hundred paces, yet they also ran away." （理雅各 译）

"Your Majesty is fond of war." said Mencius.

"May I use an analogy from it? After weapons were crossed to the rolling of drums, some soldiers fled, abandoning their armour and trailing their weapons. One stopped after a hundred paces, another after fifty paces. What would you think if the latter, as one who ran only fifty paces, were to laugh at the former who ran a hundred?"

"He had no right to," said the King, "He did not quite run a hundred paces. That is all. But all the same, he ran." （刘殿爵 译）

**王好战**

两个译本都把"王"视为直接的谈话对象并译为 Your majesty（陛下/主

---

① 若无特别说明,本章所涉及《孟子》引文均出自《孟子译注》。出处详见杨伯峻. 孟子译注. 北京:中华书局,2012.

公),既表达了对君主的敬意,又能够体现修辞者和受众的权力关系落差。亨顿译文①直接称呼梁惠王为"你",没有完整再现修辞语境中对话参与者各自话语地位这个重要参数,容易导致读者误判后续对话内容。华霭仁(Irene Bloom)译文②虽然也是以对话形式呈现的,却以"那国王"称呼梁惠王,让读者误以为修辞者是在谈论一个不在对话现场的人。"好战",两个译本都译为"爱好战争",虽然在字面上似乎比较忠实,细察之下其实不然。就语言文字角度而言,读者从译文中感受到的很可能是一个穷兵黩武的人物形象,不免有损梁惠王作为一个君主的修辞人格。就文化心理而言,好战在世界上的任何文化中几乎都不是一个正面的价值,这一译文虽然大体与原文相符,但就修辞效果而言,依然有待商榷。吴国珍译文③巧妙避开了这个文字陷阱,只提梁惠王对战争感兴趣,不容易让人产生过于负面的联想。

### 弃甲曳兵而走

刘殿爵译为"一些士兵临阵脱逃",忠实于原文表达。理雅各经过修辞考量,认为战争力量此消彼长,或是一方士气正旺,士兵大可不必逃跑,因此译为"其中一方丢盔弃甲败走",符合逻辑事理。

### 或

刘殿爵分别译为"一个""另一个",理雅各两处均译为"一些人"。从战场实况考虑,所谓兵败如山倒,失利一方如果出现逃兵,往往不是一两个人,因此使用复数更加可信。

### 以五十步笑百步,则何如

两个译文都用特殊疑问句忠实再现了原文的询问话语功能。亨顿译文④成功把握了原文精神,提炼出关键争议点,将特殊疑问句转化为一般疑问句,凸显了核心信息,从修辞效果而言是更好的翻译。

---

① 译文为:"You're fond of war."。参见 Mencius. David Hinton, trans. Berkeley: Counterpoint, 2015:5.

② 译文为:"Mencius said, 'The king is fond of war;…'"。参见 Irene Bloom. Mencius. New York: Columbia University Press, 2009:3.

③ 译文为:"Since you have interest in warfare, Your Majesty."。参见《孟子》最新英文全译全注本.吴国珍,今译、英译、英注.福州:福建教育出版社,2015:18.

④ 译文为:"Are those who run fifty feet justified in laughing at those who run a hundred feet?"。大意为:那些逃了五十步的嘲笑逃了一百步的是正当的吗?译文参见 Mencius. David Hinton, trans. Berkeley:Counterpoint,2015:5.

**不可**

"不可",刘殿爵译为"他们没有权利这么做",与原文有较大偏差。理雅各译为"他们不该这么做",比较忠实可信。万百安(Bryan W. Van Norden)译文"That is not acceptable."(那是不可以接受的),语气过于强烈,几近于愤慨,译文所投射的修辞者修辞人格与作为第三方应该展现的客观立场相去甚远。吴国珍译文"No mocking."(不许嘲笑)听起来更像是直接朝着士兵喊话,而不是对这一争议的评价。

二、曰:"臣闻之胡龁曰,王坐于堂上,有牵牛而过堂下者,王见之,曰:'牛何之?'对曰:'将以衅钟。'王曰:'舍之!吾不忍其觳觫,若无罪而就死地。'对曰:'然则废衅钟与?'曰:'何可废也?以羊易之!'不识有诸?"曰:"有之。"曰:"是心足以王矣。百姓皆以王为爱也,臣固知王之不忍也。"

王曰:"然。诚有百姓者。齐国虽褊小,吾何爱一牛?即不忍其觳觫,若无罪而就死地,故以羊易之也。"

曰:"王无异于百姓之以王为爱也。以小易大,彼恶知之?王若隐其无罪而就死地,则牛羊何择焉?"

王笑曰:"是诚何心哉?我非爱其财。而易之以羊也,宜乎百姓之谓我爱也。"

曰:"无伤也,是乃仁术也,见牛未见羊也。君子之于禽兽也,见其生,不忍见其死;闻其声,不忍食其肉。是以君子远庖厨也。"

——《孟子·梁惠王章句上·第七节》

"I heard the following incident from Hu Ho:— 'The king', said he, 'was sitting aloft in the hall, when a man appeared, leading an ox past the lower part of it. The king saw him, and asked, Where is the ox going? The man replied, We are going to consecrate a bell with its blood. The king said, Let it go. I cannot bear its frightened appearance, as if it were an innocent person going to the place of death. The man answered, Shall we then omit the consecration of the bell? The king said, How can that be omitted? Change it for a sheep.' I do not know whether this incident really occurred." The king replied, "It did," and then Mencius said, "The heart seen in this is sufficient to carry you to the royal sway. The people all supposed that your Majesty grudged the animal, but your servant knows surely, that it was your Majesty's not being able to bear the sight, which made you do as you did."

The king said, "You are right. And yet there really was an appearance of what the people condemned. But though Chi be a small and narrow State, how should I grudge one ox? Indeed it was because I could not bear its frightened appearance, as if it were an innocent person going to the place of death, that therefore I changed it for a sheep."

Mencius pursued, "Let not your Majesty deem it strange that the people should think you were grudging the animal. When you changed a large one for a small, how should they know the true reason? If you felt pained by its being led without guilt to the place of death, what was there to choose between an ox and a sheep?"

The king laughed and said, "What really was my mind in the matter? I did not grudge the expense of it, and changed it for a sheep!—There was reason in the people's saying that I grudged it."

"There is no harm in their saying so," said Mencius. "Your conduct was an artifice of benevolence. You saw the ox, and had not seen the sheep. So is the superior man affected towards animals, that, having seen them alive, he cannot bear to see them die; having heard their dying cries, he cannot bear to eat their flesh. Therefore he keeps away from his slaughter-house and cook-room."

(理雅各 译)

Mengzi said, "I heard your attendant Hu He say, while the king was sitting up in his hall, an ox was led past below. The king saw it and said, 'Where is the ox going?' Hu He replied, 'We are about to ritually anoint a bell with its blood.' The king said, 'Spare it. I cannot bear its frightened appearance, like an innocent going to the execution ground.' Hu He replied, 'So should we dispense with the anointing of the bell?' The king said, 'How can that be dispensed with? Exchange it for a sheep.'"

Mengzi continued, "I do not know if this happened." [Royal halls were typically raised off the ground, with a stairway leading up to them, so that those in the hall had a view of the courtyard below.]

The king said, "It happened." Mengzi said, "This heart is sufficient to become King. The commoners all thought Your Majesty was being stingy. But I knew that Your Majesty simply could not bear the suffering of the ox.①" The king said, "That is so. There were indeed commoners who said that. But although Qi is a small state, how could I be stingy about one ox? It was just that I could not bear its frightened appearance, like an innocent going to the execution ground. Hence, I exchanged it for a sheep."

Mengzi said, "Let Your Majesty not be surprised at the commoners taking you to be stingy. You took a small thing and exchanged it for a big thing. How could they understand it? If Your Majesty was pained at its being innocent and going to the execution ground, then what is there to choose between an ox and a sheep?"

The king laughed, saying, "What was this feeling, actually? It's not the case that I grudged its value and exchanged it for a sheep. But it makes sense that the commoners would say I was stingy." [Zhu Xi says, "This means that the ox and the sheep are both going to die although innocent. In what way does one distinguish between them and exchange the sheep for the ox? Mengzi intentionally sets up this difficulty, desiring the king to examine himself and seek his fundamental heart. The king seems unable to do so. Hence, in the end, he is unable to resolve for himself what the commoners have said."]

Mengzi said, "There is no harm. What you did was just a technique for (cultivating your) benevolence. You saw the ox but had not seen the sheep. Gentleman cannot bear to see animals die if they have seen them living. If they hear their cries of suffering, they cannot bear to eat their flesh. Hence, gentlemen keep their distance from the kitchen." [Zhu Xi comments, "On the one hand, killing the ox was something that the king could not bear to do. On the other hand, anointing the bell was something that could not be dispensed with … When he saw the ox, this heart had already been expressed and could not be repressed. But he had not yet seen the sheep, so the Pattern had not yet taken form and there were no feelings to hinder. Hence, exchanging the sheep for the ox allowed for the two (i.e., the heart and the ritual)? to be complete without harm. This is how it is a technique of

---

① Zhu Xi links this passage to 2A6: "The king saw the ox's frightened appearance and could not bear to kill it. This is just what is meant by 'the heart of compassion is the tip of benevolence.' If he can 'expand and fill it up,' then he can 'care for all within the four seas.' Hence, Mengzi refers to this, desiring the king to examine this and fill it out."

benevolence … Now, humans are the same as animals in being alive, but are different categories of things. Hence, we use animals for rituals, and our heart that does not bear their suffering applies only as far as they are seen and heard. Keeping one's distance from the kitchen is a technique used to cultivate this heart and broaden one's benevolence."

Mengzi and Zhu Xi say nothing about how slaughtering animals will affect the hearts of the commoners who work in the kitchen. Is there some hypocrisy in their willingness to allow others to do work that would damage the benevolent heart of a noble? Notice that the "Daoist" Zhuangzi uses a cook who slaughters an ox as a paradigm for human excellence. This may be an intentional jab at Mengzi.]

(万百安 译)

### 臣闻之胡龁曰

理雅各译文使用一个 incident(事件)概括了整个故事,使读者对于下文的阅读有个基本的方向性预期,同时能够给予足够的注意力和耐心。以受众为核心关注点的万百安及时为胡龁添加一个身份标签 attendant(侍从),便于读者界定人物关系,增强了译文的可读性。

### 王坐于堂上,有牵牛而过堂下者

理雅各译文使用 aloft 与 lower 体现出"堂上"与"堂下"这一对比关系,其中 aloft 还有"高高在上"的意思,巧妙地传达了梁惠王的权力地位信息,但是没有对这个"堂"做出特别的说明。万百安则对中国宫廷大殿的台阶特有的高度和视野做出说明,有助于西方读者理解中国古代宫廷文化。

### 将以衅钟

理雅各译文使用 consecrate(to officially make something holy and able to be used for religious ceremonies)翻译"衅",符合原文使钟圣化的意思。万百安译文使用 anoint(to make someone holy in a religious ceremony by putting holy water or oil on them),原意是"(在宗教仪式上)给特定人或物涂圣水(或圣油)",固然迁就西方读者,但这一修辞辞屏难免让这一译文充满了基督教文化的意味。

### 舍之

理雅各译文使用"Let it go."(放它走)固然不错,万百安等译者使用"Spare it."更符合上下文语境,可以表达"饶了它""让它免受痛苦"等多重意思。

**吾不忍其觳觫**

对于"觳觫"(恐惧发抖)的翻译,理雅各与万百安用 frightened appearance 是准确的,刘殿爵译为 shrinking with fear 则具有修辞凸显(rhetorical presence)的效果。因为 shrink(to move away from someone or something because you are frightened)更能够刻画因为恐惧而畏缩不前的现场感。亨顿译文 shivering with fear 也颇能传达瑟瑟发抖的画面。

**若无罪而就死地**

这句话的意思是"就好比没有罪过而走向受刑的地方",其中对于"死地"的翻译,理雅各使用 the place of death(死亡之地),比较宽泛,万百安使用 the execution ground(刑场),与前文 innocent(无辜)同属于一个语义场,无辜而受刑这一对比产生的修辞张力更强,更容易引发受众的同情心。亨顿译文使用 being hauled off to the executioner,更是将无辜的牛被强行拖到刽子手面前、瑟瑟发抖的画面淋漓尽致地呈现在读者面前。

**是心足以王矣**

理雅各译文重在表达不忍之心有助于建构与提升王者的人格与影响力,言简意赅。刘殿爵译文"The heart behind your action is sufficient to enable you to become a true King."(这样行为背后的那颗心足以使你成为一个真正的君主)明确指出这样的心是"王"的使能条件(enabling condition)。万百安译文望文生义,翻译成"心本身足以成为国王",在逻辑上无法自圆其说。

**百姓皆以王为爱也**

这句话中的"爱"即"吝惜",理雅各使用 grudge(to be very reluctant to part with something, perhaps because it is valuable or because one feels it is owed to them)一词,表示不情不愿地为某人或某事花费时间或金钱,与原文语义一致;万百安的 stingy(unwilling to spend money)指在金钱方面小气或吝啬。简而言之,撇开词性不论,grudge 其实是花费了,但是不情愿;"stingy"则是根本就舍不得花费。就上下文而言,stingy 并不妥帖。

**臣固知王之不忍也**

理雅各译"不忍"为"不忍目睹",万百安译进一步细化为"不忍看到牛受苦",并在注解中将其与朱熹的注解"恻隐之心,仁之端也,扩而充之,则可以保四海矣"联系起来,既阐明了这里的观点,更是升华了主题。

### 诚有百姓者

理雅各译文很详尽,既承认的确有百姓们所观察到的现象,又不失时机地指出那只是表象,同时替读者着想,补足了百姓们基于观察结果表达的指责(condemn)态度。万百安译文只提到"的确有百姓这么说",简略寡淡,修辞效果远不如理雅各译文。

### 齐国虽褊小,吾何爱一牛

从纯粹语言学角度而言,理雅各与万百安译文完全达到了忠实且通顺的翻译标准,本身无可挑剔。刘殿爵译文另辟蹊径,使用"I am not quite so miserly as to grudge the use of an ox."(我还不至于会小气到舍不得一头牛的地步),把"不至若是"的语义立体地呈现出来,不仅在内容上忠实,在风格上也成功传达了原文的特点。

### 故以羊易之也

理雅各译文使用 change(替换)是符合原文精神的,刘殿爵使用 used a lamb instead 也明确表达了"替换"这个意思,万百安译文使用的 exchange 主要是"交易"而非"替换"这个意思。

### 宜乎百姓之谓我爱也

"宜乎",理雅各译为"有理由",逻辑上是成立的。刘殿爵译为"自然"①,有"顺理成章"的意思,可谓天衣无缝。万百安译为"有道理",虽然译文本身乏善可陈,注解部分却十分精彩,指出孟子这段话的修辞意图在于通过故意设置两难情境以促使梁惠王反躬自省。

### 是乃仁术也

对于"仁术"的翻译,理雅各译为 an artifice of benevolence,其中 artifice (the clever use of tricks and devices)具有"伎俩"与"诡诈"这样的内涵,贬义色彩过于明显,无法传达对话中修辞者孟子正面肯定梁惠王的修辞意图。artifice 这一辞屏很有可能引导读者将梁惠王以羊易牛的行为解读为一种精心设计出来、意在建构个人高尚人格形象的修辞行为,排除了梁惠王的行为是出于恻隐之心的自然流露(亦即出于本心而非刻意造作)这一有助于彰显其美德的解读。刘殿爵译为 the way of a benevolent man(仁者之道),实现了原文赞誉梁惠王的

---

① 译文为:"I suppose it was only natural that the people should have thought me miserly."。参见 Mencius. D.C.Lau, trans. London:The Penguin Group, 1970.

预期话语功能。万百安译为 a technique for(cultivating your)benevolence(培育仁德的技巧或方法),虽然努力为读者解读原文增补逻辑链条,但由于未能将文本修辞意图考虑在内,终究未能避免望文生义的失误。

**闻其声**

理雅各增译为 heard their dying cries(听到它们死前的哀嚎),在逻辑上更加严密,因为并不是所有的动物叫声都会引发人类的恻隐之心。正如常言所说,鸟之将亡,其鸣也哀,动物自然死亡前的叫声就已经十分凄恻,更何况是无辜受戮的非正常死亡。dying 这一辞屏天生具有的修辞张力放大了译文的修辞效果,有助于实现译文的说服目的。万百安译为 hear their cries of suffering(听它们痛苦的惨叫)在修辞效果方面凸显了动物的悲惨遭遇,更能唤起读者的恻隐之心,从而促进读者对译文所传达的观点的认同。

**是以君子远庖厨也**

对于"君子"的翻译,理雅各翻译为 the superior man,万百安翻译为 a gentleman,均有偏颇之处。从对话语境看,华霭仁的译文 the noble person 比较适切。gentleman 主要是形容一个人有教养,品格温和谦逊;superior 更强调在社会地位如级别或职务方面高人一等;而 noble 则不仅可以形容高贵出身,也兼指高尚品格。"远",理雅各译为 keeps away from(远离),意思是到位的,万百安译为 keep their distance from(保持物理距离)也能够达意,但是亨顿的译文 stay clear of(绝不碰触)可谓后来居上。亨顿不仅传达了物理上要与庖厨拉开距离之意,还隐含了不与庖厨的任何物件或场景发生关联的意思,更能表达心灵上希望免遭玷污,想要保持那份"洁"的强烈愿望。"庖厨",理雅各细化译为 slaughter-house and cook-room(屠宰场与烹饪室),将人类屠宰动物的过程加以凸显,与前文呼应,虽然稍显烦琐,修辞效果方面倒也更有现场感。万百安译为 kitchen,简约的同时少了些许形象,但是他的注解令读者兴趣盎然:虽然他在此进一步阐发了前述关于"仁术"的误读(读者可忽略这一部分),但他对于人类自身固有局限性的思考却发人深省,也就是人类所谓恻隐之心仅限于目之所见,对于看不到的(如远处的苦难)则心安理得。① 他对孟子及其诠释者朱熹未能将屠宰场的工人的人性在日常宰杀过程所遭遇的冲击纳入考虑提出质疑,认为他们的立场不无虚伪之处,因为他们默许君子为"洁身""洁心"而远离庖厨,却支使他人替自己从事有损仁心的事。他甚至还

---

① "远处的苦难"系笔者基于行文走势的推理引申。

提到道家的庄子以解牛的庖丁为人类优秀典范这个著名的中国故事①,并将庄子的修辞意图解读为是对孟子的讥讽。

三、曰:"有复于王者曰:'吾力足以举百钧',而不足以举一羽;'明足以察秋毫之末',而不见舆薪,则王许之乎?"

曰:"否。"

"今恩足以及禽兽,而功不至于百姓者,独何与?然则一羽之不举,为不用力焉;舆薪之不见,为不用明焉,百姓之不见保,为不用恩焉。故王之不王,不为也,非不能也。"

曰:"不为者与不能者之形何以异?"

曰:"挟太山以超北海,语人曰'我不能',是诚不能也。为长者折枝,语人曰'我不能',是不为也,非不能也。故王之不王,非挟太山以超北海之类也;王之不王,是折枝之类也。老吾老,以及人之老;幼吾幼,以及人之幼。天下可运于掌。"

——《孟子·梁惠王章句上·第七节》

  Mengzi said, "Suppose there were someone who reported to Your Majesty, 'My strength is sufficient to lift five hundred pounds, but not sufficient to lift one feather. My eyesight is sufficient to examine the tip of an autumn hair, but I cannot see a wagon of firewood.' Would Your Majesty accept that?"

  The king said, "No."

  Mengzi said, "In the present case your kindness is sufficient to reach animals, but the effects do not reach the commoners. How is this different from the examples I just gave? Hence, one fails to lift a feather only because one does not use one's strength. One fails to see a wagon of firewood only because one does not use one's eyesight. The commoners fail to receive care only because one does not use one's kindness. Hence, Your Majesty fails to become King because you do not act, not because you are unable to act." [Hair is supposedly especially

---

  ① 万百安注解原文为:"The 'Daoist' Zhuangzi uses a cook who slaughters an ox as a paradigm for human excellence."。参见 Mengzi. Bryan W. Van, trans. Indianapolis:Hackett Publishing Company, Inc.,2008:10.

fine during the autumn, so it is used as an example of something hard to see. Zhu Xi comments, "People have the most valuable natures of anything in Heaven and Earth. Hence, people are in the same category as other people and are affectionate to each other. Consequently, the expression of compassion to the people is very immediate, but to animals it is slow. As one extends and broadens it through benevolent techniques, being benevolent to the people is easy, but being sparing of animals is difficult. In the present case, the king is already able to extend this heart to animals. So his failure to care for the people and become King is not because he is unable to act. It only comes from his not being willing to act."(I am less confident than Mengzi and Zhu Xi that it is easier for humans to have compassion for other humans than for nonhuman animals.)]

The King said, "How does one distinguish between concrete cases of not acting and not being able?"

Mengzi said, "Tuck Mount Tai under your arm and leap over the North Sea. If you tell others, 'I am unable', you are genuinely unable. Collect kindling for an elderly person. If you tell others, 'I am unable,' you are simply not acting, not genuinely unable. Hence Your Majesty's failure to become King is not in the category of tucking Mount Tai under your arm and leaping over the North Sea. Your Majesty's failure to become King is in the category of collecting kindling." [Zhu Xi comments, "We have this heart inherently; it does not need to be sought externally. Whether we 'expand and fill it up' lies only in ourselves. What difficulty could there be?"] Treat your elders as elders, and extend it to the elders of others; treat your young ones as young ones, and extend it to the young ones of others, and you can turn the world in the palm of your hand. （万百安 译）

Mencius said, "Suppose someone says this to you: 'I am strong enough to lift a weight of three thousand catties, but not strong enough to lift a feather; I have sharp enough eyesight to make out the tip of autumn down, but I cannot see a cartload of firewood.' Do you agree with him?"

"No."

"Now you have shown sufficient kindness to animals, but do not extend the kindness to the people. Do you know why? If a single feather is not lifted, it is because you won't use your strength; if a cartload of firewood is not seen, it is because you won't use your eyes. If the people are not protected and taken care of, it is because you won't extend your kindness to them. Therefore, if you can't be a unifier of the entire kingdom, it is because you are reluctant to do that, not because you are incapable to do it."

The king asked, "Then what is the difference between reluctance and incapacity?"

"If told to carry Mount Tai under your arm to leap over the North Sea and you say 'I am incapable', that is really incapacity," replied Mencius. "If told to bow before the elderly and you say 'I am incapable,' that is reluctance, not incapacity.

"Accordingly, your failure to be a unifier of the entire kingdom is not like the incapacity to carry Mount Tai under your arm to leap over the North Sea, but rather resembles the reluctance to bow before the elderly."

"Respect your own elders and extend such respect to those of others, cherish your own young and extend such cherishment to those of others, and you will find the entire kingdom in your grasp."

(吴国珍 译)

### 吾力足以举百钧

根据杨伯峻先生的注解，一钧等于 30 斤，百钧就是 3000 斤。万百安译为 500 磅（一磅相当于 0.9 斤）严格来说并不对等，但是从修辞效果而言取个足够大的整数倒也合理。和早前的理雅各一样，吴国珍也是译为 3000 斤，既准确也有足够分量，能够达到文本预期的修辞效果。

### 明足以察秋毫之末

和早前的理雅各一样，万百安也是用 examine（检查）翻译"察"，其实原文的意思是"发现""识别"。"检查"意味着早已知道目标的存在，只是还需要细看，而原文强调的是具备看出普通人不易察觉的东西的能力。吴国珍用 make out（看出）是十分准确的。"秋毫"，万百安注解提供了一个生物学解释，指秋天鸟兽身上新长的细毛，同时对其修辞意图做出解释，即用来比喻细微因而难以看出的事物。

### 今恩足以及禽兽，而功不至于百姓者，独何与

万百安与吴国珍都用 kindness（仁慈）翻译"恩"，很准确，但不及亨顿译文所用的 compassion（慈悲之心）更有修辞意涵。"功不至于百姓"，万百安用"effects"（效果）虽然字面与"功"对应，与前文翻译在逻辑上却不相干。读者不免感到困惑：对动物的善行与行善的结果与普通人有什么关联？吴国珍译文在逻辑上十分严密：对动物都能表现出那样的仁慈，却不能做到对人"一视同仁"。早前的译者理雅各与刘殿爵分别将此译为 no benefits are extended from it to the people 与 the benefits of your government fail to reach the people,意思都是"百姓未能得到实惠",其中 benefits(好处)虽然与"功"在字面上不对应,修辞效果倒是比较接近。后出的亨顿译文直白地说 but you do nothing for your people(你没有为百姓做一件实事),语义上是有偏差,但是从话语功能而言,其谴责的意图跃然纸上,有助于读者把握原作者的修辞意图。

"独何与",万百安翻译为"这样做和我前面举过的那些(荒谬的)例子有什么区别?",译文本身文从字顺,与前面的内容也有所关联,已经相当高明了。然而,比万译早出的刘殿爵译文①把"独何与"理解为"你的情况和这个有什么两样呢?"并将其前置,相当于将原文调整为"独何与? 今恩足以及禽兽,而功不至于百姓"。一句之易,使得这个部分与前文诸多例子得以无缝衔接,整个文势一气呵成,比万译在语篇衔接方面更紧凑。需要说明的是,以理雅各为代表的不少译者把"独何与"理解为"这是怎么回事呢"进行翻译,理雅各翻译为"How is this?",亨顿译为"And why is that?",这一诠释进路也能够自圆其说,只是在语篇衔接方面不占优势。

**然则一羽之不举,为不用力焉**

万百安翻译为"没能够举起一根羽毛是因为没有用力气",只是在描绘一个客观现象,没有涉及修辞劝说,与原文预期话语功能有偏差。吴国珍译为"区区一根羽毛却没能举起来,是因为你不愿意花力气去做这件事情",不仅阐述了一个基本判断,还隐约表达了谴责之意,与原文预期的修辞功能一致。

**百姓之不见保,为不用恩焉**

万百安翻译为"百姓没有接收到关爱",不如吴国珍译为"得到保护与关爱"合理且全面。

**故王之不王,不为也,非不能也**

"不王",万百安翻译为"不能成为众王之王或大国王",使用首字母大写的 King("'大'王")表达称霸之意,简约而含蓄。吴国珍则直白地译为"王国的统一者",让读者一目了然。"不为也,非不能也",万百安翻译为"你没有行动",存在比较大的误解,因为没有行动或许只是时机不成熟或尚未意识到重要性。吴国珍译为"你不情愿行动"则不存在造成误解的空间。

---

① 译文为:"Why should it be different in your own case? Your bounty is sufficient to reach the animals, yet the benefits of your government fail to reach the people."。参见 Mencius. D. C. Lau, trans. London: The Penguin Group, 1970:56.

### 挟太山/为长者折枝

万百安翻译为"把泰山夹在腋下",比吴国珍翻译的"抱着泰山"在实践层面难度更高也更有气势,修辞张力更强。"为长者折枝"一句中,由于"折枝"一词存在歧解①,所以各家译文也存在明显差异。万百安译文(为长者折取引火柴)大体为第一种诠释路线的翻译。

早前理雅各译文(依长者吩咐为其从树上折下一根树枝)②也是遵循这一诠释走向,但是没有交代用意何在,给读者留下不少困惑。万百安译文替读者补充了他认为的"枝"比较合理的用途,即引火柴,虽然解决了困惑,但未必忠实于原文意图。吴国珍所译"向长者弯腰行礼"为第二种诠释路线的翻译,就译文本身而言,并无不妥,但若从源语语言文化角度考虑,则未必尽然。就孟子话语所涉及的中国古代社会而言,正常人际交往中少敬长是天经地义的事情,向长者鞠躬有如家常便饭,年轻人不尊长往往被认为是大逆不道之事,将"不为长者折枝"解读为不愿意向长者鞠躬于理不通,此其一;其二则是"为"的使用,从纯语言角度而言,"为"表示有特定目的,"为了长者而鞠躬"说不通,为长者做事情则比较合理。因此,鞠躬说虽然貌似合情合理,其实可能性反而低于其他两种情况。正如前面讨论的,折树枝说法本身可行,问题在于折下之后关于其具体用途的猜测很难令人完全信服。

基于以上讨论,我们倾向于第三种解读,也就是"按摩搔痒"说,作为《孟子》研究领域权威的焦循《孟子正义》③所引东汉赵岐注解便持这一解读:折枝,案摩,折手节,解罢枝也。少者耻见役,故不为耳,非不能也。如按照这一理解,则"折枝"不妨译为 massage。

### 故王之不王,非挟太山以超北海之类也;王之不王,是折枝之类也

万百安的译文基本采取直译,将"类"理解为"属于这一类",译文忠实,但是原文真正的修辞意图没有得到明确揭示。吴国珍在把握原作以责备为主的修辞意图之后,将"类"理解并翻译为"像……一样",直接点明"王之不王"不是像"挟太山以超北海"那样因为能力不具备而难以实现,而是像"为长者折枝

---

① 关于"折枝",杨伯峻指出"古来有三种解释:甲、折取树枝,乙、弯腰行礼,丙、按摩搔痒"。杨伯峻译文取第一意,遗憾的是并未交代取舍依据。参见杨伯峻.孟子译注.北京:中华书局,2012:24.

② 译文为:"In such a matter as breaking off a branch from a tree at the order of a superior."。参见孟子.理雅各,译释.上海:上海三联书店,2014:18.

③ 焦循.孟子正义.沈文倬,点校.北京:中华书局,1987:85-86.

(向长者鞠躬)"那样轻而易举,但是因为不愿意去行动而难以实现。万百安在译文注解中还提到朱熹的观点,即作为同类,人与人之间很容易产生共情,而对于异类的动物,人的同理心就会淡漠许多。换句话说,将仁爱推己及人相对容易,德及禽兽则相对比较困难。他指出本例中梁惠王已经能够做到德及禽兽了,因此他未能恩及民众并一统天下并非因为能力不足,而是因为不愿行动。[①]这些补充讨论极大促进了读者的理解,甚至有可能激发文化比较的学术兴趣。

老吾老,以及人之老;幼吾幼,以及人之幼。天下可运于掌

"老吾老",万百安译为"把你家的老人当作老人对待",对于具体该如何对待老人并没有交代清楚,不免令读者困惑。吴国珍译为"尊敬自家老人",就很明确地提出对待老人的具体要求。之前的理雅各译为 treat with the reverence due to age the elders in your own family(给你家的老人以应该得到的尊重),不仅提出了对待的标准,还给出了善待的理由,很有说服力。"幼吾幼",万百安译为"把你家的少年当作少年对待",同样是语焉不详。吴国珍译为"爱护自家少年",同样是毫不含糊地提出了具体的要求。理雅各译文也进行了与"老吾老"类似的处理。"天下可运于掌",万百安按字面直译,比较拘泥,吴国珍译为"整个国家尽在掌握",既忠实又晓畅。

四、"何谓知言?"

曰:"诐辞知其所蔽,淫辞知其所陷,邪辞知其所离,遁辞知其所穷。"

——《孟子·公孙丑章句上·第二节》

Kung-sun Chau further asked, "What do you mean by saying that you understand whatever words you hear?" Mencius replied, "When words are one-sided, I know how the mind of the speaker is clouded over. When words are extravagant, I

---

[①] 万百安还顺带表示,他对孟子与朱熹关于"人类对同类比对非人类更容易产生恻隐之心"的观点持保留态度。其背后的原因或许是西方的宠物文化比中国发达,人与动物的关系一点都不逊色于人与人的关系,甚至有过之而无不及。这一视角对于思考中国文化对外传播的方式,特别是中国价值对外交流与推广的方式,有很大的启发意义。传播中国文化,不能一味以中国为中心,而应该做目标受众文化心理结构与基本预期调研与分析,构建受众画像并相应调整文化交流与传播策略以顺应受众,从而提高中国文化在英语受众中的接受度。万百安关于恻隐之心的讨论原文参见 Mengzi. Bryan W. Van Norden, trans. Indianapolis: Hackett Publishing Company, Inc., 2008: 11-12.

know how the mind is fallen and sunk. When words are all-depraved, I know how the mind has departed from principle. When words are evasive, I know how the mind is at its wit's end."
（理雅各 译）

"What do you mean by understanding words?" asked Kung-sun Ch'ou.

"I understand what lies hidden beneath beguiling words. I understand the trap beneath extravagant words. I understand the deceit beneath depraved words. And I understand the weariness beneath evasive words."
（亨顿 译）

知言

理雅各译为"理解所听到的任何话"，属于表层字面意思。刘殿爵译为"I have an insight into words."（对言辞有独特的洞察力），也就是懂得话语修辞机理，比较契合孟子对自己的自我界定。

诐辞知其所蔽

这句话的意思是"只呈现一面的说辞我知道它隐瞒了什么"。理雅各译为"如果话语是片面的，我就知道说话人的头脑是如何被蒙蔽了"，凸显的是心理语言学方面的认知问题而不是对偏颇表述的社会语言学分析，这一翻译充其量只说明了说话人智识缺陷导致客观上的认知局限而已，与说话人主动使用话语修辞策略掩盖某些不希望他人了解的事实并无关联。假如接受这一翻译，那么孟子在看到别人的智识缺陷时最恰当的反应应该是悲悯而非极度的自信乃至骄傲。实际情况是孟子对自己"知言"这一点十分自信并引以为傲，因此这样的翻译有待商榷。亨顿翻译为"我知道那些骗人的话语底下隐藏了什么"，虽然其对"诐辞"的翻译不如理雅各地道，但是对"蔽"的翻译明确提示读者这是修辞者主观上有意使用话语手段对事实进行掩盖。基于这一理解，孟子对其修辞机理进行剖析，对其修辞意图进行揭露，从而对自己熟稔话语运作而倍感骄傲也就顺理成章了。

淫辞知其所陷，邪辞知其所离，遁辞知其所穷

理雅各译为"言辞夸夸其谈，我知道说话人的头脑是何等沉溺"，句子读起来令人困惑。亨顿翻译为"我知道夸夸其谈之下有什么陷阱"，将言过其实理解为一种话语策略，符合语境。"邪辞知其所离"，理雅各译为"言辞邪僻，我知道说话人的头脑是何等背离正道"。亨顿翻译为"我知道邪说之下有什么欺骗的伎俩"，将邪说理解成为其他不可告人的目的打掩护的手段，能够自圆其说。

"遁辞知其所穷",李双解释为"能够辨清它理屈窘迫之处"①,蒋伯潜则指出"若能知其词之所穷,则其奸不能售也"②,也就是真正的知言者能够解构遁辞,令修辞者无所逃遁。理雅各译为"闪烁其词,我知道说话人已经束手无策了",逻辑欠通顺。亨顿翻译为"我知道说话人闪烁其词是因为倦怠",这里所谓的因果关系十分勉强,译文难以令人信服。吴国珍译文③"闪烁其词,我知道说话人处于什么样的困境中"比较妥帖:正因为有不方便的情况不愿意对外人透露,说话人才会顾左右而言他。

五、孟子曰:"矢人岂不仁于函人哉?矢人唯恐不伤人,函人唯恐伤人。巫匠亦然,故术不可不慎也。"

——《孟子·公孙丑章句上·第七节》

Mencius said, "Is the arrow-maker less benevolent than the maker of armour of defence? And yet, the arrow-maker's only fear is lest men should not be hurt, and the armour-maker's only fear is lest men should be hurt. So it is with the priest and the coffin-maker. The choice of a profession, therefore, is a thing in which great caution is required."

(理雅各 译)

Mencius said, "Is the maker of arrows really more unfeeling than the maker of armour? The maker of arrows is afraid lest he should fail to harm people, whereas the maker of armour is afraid lest they should be harmed. The case is similar with the sorcerer-doctor and the coffin-maker. For this reason one cannot be too careful in the choice of one's calling."

(刘殿爵 译)

对这一选段杨伯峻有意思十分清晰的译文:

"孟子说:'造箭的人难道比造甲的人本性要残忍吗?(如果不是如此,为什么)造箭的人生怕他的箭不能伤害人,而造甲的人却生怕他的甲不能抵御刀剑呢?做巫的和做木匠的也如此(巫唯恐自己的法术不灵,病人不得痊愈,木匠唯恐病人好了,棺材销不出去)。'可见得一个人选择谋生之术不可以不谨慎。"④

"矢人岂不仁于函人哉",理雅各译为"造箭的人难道不如造甲的人仁慈

---

① 《孟子》白话今译. 李双,译释. 北京:中国书店,1992:67.
② 沈知方四书读本. 蒋伯潜,注释. 上海:上海辞书出版社,2017:357.
③ 译文为:"When words are evasive, I know what plight the speaker is in."。《孟子》最新英文全译全注本.吴国珍,今译、英译、英注.福州:福建教育出版社,2015:70.
④ 杨伯峻. 孟子译注. 北京:中华书局,2012:85.

吗?",不如刘殿爵的译文"造箭的人难道比造甲的人残忍吗?"更有修辞冲击力。"矢人唯恐不伤人",说的是矢人唯恐所制造的箭不能够伤人,刘殿爵译文读起来的意思是"矢人亲自上阵厮杀灭敌(伤人)",与原文不一致。理雅各译出了"唯恐不会伤害(敌)人"这一点,逻辑比较严密。"巫",理雅各译为"priest"(祭司),宗教色彩过于浓厚。刘殿爵使用"sorcerer-doctor"(魔法师-医生)这个辞屏,"不无魔幻色彩"。吴国珍译为"wizard-doctor"(巫师医生)并且通过注解①对特定时代巫师与医生的关系加以说明,同时对不同职业客观上会激发从业者对同一对象截然相反的主观愿望进行解释和概括,既有细节解说又有宏观概括,不仅给读者答疑解惑,还有助于中国哲学思想对外传播。"巫匠亦然",说的是以矢人与函人的情况为参照点,巫匠的情况也是如此。理雅各译出了这一点,叙事主线比较突出。刘殿爵的译文则是以巫匠为参照点,然后比较说矢人与函人情况与此相似,淡化了叙事主线,有喧宾夺主之嫌。"故术不可不慎也",理雅各译得中规中矩,刘殿爵则充分调动英语语言工具库的表达资源,通过"cannot … too"(再怎样都不为过)强调了"择业务慎"这个原则。万百安译文则通过注解②为读者指明了原文的修辞目的,为矢人与匠进行修辞"平反",进一步消解了读者对他们可能存在的误会。

六、孟子曰:"天时不如地利,地利不如人和。"
——《孟子·公孙丑章句下·第一节》

Mencius said, "Opportunities of time vouchsafed by Heaven are not equal to advantages of situation afforded by the Earth, and advantages of situation afforded by the Earth are not equal to the union arising from the accord of Men."

(理雅各 译)

---

① 注解为:"In those days, a doctor was usually a witch or a wizard. This sentence means that the doctor usually seeks bliss for those who pray, whereas the coffin-maker usually hopes more deaths. It implies that men of different occupations usually have different mind sets." 参见《孟子》最新英文全译全注本.吴国珍,今译、英译、英注.福州:福建教育出版社,2015:82.

② 原注为:"The arrow-maker and the coffin-maker are born with the same heart of benevolence as the armor-maker and the shaman-healer. But their choices of career and way of life determine whether they want humans to live or die." 大意为:矢人与匠生来具有和函人与巫一样的仁慈之心,但是他们的职业选择与生活方式决定了他们希望人们要活着还是死去(哪一种对他们更有利)。万百安注解原文参见 Mengzi. Bryan W. Van Norden, trans. Indianapolis: Hackett Publishing Company, Inc., 2008:47.

Mengzi said, Heavenly omens are not as good as advantages of terrain. Advantages of terrain are not as good as harmony with the people. ["Heavenly omens" means simply picking an auspicious day for an attack (by divining with the *Classic of Changes*, for example). Heaven, Earth (here translated "terrain"), and people are sometimes discussed as an interrelated trio, as in the *Mean*, Chapter 22. It is possible that in this passage Mengzi is playing on this grouping.]

(万百安 译)

"天时",理雅各译为"上天给予的时间机会",虽然字面对应"天时",却没有给读者解释这个时间是如何被决定的,这一决定又是如何让人接收到的。刘殿爵译为"Heaven's favourable weather"(上天提供的有利的天气),比较有局限性。万百安翻译为"上天的兆头"并加注说明"用占卜的方法选定一出兵的吉日",给读者提供了足够的文化背景信息,使他们不仅知其然还能够知其所以然。"地利",理雅各译为"地理情境优势",有很强的兼容性,可以囊括自然地理与人文地理的各种情形(比如山川城池之固等)。万百安翻译为"有利地形",局限于纯粹自然地理,比较狭隘。"人和",理雅各译为"人心齐",比万百安模糊的"与人们关系和谐"更能够准确传递信息。

七、得道者多助,失道者寡助。
——《孟子·公孙丑章句下·第一节》

He who finds the proper course has many to assist him. He who loses the proper course has few to assist him.

(理雅各 译)

A just cause enjoys many support while an unjust cause finds little assistance.

(吴国珍 译)

得道者多助

理雅各译为"找到合适路径的人",过于具体而窄化了文本意涵。刘殿爵的译文(One who has the Way)使用带有强烈基督教文化意味的辞屏 the Way(神之道),难免让读者将这句话与只能仰视、无法把控的超自然力量联系起来,从而偏离"道"在原文语境中表示的"仁政"[①]"公义"等人类原本可以平

---

① 管晓霞是翻译为"施行仁政"。其译文为"He who carries out benevolent measures will have many to support him."。参见颜建真.孟子语录:汉英双语版.管晓霞,译.济南:山东友谊出版社,2008:18.

视并努力追求的价值这一务实层面。所谓"得道"并非得到"道",从正面而言,更多的是指符合大多数人的价值标准与契合人类命运共同体的核心利益,从反面而言,则是指不违反公序良俗,不伤天害理,不做千夫所指、人神共愤的事情。吴国珍的译文①成功避免了单独翻译"道"可能引发的误会与争议。原文还使用"enjoy"(享有)这个正面辞屏表达赞成之意,用中性的 find(找到/得到)与"寡助"搭配,从而形成一种价值差。通过给语言表达赋予不同价值,译者表达了对前者价值的认可并实现了话语预期的修辞劝说或劝阻功能。

## 八、民之为道也,有恒产者有恒心,无恒产者无恒心。

——《孟子·滕文公章句上·第三节》

"The way of the people is this:—If they have a certain livelihood, they will have a fixed heart; if they have not a certain livelihood, they have not a fixed heart."

(理雅各 译)

This is the way of the common people. Those with constant means of support will have constant hearts, while those without constant means will not have constant hearts.

(刘殿爵 译)

**民之为道也,有恒产者有恒心**

"民之为道也",理雅各译为"人们的行事方式",没有专门提到普通民众。刘殿爵译为"普通老百姓的行事方式",比较忠实于原文。"有恒产者有恒心",理雅各译为"如果他们有某种谋生手段,就会有一颗固定的心",对于什么是固定的心并没有加以解释。此外,有谋生手段只是涉及生存(survival),离富足(thriving)还有不少路要走,如何就会知足②,在逻辑上存疑。刘殿爵译为"有稳定生活来源",能够自圆其说,但将"有恒心"翻译为"有恒定的心"依然需要进一步解释。管晓霞将"有恒心"翻译为 keep the constant moral principle(守住恒常的道德原则)③,在逻辑事理上具有较高可信度,容易为读者所接受。这一译文也可以从反面得到确认,那就是"我们不可能和一群饥肠辘辘的人大谈仁义道德"。

---

① 大意为:正义的事业会获得许多支持者,不正义的事业则得不到什么帮助。
② 姑且把"固定的心"理解为知足。
③ 颜建真.孟子语录:汉英双语版.管晓霞,译.济南:山东友谊出版社,2008:18.

九、昔者有馈生鱼于郑子产,子产使校人畜之池。校人烹之,反命曰:"始舍之圉圉焉,少则洋洋焉,攸然而逝。"子产曰:"得其所哉!得其所哉!"校人出,曰:"孰谓子产智?予既烹而食之,曰:得其所哉?得其所哉。"故君子可欺以其方,难罔以非其道。

——《孟子·万章章句上·第二节》

Formerly, some one sent a present of a live fish to Tsze-ch'an of Chang. Tsze-ch'an ordered his pond-keeper to keep it in the pond, but that officer cooked it, and reported the execution of his commission, saying, "When I first let it go, it appeared embarrassed. In a little while, it seemed to be somewhat at ease, then it swam away joyfully." Tsze-ch'an observed, "It had got into its element! It had got into its element!" The pondkeeper then went out and said, "Who calls Tsze-ch'an a wise man? After I had cooked and eaten the fish, he says, 'It had got into its element! It had got into its element!'" Thus a superior man may be imposed on by what seems to be as it ought to be, but he cannot be entrapped by what is contrary to right principle.

(理雅各 译)

Formerly, someone gave a gift of a live fish to Zichan of Zheng. Zichan ordered a groundskeeper to take care of it in the pond. The groundskeeper cooked it instead. But he reported back, "When I first released it, it seemed uncertain. But in a short time it was at ease. It was satisfied and swam off." Zichan exclaimed, "He has found his place! He has found his place!" The groundskeeper left and said to himself, "Who said that Zichan was wise? When I had already cooked and eaten it, he says, He has found his place! He has found his place!" Hence, a gentleman can be deceived by what is in line with his path, but it is difficult to trap him with what is not the Way.

(万百安 译)

### 使校人畜之/校人烹之/反命/圉圉/攸然而逝

"校人",蒋伯潜解释为"管理池沼的小吏"①,理雅各译为"池塘管理员"比万百安的"运动场(或公园)管理员"更准确。"畜之",理雅各译为"养在池塘里",是很忠实的纯语言学角度的翻译。万百安翻译为"好好照料",这是符合读者心理预期的修辞性翻译。"校人烹之",万百安使用 instead(反而)比理雅各使用 but(但是)对故事进行平铺直叙更能够表达对校人监守自盗的失职与

---

① 沈知方.四书读本.蒋伯潜,注释.上海:上海辞书出版社,2017:454.

失德的谴责。"反命",万百安翻译为"回复",比较平淡。理雅各译为"报告已经执行完任务",用词庄重,显得煞有介事,与实际的欺骗行为形成强烈反差,具有很强的修辞冲击力。"圉圉",蒋伯潜解释为"困而未舒之貌"①,万百安译为"不确定",吴国珍译为 spiritless(无精打采),均不如理雅各译为"刚开始显得窘迫或不自在"恰如其分。"攸然而逝"②,理雅各译为"向远处游去",颇得原文真趣。万百安译为"鱼很满足地游走了",比较牵强,如果非要描绘鱼此刻的样态,比较恰当的当属"悠哉"。刘殿爵对这一句的翻译③虽然未必忠实于原文,从人们日常与鱼打交道的生活经验而言,倒也言之成理,从修辞性翻译的角度而言,不失为一个可选项。"得其所哉",万百安译为"它找到自己的地方了",虽然忠实但是比较局限于具体场所。理雅各译为"适得其所",不仅涉及理想场地,同时兼及与生态环境诸要素的和谐。

**故君子可欺以其方,难罔以非其道**④

理雅各译为"可以用应然之事欺骗他,但是有违正确原则的事情骗不了他",对"方"的理解很正确,但是对"非道"的理解有偏颇。刘殿爵译为"可以被合理的理由欺骗,但是不可能轻易地被错误的方法蒙骗",⑤对"方"的理解同样合理,但是把"非道"理解为"错误的方法"不免令读者困惑。即便是骗人,也要使用恰当的修辞说服手段,用不正确的手段是不可能成功说服目标受众的。万百安译为"可以被与其路径一致的东西欺骗,但是很难被不符合天道的事物所蒙蔽",将切近伦常的"道"拔高至宗教与哲学的抽象维度,属于过犹不及的翻译。

---

① 沈知方.四书读本.蒋伯潜,注释.上海:上海辞书出版社,2017:454.
② 蒋伯潜认为有两种解读,一个是"自得其乐之貌",另外一个是"迅走水深处"。笔者赞同第二种解读,理由之一是"乐"已通过"洋洋"加以表达,不必再叠床架屋,理由之二是鱼见人而远去最符合自然规律。蒋伯潜解读原文详见沈知方.四书读本.蒋伯潜,注释.上海:上海辞书出版社,2017:454.
③ 刘殿爵译文为:"'When I first let go of it,' said he, 'it was still sickly, but after a while it came to life and swam away into the distance.'"。大意为:刚开始还病怏怏(半死不活)的,不一会儿就缓过来游向远处了。刘殿爵译文参见 Mencius. D.C. Lau, trans. London: The Penguin Group, 1970.
④ 蒋伯潜解读为"可以情理之所常有者欺之,不可以情理之所必无者欺之"。见沈知方.四书读本.蒋伯潜,注释.上海:上海辞书出版社,2017:454.
⑤ 译文为:"a gentleman can be taken in by what is reasonable, but cannot be easily hoodwinked by the wrong method."。参见 Mencius. D.C.Lau, trans. London: The Penguin Group, 1970:140.

十、故说诗者,不以文害辞,不以辞害志。以意逆志,是为得之。
——《孟子·万章章句上·第四节》

Hence in explaining an ode, one should not allow the words to get in the way of the sentence, nor the sentence to get in the way of the sense. The right way is to meet the intention of the poet with sympathetic understanding. （刘殿爵 译）

Hence, in explaining an ode, do not interpret a character to the detriment of the phrase, and do not interpret a phrase to the detriment of the poem's intent. Let your own thought meet the poem's intent. In this manner you will understand it.

（万百安 译）

**不以文害辞,不以辞害志/以意逆志**

这句话的意思是"不可拘泥于文字,不可拘泥于词句"。刘殿爵译为"不应该允许词语妨碍句子,也不应该让句子妨碍意义",虽然字面意思很忠实,但是没有说明白为什么以及通过什么方式造成妨碍。万百安翻译为"不要为了解读某一个文字而损害整个短语,不要为了解读某个短语而损害整首诗的意图",交代清楚了造成妨碍的原因是为了解读某个相对局部的表达,但是究竟如何产生负面影响依然语焉不详。吴国珍译文[①]明确了执着或拘泥于表面意义是产生负面影响的根本原因。关于"志",华霭仁译文 the overall intent（总体意图）是很准确的翻译。"以意逆志",杨伯峻解读为"用自己切身的体会去推测作者的本意"[②]。万百安译为"用自己的思想去推测诗人的意图"[③],不如刘殿爵"以同情之理解去推测诗人的意图"更有可操作性。

十一、万章问曰:"敢问友。"

孟子曰:"不挟长,不挟贵,不挟兄弟而友。友也者,友其德也,不可以有挟也。"

——《孟子·万章章句下·第三节》

Wan Chang asked Mencius, saying, "I venture to ask the principles of friendship."

---

① 译文为:"Anyone who explains a poem should not cling to the literal meaning of a single word to distort the spirit of a term, nor should he cling to the literal meaning of a term to distort the spirit of the whole poem."。参见《孟子》最新英文全译全注本.吴国珍,今译、英译、英注.福州:福建教育出版社,2015:215.

② 杨伯峻.孟子译注.北京:中华书局,2012:235.

③ 要弄清对方意图自然要思考,但"思想"是个大词,比较模糊。

Mencius replied, "Friendship should be maintained without any presumption on the ground of one's superior age, or station, or the circumstances of his relatives. Friendship with a man is friendship with his virtue, and does not admit of assumptions of superiority."

(理雅各 译)

Wan Zhang asked, "May I ask about friendship?"

Mencius said, "In friendship one should not presume upon one's own seniority, high rank, or the prestige of one's family connections. To befriend someone is to befriend his Virtue, which allows for no such presumption."

(华霭仁 译)

### 万章/敢问友

关于万章的身份,两位译者都没有加以说明。万百安译为"孟子的学生",对人物身份进行说明,有利于读者重构修辞场景。"敢问友",华霭仁只是简单地直译为"想讨教关于友谊的问题",理雅各译为"冒昧问一下交友应该秉承哪些原则";结合下文回答的内容,不难发现理雅各译文更有提纲挈领的效果,有助于读者为即将进行的对话进行心理预构筑。

### 不挟长/贵/兄弟/友也者,友其德也,不可以有挟

"长",理雅各译为"优越的年龄",语焉不详。对于究竟是年轻更有优越性还是年长更有优势完全取决于具体修辞场景:当特定场景需要修辞权威时,基于"年长智深"(Age brings wisdom.)的观念预设,长者更有发言权与说服力;当特定场景需要青春活力之时,年轻则成为优势,越青春越吃香。因此,究竟是哪个方向的年龄优势应该指明。华霭仁译文使用"资深",清晰表明了长者所享有的与生俱来的权威(authority)容易被视为一种交友时可以征用的修辞资源以及原作者对其遭遇潜在滥用的忧虑。"不挟贵"的"贵",理雅各翻译为"地位",总体达意;华霭仁则准确地翻译为"高贵的社会等级"。"不挟兄弟",杨伯峻解读为"不依仗自己兄弟的富贵"[①]。理雅各将"兄弟"译为亲戚的状况,偏离了原文"兄弟"的范畴,同时"状况"有好坏各种情形,应该加以明确。华霭仁译为"其他家庭成员的声望",虽然不忠实,但从话语修辞所要产生的预期效果而言,不失为一个生动的译文。"友也者,友其德也",两个译文均译为"与某人交朋友就是与他的美德交朋友",不如刘殿爵译文[②]在逻辑上自然明

---

① 原文为"俗解谓不挟兄弟多人而友,兄弟多人,有何可挟乎? 须辨别之"。参见杨伯峻.孟子译注. 北京:中华书局,2012:260.

② 译文为:"In making friends with someone you do so because of his virtue."。大意为:与某人交朋友,是奔着他的美德而去的。刘殿爵译文参见 Mencius. D.C. Lau, trans. London: The Penguin Group,1970:152.

了。"不可以有挟",两个译文都没有译出"不可倚仗某种与品德无关的优势"这个意思,刘殿爵译文①最为清晰地表达了这一点。

十二、告子曰:"性犹湍水也,决诸东方则东流,决诸西方则西流。人性之无分于善不善也,犹水之无分于东西也。"

孟子曰:"水信无分于东西。无分于上下乎?人性之善也,犹水之就下也。人无有不善,水无有不下。今夫水,搏而跃之,可使过颡;激而行之,可使在山。是岂水之性哉?其势则然也。人之可使为不善,其性亦犹是也。"

——《孟子·告子章句上·第二节》

The philosopher Kao said, "Man's nature is like water whirling round in a corner. Open a passage for it to the east, and it will flow to the east; open a passage for it to the west, and it will flow to the west. Man's nature is indifferent to good and evil, just as the water is indifferent to the east and west."

Mencius replied, "Water indeed will flow indifferently to the east or west, but will it flow indifferently up or down?" The tendency of man's nature to good is like the tendency of water to flow downwards. There are none but have this tendency to good, just as all water flows downwards."

"Now by striking water and causing it to leap up, you may make it go over your forehead, and, by damming and leading it you may force it up a hill;—but are such movements according to the nature of water? It is the force applied which causes them. When men are made to do what is not good, their nature is dealt with in this way."

(理雅各 译)

Kao Tzu said, "Human nature is like whirling water. Give it an outlet in the east and it will flow east; give it an outlet in the west and it will flow west. Human nature does not show any preference for either good or bad just as water does not show any preference for either east or west."

"It certainly is the case", said Mencius, "that water does not show any pre

---

① 译文为:"You must not rely on any advantages you may possess."。大意为:你不可以凭借你可能拥有的那些优势(去强迫别人与你交往)。刘殿爵译文参见 Mencius. D.C. Lau., trans. London: The Penguin Group, 1970:152.

ference for either east or west, but does it show the same indifference to high and low? Human nature is good just as water seeks low ground. There is no man who is not good; there is no water that does not flow downwards."

"Now in the case of water, by splashing it one can make it shoot up higher than one's forehead, and by forcing it one can make it stay on a hill. How can that be the nature of water? It is the circumstances being what they are. That man can be made bad shows that his nature is no different from that of water in this respect." （刘殿爵 译）

### 告子

理雅各译文将告子学术身份界定为哲学家，固然使得人物形象更加丰满，但同时也不无争议。刘亚猛就曾在《从"百家争鸣"的角度理解中国先秦话语时存在的三大问题》一文中质疑西方汉学界将中国先秦诸子的学术身份界定为哲学家这一学术定论，提议将"修辞观点"引进西方汉学研究领域并将诸子重新界定为修辞批评实践者（rhetorical critics）①。其核心论点是：把先秦诸子视为以逻辑理性为主要论辩方式的哲学家是对其话语实践的简单化概括。其实诸子的话语实践远远超越了单一逻辑论辩模式，包括但是不仅限于使用修辞人格与权威（ethos）、受众情感（pathos）等一切有用、可用的修辞手段与资源以驳斥对立观点并捍卫己方立场。这一重新界定意在充分体现诸子话语总体上以及在具体论辩中的广度、深度与复杂性。基于这一见解，不妨把告子的学术身份重新界定为 sophist（哲辩师）或 rhetorician（修辞师）。

### 性犹湍水也

"湍水"，蒋伯潜解读为波流潆洄。② 刘殿爵的处理方式是进行直译；理雅各则译为"角落里回旋的水"，不仅译出原文已有的信息，还进一步补充原文没有明言却在逻辑上允许的"角落里"这一情境，为下文"决水"做了修辞铺垫，增加了文本的说服力。

---

① 原文为："At issue is also what initial assumption about the identity of Zhou masters can best help to reveal the scope, depth and complexity of their discourse in general and their disputation in particular: should they be seen as philosophers who argued with one another only when they adopted the logico-rational approach as we know it now, or could they rather be described as rhetorical critics of their time, who endeavored to distance themselves from, yet were ultimately unable to rise above, the dominant rhetorical mode of pre-Han discursive practices?"。参见 Liu Yameng. Three Issues in the Argumentative Conception of Early Chinese Discourse. *Philosophy East and West*，1996(46)：33-58.

② 沈知方.四书读本.蒋伯潜，注释.上海：上海辞书出版社，2017：478.

**人性之无分于善不善也，犹水之无分于东西也**

刘殿爵译文"正如水不会对东方或西方有偏好一样，人性对好和坏也没有偏好"，与理雅各译文"正如水不在意流向东方或西方那样，人性对善良与邪恶是漠然的"都凸显了人的主观性。华霭仁译文①不仅客观而且句法②严谨，凸显了对被比较双方的否定，实现了预期话语功能。"上下"，刘殿爵译为代表方位的"高处与低处"，不如理雅各直译为"上方与下方"更能够体现方向感。"人性之善也，犹水之就下也"，刘殿爵译文"人性是好的，就像水往低处流"中性善与水的倾向并非同一范畴，二者并没有很强的内在逻辑。理雅各译为"人性向善的倾向就像水往下流的倾向一样"，很明确地将二者具有相似倾向表达了出来。

**人无有不善，水无有不下**

刘殿爵译文为"没有人不善良，没有水不往低处流"，虽然后一句是举世公认的真理，但前一句则很容易被证伪，毕竟这个世界上不都是好人，译文因局部的武断而影响了整体的可信度。理雅各忠实翻译为"就像水没有不往低处流的倾向一样，人没有不具备向善倾向的"。万百安译文在这一处加了注解③，提醒读者注意辞格的认知功能。

**今夫水，搏而跃之，可使过颡；激而行之，可使在山**

"今夫水，搏而跃之，可使过颡"，理雅各译为"击水使其跳上额头"，刘殿爵

---

① 译文为："Human nature does not distinguish between good and not-good any more than water distinguishes between east and west."。参见 Mencius. Irene Bloom, trans. New York: Columbia University Press, 2009: 121.

② 使用 not…any more than 这一经典的否定比较句型。

③ 原注为："The key to appreciating this chapter (and the adjacent ones) is that the similes are not intended as mere rhetorical window-dressing without cognitive content. Mengzi's objection is that Gaozi's simile fails to do justice to the natural characteristics of water, and thereby presents a misleading impression of human nature. Although water is indifferent to flowing east or west, to make it flow either way, we must follow its natural disposition to flow downward. Likewise, to make humans good, we must work either with or against our natural dispositions."。大意为：解读本节的关键在于这个明喻并非纯粹装点门面的修辞格，而是要认识到它是有着实际认知内容的。孟子反对告子，认为他的明喻没有正确表述水的自然特征，因此其所表达的关于人性的印象是误导性的。尽管水不会对向东或向西流动有所取舍，我们依然必须遵循其向下流动的自然趋向才能够让它流动起来。相应地，为了让人类向善，我们必须利用或克制我们与生俱来的自然倾向。参见 Mengzi. Bryan W. Van Norden, trans. Indianapolis: Hackett Publishing Company, Inc., 2008: 144.

译为"拍水使其激越额头",二者各有得失。"击水"比"拍水"更有力道,而"激越"比"跳上"更能够体现受到外力激发所产生的不由自主的结果。"激而行之,可使在山",理雅各译为"把它壅积起来,可以流到山上去",比刘殿爵译文"迫使水停留在山上"合理得多。

**其势则然也/人之可使为不善,其性亦犹是也**

"其势则然也",刘殿爵译为"环境就是那样",逻辑不甚明了。理雅各译为"是外力的作用使它变成那样的",逻辑十分清晰。万百安译为"It is only that way because of the circumstances."(正是环境使它变成那样),把"势"由单一的"力量"拓展到更多的因素,是更加可取的译文。"人之可使为不善,其性亦犹是也",刘殿爵译为"人会因外力变坏这个事实表明其本性与水在这一方面并无二致",译文比较迂回,遮蔽了关键信息。理雅各译为"人们被迫作恶,是因为他们的本性也受外力强制",将原文观点明晰地表达了出来。

### 十三、恻隐之心,人皆有之;羞恶之心,人皆有之;恭敬之心,人皆有之;是非之心,人皆有之。

—— 《孟子·告子章句上·第六节》

"The feeling of commiseration belongs to all men; so does that of shame and dislike; and that of reverence and respect; and that of approving and disapproving."

（理雅各 译）

Compassion is a feeling shared by all men alike, so is the sense of shame; reverence is the conscience shared by all men alike, so is the sense of right and wrong.

（吴国珍 译）

"恻隐之心",理雅各译为 commiseration(a feeling or expression of sympathy for someone about some bad luck),也就是"对发生不幸者的怜悯之情",已属于忠实翻译。吴国珍译为 compassion(a strong feeling of sympathy and sadness for the suffering or bad luck of others and a wish to help them),表示不仅同情他人的不幸遭遇,尤其还有施以援手的情感冲动,更能够体现人类的共情心理。"人皆有之",理雅各译文"属于每个人"不如吴国珍的译文"同情心是所有人类都共有的",后者凸显了这一心理品质的能动性与普世性。"羞恶之心",理雅各译为"羞耻与厌恶之情感",不如吴国珍所译的"羞耻感"简约准确。"恭敬之心",吴国珍翻译为"尊敬的良知",考虑到敬意属于"礼"的范畴,与良知无涉,译文逻辑无法自洽。理雅各译为"尊敬的情感",比较恰当。"是非之心",属于智力范畴,与情感关系不大,理雅各译为"赞同与反对的情感",不妥。吴国珍翻译为"对是与非的辨识力",是很正确的解读。华霭仁译文 the mind that knows right and wrong(知道是与非的头脑)更是毫不含糊地翻译出智识能力这一点。

十四、孟子曰:"虽有天下易生之物也,一日暴之,十日寒之,未有能生者也。"

——《孟子·告子章句上·第九节》

Even a plant that grows most readily will not survive if it is placed in the sun for one day and exposed to the cold for ten. （刘殿爵 译）

Even though it may be the easiest growing thing in the world, if it gets one day of warmth and ten days of frost, there has never been anything that is capable of growing. （万百安 译）

"虽有天下易生之物也",万百安按字面进行忠实翻译,刘殿爵则将物具体化为植物,是很合理的推测。"一日暴之,十日寒之",刘殿爵译为"被拿出去放在太阳底下晒一天,接着被晾在寒冷的地方十天",强调不能够持之以恒、善始善终地恰当对待,与有始无终的人性弱点高度吻合,有很强说服力。万百安译为"得到一天的温暖,又遭受十天的霜冻",表达的是没有人为干预的客观遭遇,描绘的是物理而非人事,无法传递原文"因为疏忽或慵懒而不再坚持照料"这一情况及其附带的对类似行动的修辞劝诫功能。"未有能生者也",刘殿爵译为"活不成",过于绝对。万百安译为"无法生长",符合因为日照不足而缺乏生长后劲这一物理现实。

十五、孟子曰:"鱼,我所欲也,熊掌,亦我所欲也;二者不可得兼,舍鱼而取熊掌者也。生,亦我所欲也,义,亦我所欲也;二者不可得兼,舍生而取义者也。

——《孟子·告子章句上·第十节》

Mencius said, "Fish is what I want; bear's palm is also what I want. If I cannot have both, I would rather take bear's palm than fish. Life is what I want; dutifulness is also what I want. If I cannot have both, I would choose dutifulness rather than life." （刘殿爵 译）

Mencius said, "Fish is my favorite and so is the bear paw. If I could not enjoy both of them, I would give up fish and choose the bear paw. Life is what I desire and so is righteousness. If I could not keep both of them, I will give you a life and choose righteousness." （吴国珍 译）

鱼，我所欲也，熊掌，亦我所欲也；二者不可得兼

"我所欲也"，刘殿爵译为"是我想要的"，比吴国珍"是我最喜爱的"接近原文。"熊掌"，刘殿爵译为"熊的手掌"，不如吴国珍译为"熊爪"①合理。万百安专门就熊掌添加注解②，说明它是一种美食，给读者带来了文化新鲜感，但是与其他两位译者一样都忽略了一个因时代差异③衍生的伦理问题。那就是在动物权益保护呼声日益高涨的当下，大部分读者（包括话语原产国——中国的当代读者）已经不能对他人食用熊掌坐视不管了。如果不在译文合适部分对这些文化背景信息加以补充，英语读者难免会对孟子产生负面评价，同时对中国餐饮文化传统产生误解，进而损害中国人的集体修辞人格（collective ethos）。第一处"得兼"，刘殿爵译为 have both（拥有两个），虽然忠实却比较平淡，吴国珍用 enjoy both of them（享有两个），充分表达了说话人的价值取向。

生，亦我所欲也，义，亦我所欲也；二者不可得兼

此处"欲"，吴国珍用 desire（渴慕），比刘殿爵译的 want（想要）情感更强烈。"义"，刘殿爵译为 dutifulness（尽职尽责），不如吴国珍用 righteousness（正义）接近原文意思。第二处"得兼"，刘殿爵并未改变措辞，吴国珍则根据语境灵活调整措辞，使用 keep both of them（保住两个）进行翻译。

十六、故天将降大任于是人也，必先苦其心志，劳其筋骨，饿其体肤，空乏其身，行拂乱其所为，所以动心忍性，曾益其所不能。

——《孟子·告子章句下·第十五节》

Thus, when Heaven is about to confer a great office on any man, it first ex-

---

① 吴国珍译文 the bear paw 照理应该是 the bear's paw，不知是作者特意如此表达还是印刷过程技术失误。

② 原注为："Bear's paw was a kind of culinary delicacy."。参见 Mengzi. Bryan W. Van Norden, trans. Indianapolis: Hackett Publishing Company, Inc., 2008:153.

③ 在农业文明为主的中国古代，熊掌作为山珍之一，是猎户的合法食材，理所当然的美食，没有人会因为周边有人食用熊掌而感到不安或进行抗议。

ercises his mind with suffering, and his sinews and bones with toil. It exposes his body to hunger, and subjects him to extreme poverty. It confounds his undertakings. By all these methods it stimulates his mind, hardens his nature, and supplies his incompetencies.

（理雅各 译）

That is why Heaven, when it is about to place a great burden on a man, always first tests his resolution, exhausts his frame and makes him suffer starvation and hardship, frustrates his efforts so as to shake him from his mental lassitude, toughen his nature and make good his deficiencies.

（刘殿爵 译）

"降大任"，刘殿爵译为"给重担"，读起来像是负面的事情，理雅各译为"赋予重大职责"，比较忠实地反映了原文。"苦其心志"，刘殿爵译为"测试他的意志"，不如理雅各所译"用苦难锻炼他的头脑"准确。"劳其筋骨"，理雅各忠实地译为"用劳作锻炼他的筋骨"，刘殿爵译作"让他筋疲力尽"，有过犹不及之嫌。"空乏其身"，刘殿爵译为"让他受苦"，偏离原文且与前文语义重复，理雅各忠实地译为"使其遭受极度贫困"。"行拂乱其所为"，理雅各译为"挫败他的事业"，刘殿爵译为"挫败他的努力"，二者均成功再现了原文精神。"动心"，理雅各译作"刺激其头脑"，刘殿爵译为"让其头脑摆脱倦怠状态"，均不如吴国珍译文 to inspire his ambition（激发其雄心壮志）明晰。"曾益其所不能"，理雅各与刘殿爵均译出原文意思，万百安译为 provides those things of which one is incapable（提供他无法得到的东西），偏离了原文关于"能力"的论述。

十七、孟子曰："孔子登东山而小鲁，登泰山而小天下。故观于海者难为水，游于圣人之门者难为言。

——《孟子·尽心章句上·第二十四节》

Mencius said, "Confucius ascended the eastern hill, and Lu appeared to him small. He ascended the T'ai mountain, and all beneath the heavens appeared to him small. So he who has contemplated the sea, finds it difficult to think anything of other waters[①], and he who has wandered in the gate of the sage, finds it difficult to think anything of the words of others."

（理雅各 译）

Mencius said, "When he ascended the Eastern Mount, Confucius felt that Lu

---

① 原注为："After seeing the surging oceans, the streams are not worth being taken into account."。参见孟子.理雅各,译释.上海：上海三联书店,2014.

was small, and when he ascended Mount T'ai, he felt that the Empire was small. Likewise it is difficult for water to come up to the expectation of someone who has seen the Sea, and it is difficult for words to come up to the expectation of someone who has studied under a sage."

(刘殿爵 译)

Mencius said, "When Confucius was atop the East Hill, he found the land of Lu appear small. When he was on top of Mount Tai, he found all beneath the sky small to the eye. So those who have seen a sea will find it difficult to be impressed by other waters; those who have learned under a sage will find it difficult to be impressed by other doctrines."

(吴国珍 译)

关于本节,蒋伯潜解读如下:

"所登愈高,所望愈远,眼界亦愈大,故'登东山而小鲁,登泰山而小天下'也。所见愈广,所知愈多,眼界亦愈高,故'故观于海者难为水,游于圣人之门者难为言'也。"①

**孔子登东山而小鲁,登泰山而小天下**②

"登",理雅各与刘殿爵均使用动词强调动态的"登山",吴国珍译文凸显的是静态的结果,既"当孔子站在东山/泰山之顶时",更符合"一览众山小"的情境。"东山",理雅各译为"东部的山",并不准确。杨伯峻认为东山"当即蒙山,在今山东蒙阴县南"③,也就是一座具体的山。刘殿爵与吴国珍均使用专有名词翻译,虽然名称不准确,至少指出这是一座特定的山。吴国珍译文专门使用 Hill 以便与泰山译文所用的 Mount 形成价值阶,方便不熟悉中国文化的读者领会二者小大之别,成功再现了话语预期的修辞比较与价值判断。"鲁",理雅各与刘殿爵均没有特别说明,吴国珍补充提到鲁国的国土,为读者提供了必要的文化背景知识,使得"鲁"不至于沦为一个抽象符号。"天下",理雅各与吴国珍均译为"天底下",万百安翻译为 the world(全世界),均不如刘殿爵译的 the Empire(整个帝国),该译文准确体现了文本所指的中国。

**观于海者难为水,游于圣人之门者难为言**

"观于海",刘殿爵与吴国珍均简单翻译为"见过海",理雅各译为"凝视沉思过大海",意涵更深刻。"难为水",刘殿爵译为"难以达到对水的期望值",吴

---

① 沈知方.四书读本.蒋伯潜,注释.上海:上海辞书出版社,2017:524.

② 东山,鲁国境内之山。泰山,齐鲁两国共有之山。参见沈知方.四书读本.蒋伯潜,注释.上海:上海辞书出版社,2017:524.

③ 杨伯峻.孟子译注.北京:中华书局,2012:344.

国珍译为"很难给观者留下深刻印象",都把握了原文大意。就忠实与详尽程度而言,理雅各译文"很难对其他水体有特别的看法"及其注解"见过波涛汹涌的大海后,溪流就不值一提了"给读者提供了极为明晰充分的信息。"游于圣人之门者",理雅各译文"在圣人的大门前漫步",停留在字面,逻辑上难以自洽。刘殿爵与吴国珍均译为"求学于圣人门下",符合原文意思。

十八、孟子曰:"挟贵而问,挟贤而问,挟长而问,挟有勋劳而问,挟故而问,皆所不答也。"

——《孟子·尽心章句上·第四十三节》

Mencius replied, "I do not answer him who questions me presuming on his nobility, nor him who presumes on his talents, nor him who presumes on his age, nor him who presumes on services performed to me, nor him who presumes on old acquaintance." (理雅各 译)

"I never answer any questioner," said Mencius, "who relies on the advantage he possesses of position, superior qualities, age, merit or status as an old friend." (刘殿爵 译)

"贵",理雅各译为"高贵的身份/出身",刘殿爵译为"地位的优势",虽有侧重点的不同,均有效传达了修辞者依赖个人品德之外的身份权威制造权力势差以左右话语交流的意图。"贤",理雅各译为"才华",比较片面,因为贤固然可以指才能,但是才能是其必要而非充分条件,美德才是主要方面。刘殿爵译为"优秀的品质",比较忠实于原文,体现了修辞者想依仗品德方面的修辞人格(ethos)获取话语交流优势的意图。"有勋劳",理雅各译为"为我提供过的服务",比较有局限性,刘殿爵译为"功绩",比较妥当。"故",理雅各译为"老交情",比刘殿爵"老朋友的身份"更有内涵。

十九、孟子曰:"贤者以其昭昭,使人昭昭;今以其昏昏,使人昭昭。"

——《孟子·尽心章句下·第二十节》

Mencius said, "men of virtue and talents by means of their own enlightenment made others enlightened. Nowadays, it is tried, while they are themselves in darkness, and by means of that darkness, to make others enlightened." (理雅各 译)

Mencius said, "A good and wise man helps others to understand clearly by his own clear understanding. Nowadays, men try to help others understand by their own benighted ignorance."

(刘殿爵 译)

"以其昭昭,使人昭昭",理雅各译为"通过自己的领悟去启发别人",只提到领悟,没有对其质量进行限定,不能排除"自己的领悟"是错误的。刘殿爵译为"通过自己清晰的理解去帮助别人弄明白",逻辑清晰,一目了然。万百安译文①"用自己的洞察力帮助他人成为有洞察力的人",比原文稍微提高了标准,原文只是说让对方明白即可。吴国珍译文②"自己先领悟,再去启发别人",强调先后顺序(前者是后者的先决条件),比较独到。"以其昏昏,使人昭昭",刘殿爵译为"用自己的昏昧无知尝试去帮助别人理解",没有强调修辞者缺乏自知之明,读起来像是明知故犯。理雅各译为"自己还在昏昧之中,却用这些稀里糊涂的理解试图去启发别人",逻辑比较清晰,更容易获得读者认同。

## 本章参考的英译本

颜建真.孟子语录:汉英双语版.管晓霞,译.济南:山东友谊出版社,2008.

《孟子》.理雅各,译释.上海:上海三联书店,2014.

《孟子》最新英文全译全注本.吴国珍,今译、英译、英注.福州:福建教育出版社,2015.

Mencius. D.C. Lau, trans. London: The Penguin Group, 1970.

Mengzi. Bryan W. Van Norden, trans. Indianapolis: Hackett Publishing Company, Inc., 2008.

Mencius. Irene Bloom, trans. New York: Columbia University Press, 2009.

Mencius. David Hinton, trans. Berkeley: Counterpoint, 2015.

---

① Worthies use their own insight to make others insightful.

② The ancient virtuous enlightened themselves before trying to enlighten others.

# 第三章 《道德经》英译比较与评析

一、天下皆知美之为美,斯恶已;皆知善之为善,斯不善已。

——《道德经》第二章①

Everyone understands that which makes "beauty" beautiful,
And thus the concept of ugliness arises;②
Everyone understands that which makes 'goodness' good,
And thus the concept of badness arises.

(杨有维 译)

---

① 若无特别说明,本章所涉及《道德经》引文均出自《老子今注今译及评介》。出处详见陈鼓应.老子今注今译及评介.台北:台湾商务印书馆,1984.

② 此处原注为:"/Some scholars interpret this sentence as meaning that everyone understands that that which makes 'beauty' beautiful eventually changes to make the object ugly. Lao Tzu's intention is not to point out that the processes of change inevitably render all beautiful things ugly, but rather to explain the relativity of value judgments. If we have the concept of 'beauty', the concept of 'ugly' necessarily arises. Similarly, the second sentence, 'everyone understands that which makes "goodness" good, and thus the concept of badness arises' explains the relative nature of standards and their interdependence with their antitheses. The passage which follows these two statements on the relationship between antithetical concepts from 'being and non-being give birth to each other' to 'before and after follow each other' are six examples of this relationship. In the commentaries, there are some relatively lucid explanations, such as Fan Ying-yuan, who states that 'If we exaggerate something and consider it beautiful, boast of something and consider it good, and then cause everyone to understand this, then the concepts of ugliness and badness must follow from it.' Wu Ch'eng's commentary says, 'The designation of "beauty" and "ugliness" arise from each other.' Ch'en I-tien's commentary states, 'But in understanding that which makes "beauty" beautiful, there must also be non-beautiful things existing.' In each commentary, it is explained that the concepts of 'beauty' and 'ugliness' arise from their mutual contrast./"。参见 Chen Guying. Lao Tzu: Text, Notes, and Comments. Rhett Y.W.Young, Roger. T. Ames, Trans. Taiwan: Chinese Materials Center, 1981:59.

There seems a fundamental interconnection between opposites. There was no ugliness until humanity defined beauty. There was no bad until humanity defined good. These labels are human creations and mean nothing to Tao.

(Julian von Bargen 等 译)

天下皆知美之为美

"When the whole world knows the pleasing to be pleasing."
When the beautiful praise themselves, they put themselves on display.

斯恶已

"This ends in despising."
They are in danger of being killed.

皆知善之为善

"When all know the good to be good."
When people are known to have accomplishments and fame.

斯不善已

"This ends with what is not good."
Others compete and fight with them.

(Dan G. Reid 译)

Everyone knows how our discriminative minds frame things in pairs that seem interdependent. Awareness of the beautiful leads one to frame the ugly at the same time. Push leads to pull. Calling out the good creates headspace for the bad.

(Marc S. Mullinax 译)

这句话容许有两解:一是如汉代河上公①、宋朝司马光②等人认为其系"自我彰显"的解读,修辞目的是劝人"自我韬晦"(self-effacement);二是如宋朝苏辙③、

---

① 河上公原注为:"自扬己美,使彰显也。有危亡也。"参见河上公,等.道德经集释.北京:中国书店,2015:3.

② 司马光对这一自彰行为的修辞后果的评论原文为:"美善有迹,为众所知,非美之至者也。"参见河上公,等.道德经集释.北京:中国书店,2015:166.

③ 苏澈原著为:"天下以形名言美恶,其所谓美且善者,岂信美且善哉?彼不知有无、难易、长短、高下、声音、前后之相生相夺,皆非其正也。方且自以为长,而有长于我者临之,斯则短矣。方且自以为前,而有前于我者先之,斯则后矣。苟从其所美而信之,则失之远矣。"参见河上公,等.道德经集释.北京:中国书店,2015:283.

宋徽宗赵佶[①]、清代魏源[②]等将其理解为相对论。Reid 将"恶"往"厌恶"而非"产生恶果"方向理解并翻译为 despising（鄙视），与上下文缺乏逻辑关联，难免让读者感到困惑。但是在翻译河上公的解读时，则比较畅达。杨有维所译陈鼓应解读也是将本句理解为相对论。值得注意的是陈鼓应指出若按相对论解读此句，则本章后半部分内容与前文逻辑似乎不洽。[③] 为了对读者负责任，建议译者在译文注解中对此给目标英语读者做出说明。

即便已经在相对论这一点达成了共识，学者还是存在分歧。比如冯家福等就是从反面进行理解的，翻译为"Under heaven all can see beauty as beauty only because there is ugliness."（天下人觉得美之所以为美是因为有丑的存在），虽然也是相对论的体现，但与原文相比，倒果为因，还是有一些偏颇。

在具体措辞方面，对"知"与"斯恶已"，各家译文也颇有些不同。杨有维用 understand（理解）翻译"知"，不如韦利的 recognize（认作）更加文从字顺。理雅各将"斯恶已"译为"All in the world know the beauty of the beautiful, and in doing this they have (the idea of) what ugliness is."（形成了"丑"的概念），比韦利的 that the idea of ugliness exists（"丑"的概念存在）更加能够体现从无到有这一变化过程。杨有维使用 arise 鲜明地表达了一个观念的产生这一动态过程，Mullinax 的 lead to 则将因果清晰地呈现在读者面前，二者殊途而同归。

从作为修辞者的译者对读者（受众）的顺应来看，Bargen 等与 Mullinax 的译文对读者尽显忠恕。二者都加了导语，对下文内容进行概括与预告，是典

---

① 章安从"变化"、"修辞时机"以及审美主体的"主观性"几个角度对相对论做了说明：（"变化"）"世之所美者为神奇，所恶者为臭腐，神奇复化为臭腐，臭腐复化为神奇，则美与恶奚辨？昔之所是，今或非；今之所弃，后或用之，则善与不善奚择？"（"修辞时机"）"缘机之会，应时为当，则善不善果何择哉？"（"主观性"）"情见在人，其知不同，各徇其私，而相为彼我，则美之与恶，善之与不善，其循环无穷矣。"参见李为学.宋徽宗道德真经解义.赵佶,注.章安,解义.石曼璐,点校.上海：华东师范大学出版社,2017:9-10.

② 魏源从修辞时机的角度解释相对论的注解原文为："当其时,适其情。则天下谓之美善。不当其时,不适其情。则天下谓之恶与不善。"参见魏源.老子本义二卷.台北：汉京文化事业有限公司,1980:3.

③ 此处原注为："Up to this point, this chapter is discussing the mutual dependency of antithetical concepts. The passage which follows, however, does not seem to have any connection in either meaning or style. This would lead us to believe that the second portion of this chapter has been erroneously interpolated from another chapter."。参见 Chen Guying. Lao Tzu: Text, Notes, and Comments. Rhett Y. W. Young, Roger T. Ames, Trans. Taiwan: Chinese Materials Center,1981:59.

型的迁就英语读者阅读习惯的修辞顺应行为。Bargen 等的汉堡式(导语—主要内容—小结)译文用 these labels(这些标签)巧妙地提醒并劝说读者不要去做太多无谓的区分。Mullinax 甚至还在章节开头添加了一个很有修辞意涵的小标题 DISTINCTIONS PROMOTE CONTENTION(辨生辩),表面上在叙述一件事情或形容一个现象,实则暗含价值判断,劝说读者不要人为去做过多区分或进行价值排序,因为那样只会导致争端。

二、不尚贤,使民不争;不贵难得之货,使民不为盗;不见可欲,使民心不乱。

——《道德经》第三章

Not to value and employ men of superior ability is the way to keep the people from rivalry among themselves; not to prize articles which are difficult to procure is the way to keep them from becoming thieves; not to show them what is likely to excite their desires is the way to keep their minds from disorder. (理雅各 译)

章安认为本章第一句的核心思想是"名者争之端,利者盗之起"。[1] 魏源认为"盖君子好名,小人好利。贤与货皆可欲之具,是故人以相贤为尚。则民耻不若而至于争。货以难得为贵。则民病其无而至于盗。皆由见可欲耳"。[2] 因此,该论断本质上是基于特定修辞情境而针对具体受众的心理特征提出的修辞解决方案。

贤

理雅各翻译为 men of superior ability(才华出众者),韦利译为 persons of superior morality(道德超常者),都凸显了贤者的某一方面,同时也淡化、遗漏了另外一方面。杨有维翻译为 superior men(卓越的人),似乎想涵摄德与才两个方面,但读者若没有耐心阅读那些提示,可能会误以为指的是"高人一等"的人。Dan G. Reid 翻译为 the worthy(有道德或有价值的人)并英译河上公

---

[1] 参见李为学.宋徽宗道德真经解义.赵佶,注.章安,解义.石曼璐,点校.上海:华东师范大学出版社,2017:15.

[2] 魏源.老子本义二卷.台北:汉京文化事业有限公司,1980:4.

注解，大意是不应该推崇遵礼徇法的世俗意义上的所谓"贤人"①，基本达意。赵彦春翻译为 paragon②(a person or thing that is perfect or has an extremely large amount of a particular good characteristic)，与反对过度突出典范人物的语境契合度最高。

争

理雅各译为 rivalry among themselves(民众之间相互较劲)，韦利译为 jealousies among the people(民众之间相互嫉妒)，都很形象地描绘出百姓争名逐利的场面。郝大维等的③ contentious(好争吵的)并不符合实际，百姓并非为了一逞口舌之能，而是为了争名利。

不贵难得之货

理雅各与郝大维等的译文(Not prizing property that is hard to come by)均使用头韵修辞进行翻译，不仅传达了原文意义，而且比原文更能够给读者带来审美愉悦。

不见可欲

前文都是在说君上应该采取何种做法以便趋利避害，合理引导民众，这句话也不应例外。

理雅各译文大意是"不在民众面前展露容易激起他们的欲望的事物"，是十分到位的。亨顿翻译为"Never flaunt alluring things."（不炫耀诱惑民众的东西），flaunt(炫耀)比理雅各的 show(展露)更有主观故意，更能够体现原文的劝阻的修辞意图。韦利译为 If the people never see such things as excite desire(假如民众永远不看这些可以激起他们的欲望的事物)，将"（君上）不给

---

① Dan G. Reid 译文为："'The worthy' refers here to those who are deemed by a generation's customs to be worthy. Their mouths are eloquent and their appearances are glorious, but they leave the Dao and chase power and authority. They discard (real) substance and fabricate appearances."。河上公注为"贤谓世俗之贤，辩口明文，离道行权，去质为文也"。Dan G. Reid 译文参见 The Ho-Shang Kung Commentary on Lao Tzu's Tao Te Ching. 2nd edition. Dan G. Reid, trans. Montreal：Center Ring Publishing, 2015.河上公原注参见河上公，等.道德经集释.北京：中国书店，2015：3.

② 道德经英译.赵彦春，译.北京：高等教育出版社，2018：36.

③ 安乐哲译"使民不争"为"will save the common people from becoming contentious"。参见 Dao De Jing：A Philosophical Translation. Roger T. Ames, David L. Hall, trans. New York：Ballantine Books, 2003.

（民众）看"翻译成"（民众）自己克制不去看"，未能体现原文所隐含的修辞者（君上）与受众（民众）的关系，尤其是修辞者如何采用恰当的修辞策略去影响目标受众的思想、感情、态度和行为。

使民心不乱

"乱"，理雅各使用 disorder(an illness of the mind or body) 翻译，容易让读者误以为是生理功能（如精神方面）的错乱，Cleary 翻译为 confused（混乱的），主要是指认知方面，都偏离了原文方向。韦利译"不乱"为 remain placid and undisturbed（平静且不受干扰），很形象地描绘了那份如水般淡定的心绪。

三、企者不立；跨者不行；自见者不明；自是者不彰；自伐者无功；自矜者不长。

——《道德经》第二十四章

He who stands on his tiptoes does not stand firm; he who stretches his legs does not walk (easily).(So), he who displays himself does not shine; he who asserts his own views is not distinguished; he who vaunts himself does not find his merit acknowledged; he who is self-conceited has no superiority allowed to him.

(理雅各 译)

One who stands on tiptoe cannot stand steady;
One who protracts his stride cannot walk far;
One who manifests himself abroad cannot be illustrious;
One who asserts himself cannot be distinguished;
One who indulges in self praise is without accomplishments;
One who wallows in self conceit cannot endure.

(杨有维 译)

陈鼓应对这句话的解读如下：

"翘起脚尖的反而站不牢，跨步行走的反而不能成行；自逞己见的反而不得自明；自以为是的，反而不得彰显；自己夸耀的，反而不得建功；自我矜持的，反而不得长久。"①

刘瑞符解读如下："举踵而立，以增其高，则立不能久，越人而行，欲超其前，则行不能长。以己之所见为见，而不以天下之所共见为见，则所见者私，故不能无所不见也。以己之所是为是，而非人之所是，人亦非其所是，则不能显

---

① 陈鼓应.老子今注今译及评介.台北：台湾商务印书馆，1984：23.

扬其是于世也。有功而自居,不能谦以推人,人不尽力,则不能成其功业也。矜夸其荣显,自以为贵大,人不尊崇从其贵大,则有危殆也。"①

**企者不立,跨者不行**

原文字面意思是"踮起脚尖站不住,迈大步走不动",后期的刘殿爵译文"He who tiptoes cannot stand; he who strides cannot walk."便是忠实地按字面翻译。但是如此处理,读者恐怕会困惑:技术上这些事并非完全不可能,为什么这么说呢?早期的理雅各译文在逻辑上替读者做了修补,调整为"站不稳"与"不好走",已经很通顺,若能将"不行"处理为"走不远"则逻辑更严密。Moss Roberts 译文"How long can you stand up on your toes? How far walk with stretching stride?"不仅传达了这个意思,还使用修辞疑问将读者裹挟进译文,带动读者思考并自行得出原文作者所要传达的结论。杨有维翻译的陈鼓应评论②则更进一步为读者指出本句隐喻(反自然的行径)这一修辞本质,点明文本劝阻(反对自炫的行为)的修辞目的。闵福德(John Minford)在翻译河上公的注解③时,除了把权(political power)翻译为力(force)这一处偏差,总体是忠实通顺的。Ron Hogan 的译文④从反面着笔,大意是"除非你想脸先

---

① 刘瑞符.老子章句浅释.何晓岩,校订.北京:社会科学文献出版社,2016:163-164.

② 杨有维译文为:"The first two phrases in this chapter are metaphors for manifesting oneself abroad, indulging in self-praise and wallowing in self-conceit. This kind of behavior is unnatural and cannot be maintained for long. This chapter explains that ostentatious behavior cannot be relied upon since it is contrary to nature, and as such, will collapse from within while meeting pressure and opposition from without. Following the Tao in one's conduct does not permit of excesses."杨有维译文参见 Chen Guying. Lao Tzu: Text, Notes, and Comments. Rhett Y.W. Young, Roger T. Ames, Trans. Taiwan: Chinese Materials Center, 1981:59. 陈鼓应评论参见陈鼓应.老子今注今译及评介.台北:台湾商务印书馆,1984:23.

③ 闵福德译文为:"Whosoever chooses Force, whosoever loves Glory and strives for Fame, will never stand upright for long in the Tao. Whosoever glorifies Self and places Self above Others, whosoever straddles Others, will find the way ahead obstructed, will be unable to walk forward."河上公注为:"谓贪权冒名,进取功荣,则不可久立身行道。自以为贵而跨之于人,众共蔽之,使不得行。"闵福德译文参见 Tao Te Ching: The Tao and the Power. John Minford, trans. New York: Penguin Random House, 2018:84. 河上公译文参见河上公,等.道德经集释.北京:中国书店,2015:33.

④ Ron Hogan 译文为:"Keep your feet firmly planted unless you want to fall on your face. Learn how to pace yourself if you want to get anywhere."参见 Tao Te Ching: A Modern Interpretation of Lao Tzu. Ron Hogan, Trans. [2021-04-15]. https://beatrice.com/TAO.txt.

着地(扑倒),否则就应该脚踏实地;如果想到达任何目的地,就得学会控制自己的步调"。虽然字面意思与原文相差无几,其隐喻的修辞效果却大相径庭,读起来似乎是在讨论肢体如何协调的运动生理学技术问题①,与刘瑞符所总结的"守'不争'之道"②相去甚远。

### 自见者不明

河上公将这句话解释为"缺乏自知之明"③固然合理,章安的解释(大意为"见即有所不见")④更加富有哲理。理雅各将"见"等同于"现",译文大意是爱表现自己的人不会出众。爱表现的人往往更容易被人注意到,只是究竟有无真才实学他人不得而知罢了,因此这一译文与常理不合。陈鼓应对本句的现代文翻译是"自逞己见的反而不得自明",强调的是自己的洞察力;杨有维译成"不会有名气",重点转向了个体是否为他人所认可。Stephen Mitchell 译文"He who tries to shine dims his own light."(爱出风头的反倒遮蔽了自己的优点或使得自己暗淡无光)虽然措辞优雅精巧,但关于"不明"的翻译强调的是无法让人发现自己的优点,哲学意涵远不如"自己看不见天下之所共见"深刻。许渊冲的译文 one who sees only himself has no good sight⑤(只能看到自己的人是短视的),基本翻译出"有所不见"的意思,但是主要是说视力不佳或看得不远,意境还有待提升。陈乃扬的译文"Clairvoyant is he not, because he sees only himself.⑥"(只能看到自己的人是没有洞察力的),虽然个别措辞如 clairvoyant(未卜先知者)略显夸张,总体上与"见即有所不见"的意思比较接近。

### 自是者不彰

这句话宋常星解读为"我以己之是取胜于人,人亦以己之是取胜于我。我之见既不能信于人,终是私慧小智,不可公诸天下后世,岂非不彰乎?"⑦,从修辞话语互动角度而言,与现实情境高度契合,十分可取。理雅各与杨有维译文均

---

① 这一译文对于反思反译法的修辞功效倒是不无启发,因篇幅所限,拟另文探讨。
② 刘瑞符原注为:"欲高于人,欲超于人,皆不能长久。言当守'不争'之道也。"参见刘瑞符.老子章句浅释.何晓岩,校订.北京:社会科学文献出版社,2016:162.
③ 河上公原注为:"凡人自见其形容以为好,自见其所行以为人道,殊不自知其形丑而操行之鄙。"参见河上公,等.道德经集释.北京:中国书店,2015:33.
④ 章安原注为:"自见者,弊于一曲。不自见者,合而为明。"参见赵佶,注.章安,解义.宋徽宗道德真经解义.上海:华东师范大学出版社,2017:82.
⑤ 道德经:汉英对照.许渊冲,译.北京:五洲传播出版社,2011:30.
⑥ 英译老子:汉英对照.陈乃扬,译.上海:上海外语教育出版社,2012:49.
⑦ 刘瑞符.老子章句浅释.何晓岩,校订.北京:社会科学文献出版社,2016:164.

使用 assert [to state or declare positively and often forcefully or aggressively/to compel or demand acceptance or recognition of(something,such as one's authority)]翻译"是",不仅能够表达出 considers himself right①(认为自己是正确的)的含义,也能够传达出好将一己之见强加于人乃至时刻准备下场与人争论(combative readiness)的话语意图。但是对于"不彰",使用静态描绘(不突出、不卓越)的翻译无法将原文蕴含的追求卓越的动态过程凸显出来。Stephen Addiss、Stanley Lombardo 的译文②使用 no way to(非其道)体现了动态过程,虽然用 succeed(成功)翻译"彰"稍显宽泛,但总体上成功传达了原文的劝勉的修辞意图。许渊冲译文"Who thinks only himself right cannot be recognized."(认为只有自己才是对的,这样的人不会得到他人认可),关于"彰"的翻译不仅更具体,还更好地体现了原文暗含的"话语互动中修辞者建构的修辞人格会影响受众决定采取何种态度/行动"这一预设。因自以为是而被他人否定,这实在是再自然不过的事情。这一解读合情合理,容易为读者所接受。

### 自伐者无功

刘兆英把这句话解读为"那种只会自我吹嘘的人什么事也干不成"。虽然对于"自伐"的理解与主流解读"不以功劳与人而自居其功"还有一定距离,对于"无功"的解读则不可谓明白晓畅。理雅各译文大意为"自夸的人,他人不认可其功绩",并未否定这样的人取得成就的可能,与"无功"(不能成其功业)意思有较大偏差。韦利译文"He who boasts of what he will do succeeds in nothing."(吹嘘自己宏大计划的人往往一事无成)并未涉及与他人抢功这个问题。杨有维译文"One who indulges in self praise is without accomplishments." 与 Hogan 译文"Nobody gives credit to people who always take it."(老抢功的人,没有人会把功劳给他)比较明确地翻译出自居其功的意思,但后者问题在于他人不给抢功者记功,并没有完全否认抢功者有可能取得成就,因此与原文还有距离。

### 自矜者不长

理雅各译文"He who is self-conceited has no superiority allowed to him."(自大的人没有优势),究竟在哪方面没有优势语焉不详。杨有维使用短

---

① 刘殿爵译文为:"He who considers himself right is not illustrious."。参见道德经:英汉双语.刘殿爵,英译.章婉凝,译注.北京:中国对外翻译出版有限公司,2012:106.

② Stephen Addiss 等的译文为:"Self-assertion:no way to succeed."。参见 Lao Tzu. Tao Te Ching. Stephen Addiss, Stanley Lombardo, trans. Indianapolis:Hackett Publishing Company, Inc.,1993.

语 wallow in(纵情于),其字面意思是"(像动物一般)在(泥、沙中)……打滚",生动地传递了原文对这一行为的负面评价,但是说自大者不长久在逻辑上并不严密,严格来说应该是这样的行为没有可持续性。Julian von Bargen 等的译文"Complacency is no way to endure."(自鸣得意者不可能笑到最后)逻辑更严密。关于这个"长",翻译界有不少学者解读为"当上司/领导",如林语堂译文"He who prides himself is not chief among men."(自负的人当不了领导),Patrick Edwin Moran 译文"Those who boast on themselves will not be senior."(自夸者不可能成为上级),许渊冲译文"One who thinks himself superior cannot be a leader."(自觉高人一等的人当不了领导)。从现实角度而言,自大者短时间居上位是可能的,但是必然不能久居其位,因此从时间维度理解这个"长"远比从"身份/地位"角度理解更符合语境。

四、将欲歙之,必固张之;将欲弱之,必固强之;将欲废之,必固兴之;将欲取之,必固与之。

——《道德经》第三十六章

  When one is about to take an inspiration, he is sure to make a (previous) expiration; when he is going to weaken another, he will first strengthen him; when he is going to overthrow another, he will first have raised him up; when he is going to despoil another, he will first have made gifts to him.  (理雅各 译)

  Should you want to contain something, you must deliberately let it expand. Should you want to weaken something, you must deliberately let it grow strong. Should you want to eliminate something, you must deliberately allow it to flourish. Should you want to take something away, you must deliberately grant it.

(Thomas Cleary 译)

What seeks to shrink
must first have grown;
what seeks weakness
surely was strong.
What seeks its ruin
must first have risen;
what seeks to take
has surely given.

(勒古恩 译)

**将欲歙之,必固张之**

这句话一向有争议,至少有两种解读。一种是把它当作事物对立面互相转化的自然状态的描绘(下文姑且称之为自然说):所谓物极必反、势强必弱,张开来是闭合的一种微兆①,当事物发展到极限时,难免会朝相反的方向运转。另外一种解读则是将它看成人类有意加以使用的智谋或策略(下文姑且称之为干预说)。陈鼓应明确反对干预说的"阴谋论"解读②。

刘瑞符将本句解读为"将欲毁败敌人,必姑且使之侈大骄满,而后能败之也"。③ 显然是支持干预说。采取自然说翻译进路的冯家福等译文"That which shrinks must first expand."(要收缩的首先要膨胀)虽然大方向是对的,但是没能将译文明确指向"物之将歙,必是本来已张(实然状态)"这一排除人类干预的预设,而是留下了"物之将歙而待张(应然状态)"的误读的空间,读者会困惑为什么不能直接收缩而非要多此一举。④ 杨有维基于陈鼓应注解翻译为"If one desires to gather something up, he must first spread it out."(如果要收敛一个东西,首先要把它铺张开来),并未真正体现陈的诠释意图(将要合起来,必先张开),也就是排除人为干预,纯粹描绘客观现象或规律;倒是在翻译陈鼓应引用的董思靖的观点"物之将歙,必是本来已张,然后歙者随之"(If something is going to be gathered up it must already be spread out)时,更靠近陈的诠释。就翻译而言,勒古恩(Ursula K. Le Guin)译文最为接近自然说,不足之处是使用了 seeks(谋求),显得不够纯粹。就注解而言,Stefan Stenudd 注解指出老子本节提到的并非相反的固定状态,而是相反的方向或动作。歙与张方向相反但是如呼吸一般彼此互相依存。整个宇宙都在一刻不停

---

① 此为陈鼓应解读。参见陈鼓应.老子今注今译及评介.台北:台湾商务印书馆,1984:143.

② 陈鼓应提到:"不幸这段文字被误解为含有阴谋的思想,而韩非是造成曲解的第一个大罪人,后来的注释家也很少能够把这段话讲清楚。"参见陈鼓应.老子今注今译及评介.台北:台湾商务印书馆,1984:143.

③ 刘瑞符.老子章句浅释.何晓岩,校订.北京:社会科学文献出版社,2016:237.

④ 新世纪译者中吴千之将这句话译为:"If you want to close something, you must first open it."。吴千之译文也有类似问题:关门是一步到位的事情,为何先要把它再开大些而后行关闭之举? 吴千之译文参见吴千之.老子如是说:《道德经》新注新译.北京:外语教学与研究出版社,2013:82.

地运动变化着①。安乐哲等的译注指出这里描绘的是"反者道之动,弱者道之用"的原理②。任何具体的情境或条件最终都不免要向其对立面转化。这些注解都为读者了解原文意涵提供了极大的便利,同时提升了译文的哲学高度,对中国文化对外传播有着十分积极的意义。

采纳干预说诠释进路的译者如理雅各把这句话翻译为"When one is about to take an inspiration, he is sure to make a (previous) expiration."(当一个人要吸一口气时,他肯定要先呼出一口气)。其译句内容本身乃是举世公认的真理,观点是无懈可击的,但是结合其译文上下文则与文势明显龃龉。读者会发现理雅各译文其他句子都是针对特定对象需要采取的行动的建议,独有第一句是对人尽皆知的一个生理现象的描绘,也就是说,这一句译文更像是另外一个诠释方向的产物。林语堂译文③与Cleary译文④都凸显了人为策略

---

① Stefan Stenudd 注解原文为:"Ancient Chinese thought is often done in polarities, like yin and yang. They are not alone in that. In many traditions around the world, existence is seen as the dynamics between two opposites. They may be light and dark, high and low, hot and cold, life and death, good and bad, and so on. Lao Tzu is also fond of it, although he sees a single unity, Tao, at the very root of it all. In this chapter he mentions examples of opposite directions or actions, instead of opposite fixed states. Stretching is one direction, shrinking is its opposite. What he claims about their relation implies mutual dependence, comparable to what happens in our breathing. We must inhale before we can exhale, and exhale before we can inhale. There is no ideal middle point between exhalation and inhalation. If we remain there we suffocate. The opposites are interacting continuously. It's never just one or the other, not even a resting place between them. Things shrink or expand, they are weakened or strengthened, but never completely still. People are cherished or abolished, enriched or deprived, but never stay for long in one solid state of affairs. The whole universe is all about movement and change."。参见 Stefan Stenudd. Tao Te Ching: The Taoism of Lao Tzu Explained. Malmö: Arriba, 2011.

② 安乐哲等译注原文为:"/This chapter begins by describing the mutual implication of opposites, a phenomenon that is pervasive in our experience of the world. This is the same insight we find in chapter 40: '"Returning" is how way-making moves, and "weakening" is how it functions.' Any particular situation or condition that is most potent in its inchoate beginnings ultimately and inevitably gives way to its opposite/"。参见 Dao De Jing: A Philosophical Translation. Roger T. Ames, David L. Hall, trans. New York: Ballantine Books, 2003:133.

③ 林语堂译文为:"He who is to be made to dwindle (in power) must first be caused to expand."。(要消减某人势力,必须先让其势力膨胀)参见林语堂.老子的智慧:汉英对照.黄嘉德,译.长沙:湖南文艺出版社,2021:274.

④ 意为"如果你要遏制一个事物,就应该故意让它扩大"。

这样的解读,但是都没有对采取这样的策略的原因进行解释。安乐哲等的在译注中反对一些注者追随韩非子将本节看作是为了占上风而有意加以使用的政治谋略。他们认为"基于这一解读,慷慨大方就变成了处心积虑以颠覆他人的手段,'与'最终只是为了'取'"。其反对的主要理由就是这种利己主义的操控手段与道家的精神旨趣相冲突。① 假如不考虑安乐哲等人自身对这个话题的学术立场,其关于操控手段的解析倒是可以作为干预说诠释进路的注脚。

*将欲弱之,必固强之*

自然说译者冯家福等的译文"That which fails must first be strong."(要衰落的首先要强盛)没有出现人的因素,比较符合自然规律诠释进路,但是和前面一句的译文存在相同逻辑漏洞。译句固然可以理解为"要衰落的必定先是强盛的",但也不能排除"要衰落的必须先变得强盛"这样的解读。就现实情形而言,不少事物天生底子就薄弱,几乎是从未经历过强盛的高光时刻就衰灭了,因此这一译文很难令读者完全信服。勒古恩译文用了一个 was(一度是)明白无误地把这个先(强)后(弱)关系富有逻辑地呈现出来。

刘瑞符解读为"将欲衰敌之力,弱敌之势,必姑且先使之强梁横暴,自贻其祸(强者必遇其敌,而强者亦为众之所攻也。),而后图之也"。② 采纳智谋或策略说诠释进路的译者包括理雅各与林语堂,两者译文虽然一个采用主动语态,一个采用被动语态翻译③,但都明确翻译出提倡主动使用策略削弱对手这一点,可谓殊途同归。

*将欲废之,必固兴之*

原本持自然说的译者冯家福等将这句话翻译成"That which is cast down must first be raised."(要被推翻的首先要被抬高),和理雅各翻译第一句的失误很相似,似乎都不自觉地走向了对手的阵营。由于两处使用了被动态,读者很难再把这个表述和自然说联系起来,就译文效果而言,可以说是与原本翻译

---

① 安乐哲等注解原文为:"Some commentators follow Han Feizi in interpreting this passage as a conscious political strategy for having one's way. In wanting to accomplish great things, you initiate policy surreptitiously. On this reading, generosity is a calculated strategy used to subvert other people: You give in order to get. But such self-serving manipulation is not consistent with Daoist sensibilities." 参见 Dao De Jing: A Philosophical Translation. Roger T. Ames, David L. Hall, trans. New York: Ballantine Books, 2003: 133.

② 刘瑞符.老子章句浅释.何晓岩,校订.北京:社会科学文献出版社,2016:238.

③ 林语堂译文为:"He who is to be weakened must first be made strong."。参见林语堂.老子的智慧:汉英对照.黄嘉德,译.长沙:湖南文艺出版社,2021:274.

意图背道而驰了。勒古恩译文在兴与废的先后问题上逻辑一如既往地明晰,而且使用头韵修辞让译文读者以另外一种形式感受了原文之美,只是使用 seek 难免让读者有"事物自取灭亡"的联想,与事物自然衰亡的意思尚有一定距离。

"欲倾覆灭亡敌人,必先姑且示以推奉之诚,尊之以高名,自处以卑下,而悦其心,取其信,以懈其防而后图之也。"①持干预说的译者理雅各译文使用 overthrow,与林语堂使用 laid low②(to cause someone to be unable to do what they usually do)都是针对有权力的对手,以削弱其影响力为目标;Cleary 则依然是以事物为对象,以彻底清除(不留后患)为目标③。均能够自圆其说。

将欲取之,必固与之

持自然说的译者冯家福等翻译为"Before receiving there must be giving."(接受前总要有给予),道理自然是无懈可击,但是把主动索取(take)翻译为被动接收(receive),与原文有较大偏差。勒古恩译文"What seeks to take has surely given."(要拿走的,必然是给过的)与这一诠释进路更契合。

苏辙在技术层面是赞成从智谋角度(干预说)解读这句话的,但是觉得老子的圣人修辞人格(ethos)有可能因此受损,在情感上无法接受"圣人"老子与管仲、孙武等并无二致这一可能的结论,于是采取修辞离解(dissociation)策略,通过建构并应用"乘理"与"用智"④这一价值差将老子与其他人拉开距离,以使其鹤立鸡群,从而维护其修辞人格。刘瑞符解读为"将欲取敌,必先姑且施之与敌,迎合其贪欲之心而图之也。遣之以贿赂,献之以珠宝,赠之以美女,委之以大利,皆是也"。⑤持干预说的译者理雅各译文大意

---

① 刘瑞符.老子章句浅释.何晓岩,校订.北京:社会科学文献出版社,2016:238-239.
② 林语堂译文为:"He who is to be laid low must first be exalted to power."。参见林语堂.老子的智慧:汉英对照.黄嘉德,译.长沙:湖南文艺出版社,2021:274.
③ Thomas Cleary 译文为:"Should you want to eliminate something, you must deliberately allow it to flourish."。参见 The Essential Tao. Thomas Cleary, trans. New York: HarperOne,1993.
④ 苏辙注曰:"未尝与之而遽夺,则势有所不极,理有所不足。势不极则取之难,理不足则物不服。然此几于用智也,与管仲、孙武何异,圣人之与世俗,其迹固有相似者也。圣人乘理,而世俗用智。乘理如医药巧于应病,用智如商贾巧于射利。"参见河上公,等.道德经集释.北京:中国书店,2015:313.
⑤ 刘瑞符.老子章句浅释.何晓岩,校订.北京:社会科学文献出版社,2016:239-240.

为(要夺取①另外一个人的东西,首先就要送礼物给他),使用despoil(夺取)倒是营造了充满冲突的氛围,更能够凸显使用策略的必要性;此外,理雅各译文尤其能够表达以小换大这么一层意思。杨有维译文"If one desires to take something from others, he must first give them something."(如果有人想要从其他人那里拿到一些东西,首先就得给对方一些东西),译者两次使用something,未能体现出是两个不同价值的东西,就不如理雅各译文明晰。Thomas Cleary使用grant(准予),行政权力的意味太浓厚,反而使得原来的哲学文本扁平化。Ron Hogan翻译为"To take something, you must give it up entirely."(要得到一个东西,就必须完全放弃它),这一译文与使用策略以小博大的文本意思相去甚远。韦利译文"He who would be a taker must begin as a giver."使用名词倒是避免了纠缠"取"和"与"的对象、数量与方式的细节,但是稍显模糊,未能超越之前理雅各的译文。

五、名与身孰亲?身与货孰多?得与亡孰病?是故甚爱必大费,多藏必厚亡。

——《道德经》第四十四章

> Or fame or life,
> Which do you hold more dear?
> Or life or wealth,
> To which would you adhere?
> Keep life and lose those other things;
> Keep them and lose your life:—which brings
> Sorrow and pain more near?
> Thus we may see,
> Who cleaves to fame
> Rejects what is more great;

---

① 理雅各显然是按照"将欲夺之"这个版本翻译这句话的。学术界对究竟是"夺"还是"取"有不同看法。按陈鼓应的说法,"王弼本原作'夺',河上公本及其他古本亦作'夺',惟韩非喻老篇引作'取',范应元本及彭耜本亦作'取'。范本同于原本,应予以改正。"刘瑞符认为是"夺",同时认为"夺"等同于"取"。陈鼓应注解参见陈鼓应.老子今注今译及评介.台北:台湾商务印书馆,1984:141.刘瑞符注解参见刘瑞符.老子章句浅释.何晓岩,校订.北京:社会科学文献出版社,2016:239.

Who loves large stores

Gives up the richer state. （理雅各 译）

Fame or one's own self, which matters to one most? One's own self or things bought, which should count most? In the getting or the losing, which is worse?① Hence he who grudges② expense pays dearest in the end; He who has hoarded most will suffer the heaviest loss. （韦利 译）

### 名与身孰亲

理雅各译文大意为"名气与生命,你更重视哪一个?",译文固然忠实,但是没有对名做出充分说明,失去了一个对外传播中国文化关键词的机会。Moss Roberts 注解提到:"Ming, 'name', includes honor, face, fame, title, and rank, as well as personal terms of address—all of which register social status and function."(名包括荣誉、面子、名声、头衔和等级,以及个人称谓——这些都是社会地位和职责的象征),给读者提供了极具中国文化特色的关于名的解读,使得译文不至于流于片面。Stefan Stenudd 的注解提到"Why do we risk this life by filling it with things that we don't really need? The only real treasure is life itself. Nothing else can possibly compare to it, much less surpass it. But we easily forget that, when pursuing one or other superficial happiness."(我们为什么要冒着生命危险用我们实际上不需要的东西填充我们的生活?生命本身就是最大的财富。没有什么东西可以与它相提并论,遑论能超越它。但是我们一门心思追求这样或者那样肤浅的幸福的时候,很容易就忘记了这一点。),以最为通俗的语言为读者就本句的哲学意涵做了解读,回答了不少读者可能存在的困惑。

### 身与货孰多

陈鼓应在评论这一节时指出常人多轻生而殉名利,贪得而不顾危亡,并进

---

① 此处原注为:"i.e. which is better, to get fame and wealth but injure oneself, or to lack fame and wealth and save oneself?"。参见 Tao Te Ching. Arthur Waley, trans. Hertfordshire: Wordsworth Editions Ltd, 1997: 47.

② 原注为:"For ai in the sense "grudge"..."He who is stingy about rewards and gifts is called ai". The primary meaning of ai is to want to keep to oneself, hence the commoner meaning 'to love', which would here be out of place."。参见 Tao Te Ching. Arthur Waley, trans. Hertfordshire: Wordsworth Editions Ltd, 1997: 47.

一步点明老子的修辞意图在于"唤醒世人要贵重生命,不可为名利而奋不顾身"。① 理雅各译文"生命与财富,你追求哪一个?"是达意的。韦利译文把"货"望文生义地译为买来的货物,比较狭隘,其实应该是指物质财富。许渊冲译文"Which do you like more, health or wealth?"(健康与财富,你更喜欢哪一个?)通过押尾韵的方式让这句话朗朗上口,不仅在思想上表达了原文的意思,某种意义上还在语言审美层面对原作有所超越。Marc S. Mullinax译文"Body or wealth? Which would you give up first?"(如果非要放弃一个,你愿意先放弃哪个?是身体健康还是财富呢?),通过视角转换从反面着手进行提问,裹挟受众、引发深度反思并引导受众依照暗含的价值判断指引采取相应行动。该译文所使用的修辞疑问(rhetorical question)委婉(体现在给了受众选择权)而又不言自明地(几乎所有稍具理想的人都知道面对这样的问题该如何取舍)传递了原文的价值取向,比起平淡无奇地从正面去翻译这个问题要成功得多。

### 得与亡孰病

刘瑞符解释道:得到名利与伤亡生命相比较,何者为害?② 告诫人们不要以身殉名/利。理雅各译为"保有生命而失去名利或是得到名利而失去生命,这两种选择哪一个更容易带来悲哀与痛苦?",在逻辑上滴水不漏,读者看了很容易对译文产生认同感。韦利译为"得到或者失去,哪一个更糟糕?",本身令人困惑,但是注解(从另外一个角度解读)倒是令人豁然开朗:得到名利而损害自身与失去名利但保全性命,哪一个更好? 林语堂翻译为"Loss(of self) or possession(of goods), which is the greater evil?"(丢掉性命或拥有财富,哪一个更不利?),则不免令对道家哲学不甚了知的读者感到困惑:丢掉性命固然不妙,拥有财富又有什么不好呢?

### 是故甚爱必大费,多藏必厚亡

刘瑞符对这一句的解读是:"不知生之重于名,而热衷于名,不知所止,劳

---

① 杨有维英译为:"Lao Tzu observes that many people tend to disregard their own persons in the pursuit for reputation and personal advantage. They are avaricious while remaining wholly unaware of the sacrifices they must make in order to obtain these things. They fail to consider the price they must pay and the dangers which they bring upon themselves."。参见 Chen Guying. Lao Tzu: Text, Notes, and Comments. Rhett Y. W. Young, Roger T. Ames, Trans. Taiwan: Chinese Materials Center, 1981:214.

② 刘瑞符.老子章句浅释.何晓岩,校订.北京:社会科学文献出版社,2016:290.

心费神,而损及生命,所损甚大也。不知生之重于货,蓄积贮藏,不知所足,贪而无厌,致损及生命,所失甚大也。"①

　　理雅各译"甚爱"与"多藏"是到位的,但是使用带有意志与情感色彩、表达主动选择行为的"拒斥"(reject)与"放弃"(give up)翻译"必"则与原文精神相悖,原文恰恰是要表达即便名与利的追求者想长期保有它们,也是必然要失去的,这是难以抗拒、无可奈何的现实,绝非可以主动选择的。韦利译把"爱"理解为"舍不得""小气",与"热衷(于名)"的意思差距较大。冯家福等的译文"He who is attached to things will suffer much."使用 attached(依恋,喜爱),把无法割舍的状态体现得淋漓尽致,同时(与韦利一样)使用 suffer 明确表达了遭受损失这一客观结果。对于"多藏必厚亡",闵福德译文"Hoarding entails heavy loss."言简意赅,同时还使用头韵修辞格传递了原文的意义。刘殿爵译文"Too much store is sure to end in immense loss."用"落得"(end in)翻译"必",巧妙传达了原作对这个行为的否定态度。

## 本章参考的英译本

英译老子:汉英对照.陈乃扬,译.上海:上海外语教育出版社,2012.

林语堂.老子的智慧:汉英对照.黄嘉德,译.长沙:湖南文艺出版社,2021.

道德经:英汉双语.刘殿爵,英译,章婉凝,白话文翻译、注释.北京:中国对外翻译出版有限公司,2011.

吴千之.老子如是说:《道德经》新注新译.北京:外语教学与研究出版社,2013.

道德经:汉英对照.许渊冲,译.北京:五洲传播出版社,2011.

道德经英译.赵彦春,译.北京:高等教育出版社,2018.

Chen Guying. Lao Tzu:Text, Notes, and Comments. Rhett Y. W. Young, Roger T. Ames, Trans. Taiwan:Chinese Materials Center,1981.

Dao De Jing:A Philosophical Translation.Roger T. Ames, David L. Hall, Trans. New York:Ballantine Books,2003.

Dao De Jing:The Book of the Way.Moss Roberts,Trans. Berkeley:University of California Press,2004.

---

① 刘瑞符.老子章句浅释.北京:社会科学文献出版社,2016:291.

Dao De Jing: The Way and Its Power. Patrick Edwin Moran, Trans. Washington: University Press of America, 2009.

Lao Tzu. Tao Te Ching. Stephen Addiss, Stanley Lombardo, Trans. Indianapolis: Hackett Publishing Company, Inc., 1993.

Ursula K. Le Guin. Tao Te Ching: A Book about the Way and the Power of the Way. Boston: Shambhala Publications, 1997.

Stefan Stenudd. Tao Te Ching: The Taoism of Lao Tzu Explained. Malmö: Arriba, 2011.

Tao Te Ching. Gia Fu Feng et al., Trans. London: Vintage Books, 1974.

The Essential Tao. Thomas Cleary, Trans. New York: HarperOne, 1993.

Tao Te Ching. Arthur Waley, trans. Hertfordshire: Wordsworth Editions Ltd., 1997.

Tao Te Ching: A New English Version. Stephen Mitchell, Trans. New York: Harper Perennial Modern Classics, 2006.

Tao Te Ching or The Tao and Its Characteristic. James Legge, Trans. Auckland: The Floating Press, 2008.

The Ho-Shang Kung Commentary on Lao Tzu's Tao Te Ching: 2nd Edition. Dan G. Reid, Trans. Montreal: Center Ring Publishing, 2015.

Tao Te Ching: A Modern Interpretation of Lao Tzu. Ron Hogan, trans. [2021-04-15]. https//beatrice.com/TAO.txt.

Tao Te Ching: The Tao and the Power. John Minford, Trans. New York: Penguin Random House, 2018.

Tao Te Ching: Power for the Peaceful. Marc S. Mullinax, Trans. Minneapolis: Fortress Press, 2021.

Tao Te Ching. Julian von Bargen et al., Trans. [2024-10-25]. https//z-lib.org.

# 第四章 《庄子》英译比较与评析

一、罔两问景曰:"曩子行,今子止;曩子坐,今子起;何其无特操与?"景曰:"吾有待而然者邪?吾所待又有待而然者邪?吾待蛇蚹蜩翼邪?恶识所以然!恶识所以不然!"

——《庄子·齐物论》①

The Penumbra said to the Umbra, "At one moment you move; at another you are at rest. At one moment you sit down; at another you get up. Why this instability of purpose?" "I depend," replied the Umbra, "upon something which causes me to do as I do; and that something depends in turn upon something else which causes it to do as it does. My dependence is like that of a snake's scales or of a cicada's wings, which do not move of their own accord. How can I tell why I do one thing, or why I do not do another?"

(Showing how two or more may be the phenomena of one.)　(翟里斯 译)

The Penumbra asked the Shadow, saying, "At one moment, you move; at another, you are at rest. At one moment, you sit down; at another, you stand up. Why this instability of purpose?"

"Do I have to depend upon something else," replied the Shadow, "in order to be what I am? Does that something upon which I depend still have to depend upon something else in order to be what it is? Do I have to depend upon the scales of a snake or the wings of a cicada? How can I tell why I am so, or why I am not otherwise?"

This shows that everything is spontaneously what it is. One needs only to fol-

---

① 若无特别说明,本章所涉及《庄子》引文均出自《庄子今注今译》。出处详见陈鼓应.庄子今注今译.北京:商务印书馆,2016.

low one's nature and not to ask why one is so and not otherwise.—Tr.

(冯友兰 译)

Penumbra said to Shadow, "A little while ago you were walking and now you're standing still; a little while ago you were sitting and now you're standing up. Why this lack of independent action?"

Shadow said, "Do I have to wait for something before I can be like this? Does what I wait for also have to wait for something before it can be like this? Am I waiting for the scales of a snake or the wings of a cicada? How do I know why it is so? How do I know why it isn't so?"① (华兹生 译)

王叔岷对这节的解读是:"物各自然,各不相待,虽影亦不待形,有待则言辩无穷,不能齐矣。"②

罔两③问景

翟里斯(Herbert A. Giles)翻译使用 The Penumbra said to the Umbra(半影问本影),penumbra④ 与 umbra⑤ 在表达明暗差异上无疑是准确的,并

---

① 此处原注为:"That is, to ordinary men the shadow appears to depend upon something else for its movement, just as the snake depends on its scales(according to Chinese belief)and the cicada on its wings. But do such causal views of action really have any meaning?"。参见 Chuang Tzu: Basic Writings. Burton Watson, trans. New York: Columbia University Press,1964:44.

② 王叔岷.庄子校诠.北京:中华书局,2007:95.

③ 严复解释道:"凡物之非此非彼者曰'罔两'。魑魅罔两之'罔两',介于人鬼物魅之间。间影之'罔两',介于光阴明暗之间,天文家所谓'暗虚'。室中有二灯,则所成之影皆暗虚,必两光之所不及者,乃为真影。"崔大华.庄子歧解.北京:中华书局,2012:102.

④ penumbra 在词典中主要有四个定义:"1.the partially shaded outer region of the shadow cast by an opaque object[(不透明物体投射的)阴影的外围半阴暗部分]。2.(Astronomy)the shadow cast by the earth or moon over an area experiencing a partial eclipse{[天文](日食、月食的)半影}。3.(Astronomy)the less dark outer part of a sunspot, surrounding the dark core{[天文]半影(太阳黑子周围较淡的部分)}。4.Any area of partial shade(半阴影)。"。参见 Judy Pearsall, Patrick Hanks, Catherine Soanes, et al.新牛津英汉双解大词典.本词典编译出版委员会,编译.上海:上海外语教育出版社,2007:1575.

⑤ umbra 在词典中主要有三个定义:"1.the fully shaded inner region of a shadow cast by an opaque object, especially the area on the earth or moon experiencing the total phase of an eclipse(暗影;本影)。2.(Astronomy)the dark central part of a sunspot{[天文](太阳黑子中心)}。3.chiefly poetic/liter. any shadow or darkness(〈主诗/文〉荫,阴影)"。参见 Judy Pearsall, Patrick Hanks, Catherine Soanes, et al.新牛津英汉双解大词典.本词典编译出版委员会,编译.上海:上海外语教育出版社,2007:2294.

因为押尾韵而显得十分优美,但同时也因为天文学术语这一辞屏将读者的注意力导向科学问题,从而偏离了源文本的哲学方向。Brook Ziporyn 使用押头韵的 shade[comparative darkness or obscurity owing to interception of the rays of light/shelter(as by foliage)from the heat and glare of sunlight]和 shadow(the dark figure cast upon a surface by a body intercepting the rays from a source of light/partial darkness or obscurity within a part of space from which rays from a source of light are cut off by an interposed opaque body/an inseparable companion or follower),虽然在语言表达上同样很优美,也表达了不同的黑暗程度,但是因为两词经常在宽泛意义上作为同义词使用,读者很难读出语义方面的差异,也就体会不到原文的修辞意图。理雅各的及后出的冯友兰等的译本使用 the Penumbra 与 the Shadow,既能够体现"影外之微影"与"影"的差异,又借助通俗易懂的常见词语 shadow 避免了拒读者于千里之外。

囊子行,今子止;囊子坐,今子起,何其无特操与

"特操",王叔岷①考证认为是"持操",文从字顺。华兹生重复使用 a little while ago(刚才/不久前)与 and now(现在)进行对比,从修辞方面成功再现了"景"反复无常的"无特操"行为。"无特操",华兹生译为"缺乏独立行动能力",也就是"没主见"的意思,更多是能力的问题而非品格的问题。Mair 翻译为"Why are you so lacking in constancy?",表达了对"景"缺乏定性、善变的质疑。Palmer 翻译为"Why can't you make up your mind?"(你为什么举棋不定/摇摆不定?),主要还是责备"景"缺乏决断力。

吾有待而然者邪? 吾所待又有待而然者邪?

翟里斯把这个修辞疑问句翻译为肯定句,虽然语义接近,但是效果大不相同。就本句上下文语境而言,使用修辞疑问可以定向指派话语责任,有助于将读者裹挟进来一起思考哲学命题,形成一个哲学对话。而使用肯定句则变为自说自话,不仅疏离受众还容易因为没有给予足够论据支撑观点而让人怀疑修辞者太过武断。理雅各把"有待而然"译为"I wait for the movements of something else to do what I do."(等待别的东西的动作以决定自己的行动),不如冯友兰"依赖别的事物以成就自己的存在"更能再现原文的哲学意味。华兹生译文增加一个"have to"(不得不),比理雅各客观一些,但依然是望文生义地将"待"翻译为"等待"而非"取决于";用"像这样"翻译"然"不如冯友兰的"我的存在"深刻。

---

① 王叔岷.庄子校诠.北京:中华书局,2007:95.

## 吾待蛇蚹蜩翼邪

王叔岷认为"此文待疑本作似",陈鼓应翻译为"就像蛇有依靠于腹下鳞皮、蝉有待于翅膀",这一解读在逻辑上很合理。翟里斯就是顺着"似"这个思路翻译,但在翻译内容方面是从相反方向落笔:我的有所待就好比蛇皮与蝉翼依附在蛇与蝉身上一样,译文进一步增补说明皮与翼均无法自主行动。译文还漏译了"邪",使得修辞疑问变成了肯定,问题如前句分析,在此不赘。Ziporyn 也是顺着"似"这个思路翻译①,但是把蜩翼翻译为蜩甲(shell),总体上无伤大雅。冯友兰译文大意是"我需要依靠蛇皮蝉翼吗?",与前文逻辑存在断层,因而缺乏对读者的说服力。华兹生译文大意是"我在等待蛇皮蝉翼吗?",在上下文中显得突兀且令人困惑。

## 恶识所以然!恶识所以不然!

翟里斯译文大意是"我怎么能知道为什么会去做一件事情,或者为什么不做另一件事情呢?",强调的是行为而非状态,与原文有差距。但是注解则替读者提炼了话语的修辞意图:"多个现象在本质上可以是同一的"。冯友兰译文大意是"我怎么能明白自己为什么会是这样的存在而不是以另外的状态存在?",并增加注解说"万类皆自尔",人人只需顺其本性,不必追问为什么是这样的状态而不是那样的状态。华兹生译文为"我怎么能知道它为什么是这样,为什么不是这样?",与前文句子存在逻辑裂纹;但是其注解②对关于行为的因果观的解构与原文的话语修辞意图是吻合的。Mair 的译文最为简洁明了——"How can I tell why I am what I am? How can I tell why I'm not what I'm not?",其中"我之所以是我"颇有哲学意味,成功传达了原文精神。

二、昔者庄周梦为胡蝶,栩栩然胡蝶也,自喻适志与!不知周也。俄然觉,则蘧蘧然周也。不知周之梦为胡蝶与,胡蝶之梦为周与?周与胡蝶,则必有分矣。此之谓物化。

——《庄子·齐物论》

---

① 译文为:"Do I depend on it as a snake does on its skin, or a cicada on its shell?"。参见 Zhuangzi: The Essential Writings with Selections from Traditional Commentaries. Brook Ziporyn, trans. Indianapolis: Hackett Publishing Company, Inc., 2009:21.

② "换言之,在普通人看来,影子的运动依赖于其他事物的运动,就像蛇依赖皮得以爬行(这是中国人的一种观念)、蝉依靠翅膀才得以飞行一样。但是关于行为的这种因果观真的有意义吗?"

Once upon a time, I, Chuang Tz, dreamt I was a butterfly, fluttering hither and thither, to all intents and purposes a butterfly. I was conscious only of following my fancies as a butterfly, and was unconscious of my individuality as a man. Suddenly, I awaked, and there I lay, myself again. Now I do not know whether I was then a man dreaming I was a butterfly, or whether I am now a butterfly dreaming I am a man. Between a man and a butterfly there is necessarily a barrier. The transition is called Metempsychosis.

(Showing how one may appear to be either of two.) （翟里斯 译）

Once upon a time, Chuang Chou dreamed that he was a butterfly, a butterfly flying about, enjoying itself. It did not know that it was Chuang Chou. Suddenly he awoke and veritably was Chuang Chou again. We do not know whether it was Chuang Chou dreaming that he was a butterfly or whether it was the butterfly dreaming that it was Chuang Chou. Between Chuang Chou and the butterfly, there must be some distinction. This is a case of what is called the transformation of things.

This shows that, although in ordinary appearance there are differences between things, in delusions or in dreams one thing can also be another. "The transformation of things" proves that the differences among things are not absolute——Tr.

（冯友兰 译）

昔者庄周梦为胡蝶

翟里斯把庄周梦蝶当作是作者庄子自述，因此使用第一人称翻译，内容总体以主观定调。冯友兰把庄周梦蝶当作是庄子以第三方视角讲述的一个关于庄子的故事，因此使用旁观者的客观立场，里面提到庄周均使用第三人称。

栩栩然胡蝶也

翟里斯用"飞到东来飞到西"形容蝴蝶翩翩飞舞的动态，很适切，比冯友兰的"到处飞"更加形象。华兹生的 flitting and fluttering around[①] 也颇有音韵

---

① flit 在词典中与本话题相关的主要意思为："Move swiftly and lightly（轻快地移动）."参见 Judy Pearsall, Patrick Hanks, Catherine Soanes, et al.新牛津英汉双解大词典.本词典编译出版委员会，编译.上海：上海外语教育出版社，2007：805.flutter 在词典中与本话题相关的主要意思为："(of a bird or other winged creature) fly unsteadily or hover by flapping the wings quickly and lightly[（鸟或其它有翼动物）拍翅而飞，振翼，盘旋]."参见 Judy Pearsall, Patrick Hanks, Catherine Soanes, et al.新牛津英汉双解大词典.本词典编译出版委员会，编译.上海：上海外语教育出版社，2007：811.

之美,从修辞效果而言比较接近原文"栩栩然"的神韵。

**不知周也**

翟里斯译为"(蝴蝶)没有意识到自己其实是一个人",冯友兰译为"(蝴蝶)不知道它自己就是庄周",基本都能达意。Hamill 等译为 unaware of a Chuang Chou(不知道有一个庄周),则已经不是在蝴蝶与(梦见自己是蝴蝶的)庄周之间周旋,而是跟一个莫名其妙的叫作庄周的家伙打交道了,因此比较明显地偏离了原文意思。

**蘧蘧然周也**

翟里斯译为"躺在那里,还是原来的自己",基本达意,但是修辞效果不够明显。冯友兰译为"又变回不折不扣的庄周了",华兹生译为 solid and unmistakable Chuang Chou(的的确确是庄周),Mair 译为 palpably Chou(分明是庄周),都强调梦醒之后发现自己还是如假包换的庄周。大部分译本不足之处就是忽略了对"蘧蘧然"(惊视貌)的翻译。Hamill 等使用 looking a little out of sorts 翻译,意思是"有些不舒服/不高兴"(to be slightly ill or slightly unhappy),虽然不完全忠实,但是大体表达了梦醒时分的迷糊状态。Ziporyn 翻译为 the startled Zhuang Zhou in the flesh(吓了一跳的现实中的庄周),比较全面地传达了原文的意思。

**不知周之梦为胡蝶与,胡蝶之梦为周与?**

翟里斯译文大意是"我不知道刚才只是梦见自己是蝴蝶,还是我现在其实就是蝴蝶,只不过正梦见自己是人罢了",很准确地传达了原文的哲学内涵。冯友兰译文大意是"我们不知道究竟是庄周梦见他自己是蝴蝶,还是蝴蝶梦见自己是庄周"。虽然表面看来相差不大,但从修辞受众角度而言则大相径庭。使用"我们"(而不是"我"),在这一特定语境中意味着是第三方的观察者视角,前面的文字已经向读者明白无误地交代了庄周做梦(梦见自己是蝴蝶),梦醒后发现自己依然是个人(而不是蝴蝶)。庄周本人在特定语境/梦境中可以迷糊,但是如果作为观察者的"我们"在这种情况下也不明所以,是很难向读者交代的。汪榕培译文"Did Zhuang Zhou dream of the butterfly or did the butterfly dream of Zhuang Zhou?"(究竟是庄周梦见了蝴蝶还是蝴蝶梦见了庄周?),虽然在字面上几乎是一一对应原文,但是未能给读者交代清楚主体与客体相互转化的问题,不免让读者误以为不过就是庄周(如大多数普通人一样)梦见了蝴蝶这种司空见惯的事情,或者是蝴蝶居然在其梦境中遇到了庄周这么虚幻的事情。如果能够点明庄周梦见自己化身为蝴蝶以及蝴蝶在其梦境中化身为庄周,则读者更能够看出里面的哲学意涵,即人类对于自身存在的思考。

**则必有分矣**

翟里斯译文用 barrier(障碍),未能表达原文"分别"的意思,冯友兰译文用 distinction 则清晰地传达了原文意思。Ziporyn 译文"Surely, Zhou and a butterfly count as two distinct identities!",不仅表达出二者的区别,更进一步指出二者是不同的实体,为下文物化概念做了充分铺垫。

**此之谓物化**

"物化",万物变化而相通。翟里斯译文用 Metempsychosis(灵魂转世说,轮回),过于玄奥。

冯友兰和之前的理雅各一样,使用 the transformation of things(事物的转化)进行翻译,并加注解说尽管事物在表面上有差异,在幻想或梦境中彼此是可以转化的。事物可以转化这个现象说明事物之间的差异并非绝对。这一说明在逻辑上无法说服理性的读者,因为从虚幻意义上的转化并不能推导出事物在实际上可以相互转化,唯一可以说明的是在想象意义上,事物彼此的差异是可以被淡化乃至消除的,问题是这实际上是人类常识,谈不上是新鲜的理论视角。庄周的物化理论并非局限于抽象或想象领域,因此这一解读是有偏颇的。赵彦春用 metamorphosis(变态/蜕变),虽然凸显了"变化",但是因为这一辞屏的生物学意义过于明显,容易将庄子的概念窄化。

**三、吾生也有涯,而知也无涯。以有涯随无涯,殆已;已而为知者,殆而已矣!**

——《庄子·养生主》

My life has a limit, but my knowledge is without limit. To drive the limited in search of the limitless, is fatal; and the knowledge of those who do this is fatally lost.

(翟里斯 译)

There is a limit to our life, but to knowledge there is no limit. With what is limited to pursue after what is unlimited is a perilous thing; and when, knowing this, we still seek the increase of our knowledge, the peril cannot be averted.

(理雅各 译)

The flow of my life is bound by its limits; the mind bent on knowledge, however, never is.①

If forced to follow something limited by no bounds, the bounded [current of life] is put in danger. And to meet this danger by enhancing knowledge even further—that merely exacerbates the danger.

(Brook Ziporyn 译)

*吾生也有涯，而知也无涯*

翟里斯等早期译者基本都是把"生"翻译为"life"。与葛瑞汉（A. C. Graham）②类似，Ziporyn 根据整体语境中"涯"所涉及的海岸线、水流等意象将其相应翻译为"生命之流"并通过注解明确其诠释依据与翻译选择，从修辞美学角度而言是很有感染力的。翟里斯将"知"理解为知识，是一种主流的诠释进路，但是凭空加了一个"我的（知识）"，让译文在逻辑上显得可疑，读者会困惑为什么一个人的知识会是没有界限的。理雅各译文则很清晰地传达了"知识本身是无限的"这一意思。Ziporyn 则从"智识"角度解读"知"，并在注解中对 faculty of knowing（认知之官能）与 field of things to be known（有待人类认知的领域）这两类"知"进行了区分。

---

① 此处原注为："This sentence is often interpreted to mean, 'My life is limited, but knowledge is unlimited.' On this reading, 'life' refers to the duration of a human life span, while 'knowledge' is interpreted as 'the body of knowable things to be learned.' The point would then be that my life span is too short to learn all there is to learn, and hence the pursuit of learning is a futile, even dangerous endeavor. But this reading of both sheng(life) and zhi(here translated as 'the mind bent on knowledge') is not consistent with the usage of those words in the rest of the Inner Chapters, nor the usual usage in texts of this period generally, where the former refers to the process of coming to be, and the latter primarily to the faculty of knowing rather than the field of things to be known. See Glossary SHENG.[Becoming, Birth, Life, the Life in Us, the Life Process, the Process of Life, the Flow of Life. The term means both 'birth, becoming, coming into existence,' whether of a state or condition or of a living entity, and 'life' in the sense of being alive. Hence, 'life process' is sometimes used as a translation, sometimes 'generation', 'production', or the like. In the opening lines of chapter 3(3:2), in accordance with the 'shoreline' and 'current' imagery used, it is translated as 'flow of life.'](该部分是书末 Glossary 部分中的，旨在总结与解释译者对术语的翻译。)Nonetheless, something of this sense of the inexhaustibility of knowables is not irrelevant to the points being made in this chapter."。参见 Zhuangzi: The Essential Writings with Selections from Traditional Commentaries. Brook Ziporyn, trans. Indianapolis: Hackett Publishing Company, Inc., 2009.

② 译文为："My life flows between confines.（我的生命之流在有限的边界内流动。）" 参见 Chuang-tzs: The Inner Chapters. A.C. Graham, trans. London: Unwin Paperbacks, 1989: 62.

**殆已**

"殆",王叔岷赞成车柱环的解读"以其至小,求穷其至大之域,是故迷乱而不能自得"①。与此相类,陈鼓应将其解读为"疲困"(穷于应付、疲于奔命的结果),逻辑上与语境吻合。翟里斯将"殆"翻译为致命的,理雅各译为"非常危险的",均有夸张之嫌。葛瑞汉译为"(生命之流)会干涸"②,Ziporyn译为"会置(生命之流)于险境",使用隐喻进行翻译,虽然颇有修辞意境,但是依然没有离开"有性命之虞"这个诠释方向,与原文存在偏差。汪榕培使用 fatiguing(令人疲倦的)比较符合文势。

**殆而已矣**

翟里斯误解为"知识本身浪费了",包括理雅各在内的大部分译者翻译为"危险的",不无偏颇。汪榕培翻译为 fatal(致命的),与 fatiguing 一起构成了头韵修辞格且暗含比较,就语言表达本身而言是很精妙的,但从内容的忠实角度来看,严重程度有"过"之嫌。与此相反,Palmer 翻译为 we will run into trouble(我们会遇到麻烦),则明显是"不及"。过与不及,本来就是走钢丝般的翻译工作中"钢丝"的两端,译者如何在此间保持平衡,是翻译工作永恒的课题。

**四、始臣之解牛之时,所见无非牛者;三年之后,未尝见全牛也。**

——《庄子·养生主》

"When I first began to cut up bullocks, I saw before me simply whole bullocks. After three years' practice, I saw no more whole animals③."(翟里斯 译)

When I first began to cut up an ox, I saw nothing but the entire carcase. After three years I ceased to see it as a whole.

(理雅各 译)

"When I first began

To cut up oxen

---

① 王叔岷.庄子校诠.北京:中华书局,2007:100.
② 译文为:"there is danger that the flow will cease"。参见 Chuang-tzs: The Inner Chapters. A.C. Graham, trans. London: Unwin Paperbacks, 1989: 62.
③ 此处原注为:"Meaning that he saw them, so to speak, in sections."。参见 Chuang Tzu: Mystic, Moralist, and Social Reformer, Herbert A. Giles, trans. London: Bernard Quaritch, 1889: 34.

I would see before me

The whole ox

All in one mass.

'After three years'

I no longer saw this mass.

I saw the distinctions.".

(Thomas Merton 译)

翟里斯译文考虑到受众可能的困惑,对目无全牛有个注解,提到经过三年实践之后,眼中看到的是牛的各个局部。其中对牛的翻译使用 bullock(a young male cow, especially one that has had its testicles removed),也就是小阉牛,与实际情形不符。理雅各译文"刚开始宰牛时,眼里只能看见整个一大块的牛的躯体。三年后,不再把它看作一个整体了",不提活牛而是使用 carcase(the dead body of an animal, especially one slaughtered for food),也就是大型的动物尸体,倒是避免了究竟是哪种牛的争论(这不是文本的重点)。两个译文都提到字面意义上的"目无全牛",但有鉴于西方也有"见叶不见林"(或"见树不见林")这类的文化常言,这样究竟是褒是贬,读者并不是很清楚。Merton 译文"当我刚开始宰牛时,我看到的只是一整头牛,一个浑然大块。三年后,我眼里看到的不再是一个整体,而是有区分的各个部位",准确传达了原文意思,"目无全牛"真正的修辞意涵也清晰地予以呈现出来。Palmer 译文视角独特:"I had learnt not to see the ox as whole."(我终于学会了不再把牛看作一个整体),没有任何误会的空间,明白无误地肯定了"目无全牛"是一种目标、能力乃至境界。Hamill 等译文"When I first butchered an ox, I saw nothing but ox meat. It took three years for me to see the whole ox."(刚开始宰牛时,我满眼看到的都是牛肉,我整整花了三年才学会把牛看作一整头),明显是受到"不可只见树木,不见森林"观点的影响,把自己的文化前见(pre-occupation)带入翻译过程而造成的错误。

五、良庖岁更刀,割也;族庖月更刀,折也。

——《庄子·养生主》

"A good cook changes his chopper once a year,—because he cuts. An ordinary cook, once a month,—because he hacks." (翟里斯 译)

"A good cook changes his knife every year;— (it may have been injured) in cutting; an ordinary cook changes his every month;—(it may have been) broken."

(理雅各 译)

"A good cook needs a new chopper
Once a year—he cuts.
A poor cook needs a new one
Every month—he hacks!"

(Thomas Merton 译)

"良庖"与"族庖",翟里斯与理雅各译为好厨师与普通厨子,基本达意。华兹生用 mediocre(平庸的),Merton 用 poor(拙劣的)均能够体现二者专业素养方面的阶梯差。Hamill 等用 awkward(笨手笨脚的)也颇为形象。"更",翟里斯与理雅各均使用主动意义上的 change(更换);Merton 使用 need(需要)表达的是客观上需要;Palmer 用 has to change(不得不换),把迫不得已的修辞情势清晰地表达出来。"庖",大部分译者都是使用"cook"(厨子),汪榕培使用 butcher(屠夫)翻译,显然是注意到这个语境是屠宰场所而非厨房,是很准确的翻译。"刀",翟里斯使用 chopper(砍刀)是比较准确的。正如民间说法"杀鸡焉用牛刀"所提到的那样,杀鸡固然不用牛刀,但宰牛对刀是有一定规格方面的要求的。理雅各译的 knife(小刀)并不适合这样的场景。Mair 翻译为 cleaver(a heavy knife with a large square blade),也就是"大砍刀,剁肉刀",是很应景的翻译。

"割"[1],在本句是"以刀割肉"的意思。翟里斯使用 cut 表达"切,割",虽然字面上忠实,但是还欠些火候。Hamill 等补充翻译为 cuts cleanly(切得干净利落),则点明了为什么一把刀可以撑一年之久。

"折"[2],在本句中表示"刀折骨"(用刀直接剁牛骨头)而非"骨折刀"(牛骨把刀给弄折了)。翟里斯使用 hack(to cut into pieces in a rough and violent way, often without aiming exactly)表达"砍,劈",这是很适切的选词,但是与对"割"的翻译一样没有真正向读者说明为什么二者更新刀具的时间会不一样。理雅各译文补充说因为磨损而一年一度要更换,因为断了[3]所以每月都要换一把。这一理解有偏差,因为按照原文说法,二者均有磨损,只是使用的方式/技巧不同而造成不同磨损率而已。汪榕培的译文最是替读者考虑,明确

---

[1] 关于"割"的解释,郭庆藩引司马彪注解为:"以刀割肉,故岁岁更作。"参见郭庆藩.庄子集释.王孝鱼,点校.北京:中华书局,2004:122.

[2] 关于"折"的解释,郭庆藩引俞樾注解为:"折,谓折骨,非谓刀折也。"参见郭庆藩.庄子集释.王孝鱼,点校.北京:中华书局,2004:122.

[3] 理雅各对"折"的解读有望文生义之嫌,很可能是按"骨折刀"的思路翻译的。

补充说 cuts the flesh(切肉)与 hacks the bones(剁骨),二者为何磨损率不同也就一目了然了。

六、泽雉十步一啄,百步一饮,不蕲畜乎樊中。神虽王,不善也。
——《庄子·养生主》

"Now, wild fowl get a peck once in ten steps, a drink once in a hundred. Yet they do not want to be fed in a cage. For although they would thus be able to command food, they would not be free."

And had our friend above kept out of the official cage he would still have been independent as the fowls of the air.
(翟里斯 译)

A pheasant of the marshes has to take ten steps to pick up a mouthful of food, and thirty steps to get a drink, but it does not seek to be nourished in a coop. Though its spirit would (there) enjoy a royal abundance, it does not think (such confinement) good.
(理雅各 译)

The little marsh pheasant

Must hop ten times

To get a bite of grain.

She must run a hundred steps

Before she takes a sip of water.

Yet she does not ask

To be kept in a hen run

Though she might have all she desired

Set before her.

She would rather run

And seek her own little living

Uncaged.
(Thomas Merton 译)

陈鼓应认为《韩诗外传》中大泽中雉"乐其志"与"不得其志"时的不同状态①可作为本文的注解。翟里斯把"啄"按字面翻译为 peck,没有能够传达出

---

① 《韩诗外传》云:"君不见大泽中雉乎?五步一啄,终日乃饱;羽毛泽悦,光照于日月,奋翼争鸣,声响于陵泽者,何?彼乐其志也。援置之困仓中,常啄粱粟,不旦时而饱;然独羽毛憔悴,志气益下,低头不鸣,夫食岂不善哉?彼不得其志故也。"参见陈鼓应.庄子今注今译.北京:商务印书馆,2016:123.

自行获取食物之不易。理雅各译文通过"不得不"以及"一口（的量）"体现泽雉生活之不易：只能自行觅食且收获菲薄。Merton 译文大意是"为得到一小口，必须跳跃十趟"，比理雅各更能凸显谋存之不易。但是两个译文都只翻译出客观上的不得已，却没有体现出主观上的选择与努力，也就是无法体现泽雉及其所隐喻的人宁愿自力更生（以求自由自在）也不愿寄人篱下过锦衣玉食的生活的修辞人格。Palmer 用 manages one peck every ten paces（克服种种困难、想方设法地"一啄"）虽表达出个体自身的努力，但是意愿或意志尚未得到足够凸显与呈现。Hamill 等译文①"宁愿走十步以获得菲薄的'一啄'（也不愿意被人圈养）"，立体地呈现了"泽雉"宁愿自食其力也决不仰人鼻息的气节。值得一提的是，Hamill 等用 sip（啜／抿一小口）翻译"饮"，比大多数译者的 drink 都更加细致入微。

**不蕲畜乎樊中**

翟里斯翻译为"不想被关在笼中喂食"，其他两个译文也基本达意。Hamill 等译文②另辟蹊径，翻译为"一旦被关进樊笼里，（因泽雉性情刚烈、视死如归）就是求它，它也决不会碰一口食物的"。

**神虽王，不善也**

翟里斯译文大意为"尽管这样会保管饮食无忧，却是不自由的"，华兹生译文③为"虽然你把它当作国王一样伺候，它（因为不得自由）在精神上还是不会满足"。二者虽然逻辑上倒也能够自圆其说，但并未按照原文意思翻译，属于自行想象发挥。理雅各译文"虽然精神上可以享受皇家富足的物质供应，但它并不觉得这样的约束是好事"，虽然后半句译文是对的，但是前半句与后半句无法自圆其说，缺乏合理逻辑关联。Merton 译文"尽管她可以得到所想要的（除了自由之外的）世间万物，她宁愿逃离樊笼去过那种无拘无束的小日子"总

---

① 译文为："The march pheasant will go ten steps for a single peck of food and a hundred for a single sip of water."。参见 The Essential Chuang Tzu. Sam Hamill, J. R. Seaton, trans. Boston: Shambhala Publications, Inc., 1999:21.

② 译文为："but you cannot beg him into eating once he's caged."。参见 The Essential Chuang Tzu. Sam Hamill, J.R. Seaton, trans. Boston: Shambhala Publications, Inc., 1999:21.

③ 译文为："Though you treat it like a king, its spirit won't be content."。参见 Chuang Tzu: Basic Writings. Burton Watson, trans. New York: Columbia University Press, 1964:48.

体话语逻辑是合理的,但是前半句有自行发挥的成分。Ziporyn 译文①的大意是"精神状态虽然极好(因为被圈养而饮食充足),但是(因为不得自由)优越的生活条件终究没能够给它带来多大好处",虽然后半句有些许偏差,但是基本传达了原文的意思。

七、且德厚信矼,未达人气;名闻不争,未达人心。而强以仁义绳墨之言炫暴人之前者,是以人恶育其美也,命之曰菑人。菑人者,人必反菑之,若殆为人菑夫!且苟为悦贤而恶不肖,恶用而求有以异?若唯无诏,王公必将乘人而斗其捷。而目将荧之,而色将平之,口将营之,容将形之,心且成之。是以火救火,以水救水,名之曰益多。顺始无穷。若殆以不信厚言,必死于暴人之前矣!

——《庄子·人间世》

"Besides, those who, before influencing by their own solid virtue and unimpeachable sincerity, and before reaching the heart by the example of their own disregard for name and fame, go and preach charity and duty to one's neighbour to wicked men,—only make these men hate them for their very goodness' sake. Such persons are called evil speakers. And those who speak evil of others are apt to be evil spoken of themselves. That, alas! will be your end.

"On the other hand, if the Prince loves the good and hates the bad, what object will you have in inviting him to change his ways? Before you have opened your mouth to preach, the Prince himself will have seized the opportunity to wrest the victory from you. Your eye will fall, your expression fade, your words will stick, your face will change, and your heart will die within you. It will be as though you took fire to quell fire, water to quell water, which is popularly known as 'pouring oil on the flames.' And if you begin with concessions, there will be no end to them. Neglect this sound advice, and you will be the victim of that violent man."

(翟里斯 译)

---

① 译文为:"For though his spirit might there reign supreme, it does not do him any good."。参见 Zhuangzi: The Essential Writings with Selections from Traditional Commentaries. Brook Ziporyn, trans. Indianapolis, Cambridge: Hackett Publishing Company, Inc., 2009:23.

"Supposing one's virtue to be great and his sincerity firm, if he does not comprehend the spirit of those (whom he wishes to influence); and supposing he is free from the disposition to strive for reputation, if he do not comprehend their minds;—when in such a case he forcibly insists on benevolence and righteousness, setting them forth in the strongest and most direct language, before the tyrant, then he, hating (his reprover's) possession of those excellences, will put him down as doing him injury. He who injures others is sure to be injured by them in return. You indeed will hardly escape being injured by the man (to whom you go)!

"Further, if perchance he takes pleasure in men of worth and hates those of an opposite character, what is the use of your seeking to make yourself out to be different (from such men about him)? Before you have begun to announce (your views), he, as king and ruler, will take advantage of you, and immediately contend with you for victory. Your eyes will be dazed and full of perplexity; you will try to look pleased with him; you will frame your words with care; your demeanour will be conformed to his; you will confirm him in his views. In this way you will be adding fire to fire, and water to water, increasing, as we may express it, the evils (which you deplore). To these signs of deferring to him at the first there will be no end. You will be in danger, seeing he does not believe you, of making your words more strong; and you are sure to die at the hands of such a tyrant."

(理雅各 译)

### 且德厚信矼，未达人气；名闻不争，未达人心

本句有两大争议点。是将本句当作自成一体的论述还是（从整段考虑）当作下一句的前提是本句争议点之一。"（自己去）了解别人"还是"（让）别人了解（自己）"则是关于本句的争议点之二。基于本章主旨与本段上下文[①]以及西方古典修辞学泰斗亚里士多德关于修辞人格是说服中的主导因素的论述，将本句（从整段考虑）作为下一句的前提以及"（让）别人了解（自己）"当为更合理的解读。翟里斯（从整段考虑）将本句当作下一句的前提，选择"（让）别人了解（自己）"这种诠释进路进行翻译。理雅各也是将本句当作下一句的前提，但是选择"（自己去）了解别人"这种诠释进路进行翻译，为此还从修辞受众角度

---

① 下文"若殆以不信厚言，必死于暴人之前矣！"便是告诫进言者（在修辞权力严重不对等的情况下）务必警惕"交浅而言深"的失误，也就是首先要考虑在说服中占据极大比重的修辞人格分量是否足够撬得动/影响目标受众的信念/观点，再决定是否向其进言。

专门补充说"人气"中的"人"就是"他想影响的那些人"。Mair 的译文①将本句当作自成一体的论述,大意是"修辞者的懿德嘉行未必是修辞说服话语无往不利的通行证,品德再高尚、为人再低调都不足以确保获得他人的认可"这么一个论断。论断本身没有问题,但是和下文逻辑存在断层,因此不足取。

**而强以仁义绳墨之言炫暴人之前者**

这个"而"是比较明显的转折,冯友兰使用 notwithstanding,葛瑞汉使用 yet 均准确地体现了上下句逻辑关系。Ziporyn 别出心裁地使用 unless(除非)把前文原本貌似自成一体(self-contained)的句子转化为必要条件提出,同时在前后文字中分别辅以 even if(即便)与 just(不过是),淡化修辞者的修辞人格与具体修辞行为的价值,凸显了受众在决定具体修辞行为成败方面的重要性②。撇开上下文语境不谈,这个译文的观点本身倒是与西方经典修辞理论严丝合缝。从翻译忠实于原文角度而言,Ziporyn 译文自然是谈不上合格,但是从修辞效果而言,他对连接词的使用在现有大多数版本中可谓鹤立鸡群,使得译文有很强的文字方面的黏合力、凝聚力及文化与修辞方面的说服力。这种将原文话语部件打乱、进行系统性重置整合以服务于特定修辞目的的翻译方法令人耳目一新,为典籍翻译打开了新思路。

句中的"强",主要是"勉强"而非"强行"之义,其修辞意图在于表达这一行为在条件不具备的时候是不恰当的。理雅各翻译为"强加于人",重点强调"强势推进",虽然字面上貌似忠实,其实与原文的修辞意图有很大偏差。"炫",翟里斯使用 preach(鼓吹;说教;布道),虽然并不忠实于原文"夸耀"的意思,但是由于这个辞屏的负面色彩,修辞者对这一行为的反对态度跃然纸上,修辞劝阻意图

---

① 译文为:"A person of substantial integrity and solid trust may still not gain the approval of others; a person who does not contend for name and fame may still not gain the acquiescence of others."。参见 Wandering on the Way: Early Taoist Tales and Parables of Chuang Tzu. Victor H. Mair, trans. New York: Bantam Books, 1994.

② Ziporyn 对本句及其上文的处理与翻译:"But even if your Virtuosity were ample, reliable, and firm, and you engaged in no contention for the sake of a good name, unless you somehow attained perfect comprehension of his mind and disposition, your high-handed display of regulating words about Humanity and Responsibility in the face of such a tyrant would just be a way of showing off your beauty at the expense of his ugliness."。参见 Zhuangzi: The Essential Writings with Selections from Traditional Commentaries. Brook Ziporyn, trans. Indianapolis: Hackett Publishing Company, Inc., 2009:25.

得以有效实现。华兹生的译文①思路与翟里斯很接近，大意为"强迫暴君听讲关于仁义规矩的布道"，虽然对于"强迫"理解有误，但是"布道"这种自带否定意义的辞屏很容易引起读者对这一行为的反感，其修辞劝阻意图也就不言自明了。Mair 译文②的 flaunt（to show or make obvious something you are proud of in order to get admiration）有夸示、卖弄之义，与原文的精神一致。

### 是以人恶育其美也

翟里斯与理雅各都把原本应该当作名词解读的"恶"（缺点）误解为动词"厌恶"，而华兹生准确把握了"恶"作为"缺点"的意思，将这句话译为"This is simply using other men's bad points to parade your own excellence."（用别人的缺点来彰显/烘托、炫耀你自己的长处），尤其是用 parade（to show something in an obvious way in order to be admired）形象地表达了原文"炫耀"的意思。葛瑞汉翻译这句话为"This amount to taking advantage of someone's ugliness to make yourself look handsome."（这相当于利用别人的丑陋来衬托你的俊美），虽然关于美丑的翻译比较僵直，有望文生义之嫌，但是其余部分的理解与表述都是很到位的。Mair 的译文 to glorify oneself at the expense of another's failings（以别人的缺点为衬托美化自己）既准确又简约，干净利落地体现了原文"用别人的丑行来显示自己的美德"的意思。

### 命之曰菑人

翟里斯译为"说坏话的人"，理雅各译为"给（暴君）造成伤害"，虽然在语义大方向上没有出错，但是与前后文字的关联并不紧密。葛瑞汉翻译为 making a pest of oneself（使自己被人讨厌），从修辞上讲颇能说得通。Hamill 等译为"He'll charge you with injuring his reputation."（他会指控说你损害了他的名声），既巧妙地变换了说法，表达了和原文大致的意思，又能够在逻辑上与前文环环相扣。

### 菑人者，人必反菑之，若殆为人菑夫

翟里斯译文大意是"说别人坏话的人，别人也会说他坏话，这是难免的结

---

① 译文为："force him (the tyrant) to listen to sermons on benevolence and righteousness, measures and standards"。参见 Chuang Tzu: Basic Writings. Burton Watson, trans. New York: Columbia University Press, 1964:51.

② 译文为："forcibly to flaunt talk about humaneness, righteousness, and codes of conduct before a tyrant"。参见 Wandering on the Way: Early Taoist Tales and Parables of Chuang Tzu. Victor H. Mair, trans. New York: Bantam Books, 1994:30.

局",单独听起来固然正确(因为这是普世真理),但是与当前话语语境契合度很低,修辞意图很模糊。理雅各译文大意是"伤人者必为人所伤,你(去找暴君)很难避免为其所伤",在逻辑衔接方面比起翟里斯译文有明显提升。Hamill 等的译文"Who speaks evil of others will have evil done against himself."(言人恶者人必害之)并没有像前面两个译文那样("言人恶"/"人恶言"与"伤人"/"人伤之")机械对称翻译成 speak evil of others/be evil spoken of themselves,而是灵活调整为 speaks evil of others/have evil done against himself(言语上触犯他人/性命遭他人伤害)。这样的翻译浅层上固然有违原文,深层意义上其实更能体现原文关于"谨言"的主旨。

且苟为悦贤而恶不肖,恶用而求有以异

这句话的修辞情境是颜回基于老师孔子"乱国就之"(对危乱的国家应该前去帮助治理)的教导"愿以所闻思其则"(希望根据老师的学说去纠正),修辞目的是"庶几其国有瘳乎"(让卫国恢复元气)。孔子基于种种考虑觉得不可行,试图通过排除法推理劝阻(dissuade)颜回。孔子的理路大致如下:卫国的国君如果不是欣赏贤人(同时也会远离佞人),那就很可能是喜欢亲近小人(同时也会疏远君子)。如果是前者,"哪里还用得着等待颜回去才有所改变?"①,换言之,"颜回何必去显异于人?"②。如果是后者,贸然谏言必然是徒劳且危险,因此也是不可取的。翟里斯译文"你让卫君改变什么呢?"与理雅各译文"你让自己显得与卫君身边的人不一样有什么意义呢?"大体上体现了基于前一种可能性的两种不同视角(一个着眼于卫君,一个着眼于颜回)的解读,但是还不是那么直白明晰,对受众的修辞冲击力有限。华兹生的译文③"他怎么还需要你去改变?"与葛瑞汉译文"Will it do you any good to try to be especially clever?"(去卖弄你的聪明有什么好处呢?)则明白无误地表达出了孔子对这一行为的反对甚至是批评。Ziporyn 的译文交代得最为清楚,推理过程十分严密:"If he happens to be the type who takes delight in worthy men such as yourself while despising men of lesser quality, why would you want to change him in the first place?"(如果卫君碰巧是喜欢像颜回你这样的贤人而

---

① 雷仲康译文。参见庄子.雷仲康,译注.太原:山西古籍出版,1999:46。
② 陈鼓应译文。参见陈鼓应.庄子今注今译.北京:商务印书馆:2016:134.
③ 译文为:"And suppose he is the kind who actually delights in worthy men and hates the unworthy—then why does he need you to try to make him any different?"。参见 Chuang Tzu: Basic Writings. Burton Watson, trans. New York: Columbia University Press, 1964:51.

不喜欢小人,你为什么还要去改变他呢?)。译文中这一推理的结论在逻辑上无懈可击,让人很难辩驳,因此有很强的修辞说服力。

**若唯无诏,王公必将乘人而斗其捷**

王叔岷支持将这句话增补解读为"汝唯有寂然不言耳,言则王公必乘人以君势而角其捷辩,以距谏饰非也"。换言之,"汝除非不言耳,言则卫君必将以君人之势乘人而角其捷辩"。① 翟里斯与理雅各均漏译了"若唯无诏"。冯友兰译文②首先在语境上承接上文推理的第二种可能,即"如果卫君不是贤明之人",颜回就只能保持缄默,否则,一旦开口进言,就容易遭到卫君的修辞反噬。华兹生译文③大意是"你最好把建议留给自己,因为君主总是喜欢将权势凌驾于他人头上以便确保在争论中能够占上风",把原文的条件关系转化为因果关系,虽然凸显了君主好用其得天独厚的修辞权威这一重要观点,却扭曲了原文的逻辑面貌。同样在凸显君主好用其修辞权威这一点上,葛瑞汉的译文④尤为出众,不仅提到卫君会与颜回斗智,还提到卫君会利用其身份权威作为杠杆撬动颜回的观点。Mair 误解了"若唯无诏",将"理应保持沉默"变成 If you do not offer your views(如果你不表态的话);不过在翻译"王公必将乘人而斗其捷"时相当出彩,其译文"The prince will certainly take advantage to display his own eloquence."(卫君必然会抓住这个机会展示其滔滔雄辩)不仅成功传达了"乘"的意思,也具体指出了"捷"在何处,不足之处是忽略了对隐含的身份权威的翻译。

**而目将荧之,而色将平之,口将营之,容将形之,心且成之**

这句话的意思是"你必将因为卫君的修辞攻势而眼目眩惑,不得不强装镇定,口中只顾得营营自救,于是容颜将被迫俯就(调低姿态),内心无主,也就难

---

① 王叔岷.庄子校诠.北京:中华书局,2007:122.

② 译文为:"If he does not so, you can only be silent. If you are not so and begin to announce your views, the prince will take the opportunity to contend with you for victory."。参见 Fung Yulan. Chuang Tzu: A New Selected Translation with an Exposition of the Philosophy of Kuo Hsiang. Heidelberg: Springer, 2016:26.

③ 译文为:"You had best keep your advice to yourself! Kings and dukes always lord it over others and fight to win the argument."。参见 Chuang Tzu: Basic Writings. Burton Watson, trans. New York: Columbia University Press, 1964:51.

④ 译文为:"Pit his wits against one's own with the whole weight of his authority behind him."。参见 Chuang-tzs: The Inner Chapters. A.C. Graham, trans. London: Unwin Paperbacks, 1989:67.

免要依顺卫君的主张（或所作所为）了"。① 这是一个充满修辞张力的经典场景，庄子笔下的孔子构想了一个具备高尚修辞人格但是人格权威尚未被论辩对手认可的修辞者在与具有政治权威优势的对手进行话语交锋时，甫一交手便丢盔弃甲、溃不成军的场面。翟里斯译文基本都在描绘修辞者自己这一方的种种负面变化，却没有将其与修辞对手关联起来论述，让人很难感受到这是一场修辞冲突导致的结果。葛瑞汉译文②则明确指出颜回之所以会如此狼狈，主要是因为被修辞对手所影响，连续使用五个"he"（也就是卫君），凸显了影响力的来源；特别是使用 cow（to frighten someone into doing something, using threats or violence），形容卫君可能会利用其政治地位或权势威吓颜回，并使用 manage（掌管）、shape（形塑）等一系列辞屏引导读者想象这一"人为刀俎，我为鱼肉"的修辞场景。从忠实角度而言，该译文还有不少偏差，但就修辞效果而言，已经足以让读者感受到颜回将会面临的不利局面。值得一提的是，由于葛瑞汉在排版方面也深谙西方古典修辞五大部门之一的发表（delivery）之道，他特意将这一部分独立出来，另起一段并将其纵向叠拼，形成强烈的排比视觉修辞效果，给读者造成足够的感官冲击。"目将荧之"，理雅各翻译基本到位，华兹生译文"You will find your eyes growing dazed."更能表现这种遭受修辞冲击之后的变化过程。Ziporyn 译文"Your eyes will be dazzled by the struggle."增加了"挣扎"，让颜回所遭受的煎熬更有画面感。"色将平之"，理雅各翻译为"努力表现出愉悦的样子"是很生动的。汪榕培翻译为 but you will pretend to be calm（强装镇定）是完全忠实于原文精神的。Hamill 等译文"You'll turn pale as you try to pacify him."（为了缓和剑拔弩张的对话气氛着急得脸都变白了），有不少译者自行发挥的成分，虽然在修辞上也颇为形象生动，但明显属于过度诠释。"口将营之"，理雅各译文对为何颜回需要"小心翼翼、字斟句酌地发言"语焉不详，冯友兰译文"Your mouth will frame words to excuse yourself."点明了原因：为了寻找摆脱困境的托词。华兹生更是生动地指明 your mouth working to invent excuses（嘴里试图从修辞上发明出一个借口）。Palmer 译文为 and your mouth trying to find words to apologize with（寻找致歉的说辞）。但是这些译文都还没有真正解开读者的困惑，就是

---

① 参考了王叔岷、陈鼓应译文部分观点。
② 译文为："Your eye he'll dazzle, Your look he'll cow, Your mouth he'll manage, Your gesture he'll shape, Your heart he'll form."。参见 Chuang-tzs: The Inner Chapters. A.C. Graham, trans. London: Unwin Paperbacks, 1989: 67.

为什么要寻找借口。Hamill 等译文"Your mouth will work at placating[①] him."(安抚卫君)比较明确地指出、解释了该行为的修辞目的。"容将形之",理雅各译文"神态举止迁就卫君"基本达意,冯友兰译文"Your manner will express your inner confusion."(举止暴露了你内心的混乱)虽然在本段主旨的大方向上并无龃龉之处,对照原文却并非忠实的译文,在现有语境中也无法在文势上一气呵成。华兹生译文 Your attitude becoming more and more humble(你的态度变得越来越谦卑)只是对原文意思的概括,而非对原文的准确翻译。Palmer 译文"You will bend in contrition."(你将因为悔恨而屈服),说明了态度变化的部分原因,但是忽略了对为什么悔恨的交代。Hamill 等译文"Your face will twist into false expressions."(脸上违心地挤出一副迎合的表情)充满了修辞既视感,把身不由己的样子体现得淋漓尽致。"心且成之",理雅各只是平淡地翻译出"你会赞成卫君的观点",既没有翻译出不情愿,也没有点明不得已,无法实现劝阻的修辞功能,缺乏原文应有的修辞张力。冯友兰译文"Your mind will tend to confirm what he said."(内心会变得倾向于赞成卫君观点),预测了一种走势而非直接断言说就是那样,比较客观。华兹生译文"Until in your mind you end by supporting him."(最终会沦落到去支持卫君的观点),表达了一种遗憾的态度。Hamill 等译文 while your heart and mind struggle to find an angle from which to agree with his arguments(绞尽脑汁地搜寻一个角度去表达对卫君观点的赞许)形象地描绘出修辞者"偷鸡不成蚀把米"(go for wool and come back shorn)的反讽结局。

**是以火救火,以水救水,名之曰益多**

这句话的意思是"这样做就像是用火救火,用水救水,可以称之为错上加错"。"以火救火,以水救水",翟里斯与理雅各译忠实地进行了翻译。"名之曰益多",翟里斯翻译不仅忠实,还形象,通过"火上浇油"有效传达了"错上加错"的意思。理雅各译文意思相当于"助纣为虐",也是很成功地实现了预期的修辞劝阻功能。葛瑞汉译为 going from bad to worse(每况愈下),只能表达事态本身朝与人们期待的相反的方向发展,却无法体现这是人的错误决策造成的不良后果,因此徒具描绘的话语功能,却不具备劝阻的修辞效果,与原文预

---

[①] 意为"to stop someone from feeling angry",平息,安抚。

期话语功能相去甚远。Ziporyn 译文①并没有忠实地翻译"以水救水",而是使用"向溺水的人继续倒水"表达了"雪上加霜"的意思,后面再评论说"这是'为已甚'之举",整体修辞效果丝毫不逊色于完全忠实的翻译。

**顺始无穷**

这句话意思是"有了依顺他的开始,以后顺从他的旨意的事情便会没完没了"。翟里斯与理雅各译文基本按字面忠实地传达。华兹生译文"If you give in at the beginning, there is no place to stop."(你一旦开始让步了,后面就只能步步退让,无法收住脚步)比较形象地表达了"有了初一,就会有十五"这样的修辞走势。Palmer 译文"Once you do this, you will be unable to argue with him again."(你一旦这么做,就无法再与卫君争辩了),把这一修辞后果与整个讨论的主题进行挂钩,能够替读者考虑,因而更容易让读者接受(reader-friendly)。

**若殆以不信厚言②,必死于暴人之前矣**

这句话的意思是"假如你未能取信便推心置腹进言,那么一定会死在这个暴君面前"。翟里斯正确地将"不信厚言"断句为"不信/厚言",但是将"暴人"(暴君)误解为"暴力之人",因此译文出现了偏差。理雅各译文虽然颇有修辞意识,译为"不可罔顾君主心态固执地推进自己的观点",与原文直接点明"要首先建构可信的话语修辞人格再向君主进言"还有些"隔"。冯友兰译文③把"不信"的重点放在颜回推出的观点而非修辞者颜回的修辞人格方面,华兹生译文④"既然你热心的建言注定不会被接受",关注的是进言的结果而非进言

---

① 译文为:"Then it will be like using fire to put out a fire, or pouring water on a drowning man—I'd call that augmenting the excessive."。参见 Zhuangzi: The Essential Writings with Selections from Traditional Commentaries. Brook Ziporyn, trans. Indianapolis: Hackett Publishing Company, Inc., 2009:25.

② 王叔岷的解释为:"'不信厚言',犹言'交浅言深'。"参见王叔岷.庄子校诠.北京:中华书局,2007:124.

③ 译文为:"If you insist on your own good words which he does not believe, you will die in the hand of the tyrant."。参见 Fung Yulan. Chuang Tzu: A New Selected Translation with an Exposition of the Philosophy of Kuo Hsiang. Heidelberg:Springer, 2016:26.

④ 译文为:"Since your fervent advice is almost certain not to be believed, you are bound to die if you come into the presence of a tyrant."。参见 Chuang Tzu: Basic Writings. Burton Watson, trans. New York: Columbia University Press,1964:51.

的条件,二者与原文均有较大偏差。汪榕培译文①(未取信于人却一再进言)不仅解读方向对路,译文也成功地呈现了译者所解读出的原作意思。

八、夫传两喜两怒之言,天下之难者也。夫两喜必多溢美之言,两怒必多溢恶之言。凡溢之类妄,妄则其信之也莫,莫则传言者殃。故法言曰:"传其常情,无传其溢言,则几乎全。"且以巧斗力者,始乎阳,常卒乎阴,泰至则多奇巧;以礼饮酒者,始乎治,常卒乎乱,泰至则多奇乐。凡事亦然。始乎谅,常卒乎鄙;其作始也简,其将毕也必巨。
——《庄子·人间世》

Now the transmission of messages of good- or ill-will is the hardest thing possible. Messages of good-will are sure to be overdone with fine phrases; messages of ill-will with harsh ones. In each case the result is exaggeration, and a consequent failure to carry conviction, for which the envoy suffers. Therefore it was said in the *Fa-yen*, "Confine yourself to simple statements of fact, shorn of all superfluous expression of feeling, and your risk will be small." In trials of skill, at first all is friendliness; but at last it is all antagonism. Skill is pushed too far. So on festive occasions, the drinking which is in the beginning orderly enough, degenerates into riot and disorder. Festivity is pushed too far. It is in fact the same with all things: they begin with good faith and end with contempt. From small beginnings come great endings.

(翟里斯 译)

To transmit words that are either pleasing to both parties or infuriating to both parties is one of the most difficult things in the world. Where both parties are pleased, there must be some exaggeration of the good points; and where both parties are angered, there must be some exaggeration of the bad points. Anything that smacks of exaggeration is irresponsible. Where there is irresponsibility, no one will trust what is said, and when that happens, the man who is transmitting the words will be in danger. Therefore the aphorism says, "Transmit the established facts; do not transmit words of exaggeration." If you do that, you will probably

---

① 译文为:"If you give repeated admonishments while you are not trusted, you will certainly fall victim to the tyrant."。参见庄子.汪榕培,任秀桦,英译.秦旭卿,孙庸长,今译.长沙:湖南人民出版社,1997:59.

come out all right. "When men get together to pit their strength in games of skill, they start off in a light and friendly mood, but usually end up in a dark and angry one, and if they go on too long they start resorting to various underhanded tricks. When men meet at some ceremony to drink, they start off in an orderly manner, but usually end up in disorder, and if they go on too long they start indulging in various irregular amusements. It is the same with all things. What starts out being sincere usually ends up being deceitful. What was simple in the beginning acquires monstrous proportions in the end.

(华兹生 译)

### 夫传两喜两怒之言,天下之难者也

"传",翟里斯翻译为"传输",显得比较客观,而这句话却是要表达传话人的主观能动性。理雅各译为 convey,葛瑞汉译为 pass on,都容许传话人有修饰调整的空间,较为妥当。"两喜之言"是赞誉之言,"两怒之言"是诽谤之言。翟里斯译文大意为"带有善意与敌意的消息",主要是从修辞者一方去选择措辞,表达很准确,没有误会的空间。华兹生译文从受众一方去选择措辞,但是存在歧义:一种理解是同时向双方传达令人愉悦或愤怒的话,这就意味着有个作为话语源头的第三方,显然与"充当甲乙双方传声筒"的文意不符;另外一种解读就是交替地为甲乙双方带话(善言或恶语),这个是符合实际情况的。汪榕培译文(messages of the rulers' pleasure or anger)不像大部分译文那样泛泛而论双方,而是特别指出修辞者身份是君主,有助于读者理解在话语权力不对等情况下"言媒"面临的潜在风险。"难",大部分译者翻译为"困难",忠实但是不生动,Palmer 翻译为 the most thankless task under Heaven(天底下最吃力不讨好的活),成功实现了话语预期的修辞劝阻功能。

### 夫两喜必多溢美之言,两怒必多溢恶之言

王叔岷赞同《论衡·艺增篇》对此的解读:"誉人不增其美,则闻者不快其意;毁人不益其恶,则听者不惬于心。"[①]不难发现,"溢"不仅是一种客观现象,更是一种主观修辞需求。正所谓人同此心,心同此理,这个观察从比较修辞角度而言具有普世意义,在翻译时不存在文化鸿沟,找到对等的措辞直译便可以成功传达原意。翟里斯译文很忠实地传达了原文意思。Ziporyn 译文"The esteem gets exaggerated into flattery and the anger into insult."(敬重过头变成无原则的恭维,发怒升格为不顾脸面的辱骂),用"敬重"翻译"喜"虽然欠准

---

① 王叔岷.庄子校诠.北京:中华书局,2007:140.

确,却能够通过不同词语语义轻重的"级别差"成功体现"溢"的后果,比翟里斯译文更能够给读者带来明显的修辞冲击。

**凡溢之类妄,妄则其信之也莫,莫则传言者殃**

原句为顶真修辞,翟里斯虽然没有使用相同修辞手段进行翻译,却充分利用了英语形合语言手段使得逻辑环环相扣,译文成功再现了严密的逻辑推理过程,对读者而言很有说服力。与翟里斯译文凸显"无法取信于人"的客观结果不同,理雅各译文"When this distrust arises, woe to the internuncio."强调君主主观上的不信任使得传言者遭殃,二者殊途同归,都成功实现了既定的话语功能。"殃",葛瑞汉理解为"必死无疑",死亡的确是传言者可能遇到的最坏的结果,但是也有很大可能是遭遇其他非致命的困难,这一译文把其他可能的情况排除了,与实际情况不尽相符。

**故法言曰:"传其常情,无传其溢言,则几乎全。"**

"法言"①,翟里斯使用音译,且顺便提到它是一部古书,但是并没有为读者介绍书的主要内容。理雅各把它翻译为 the Rules for Speech(言语的规则)并对其内容进行推测,认为可能是当时的一本指南。理雅各译文把书名调整了顺序,《法言》(法之言)变成了《言法》(言之法),使得包括但是不限于言语规则在内的指南,看起来更像是一本演说或写作指南,将原本可以包罗万象的话题局限于言语一科。华兹生撇开具体书名,直接使用 the aphorism(格言)进行翻译,显然是采纳了"'格言'说"的解读。葛瑞汉译为 the book of rules(规则之书),遵循"《法言》说"解读路径,大体传达了字面意思。Mair 翻译为 the Legal Counsels(法律建议;律师),则不免有些望文生义了。Palmer 加注解说 a book of rules and proverbs.(一本关于规则与谚语的书),似乎意在调和"'格言'说"与"《法言》说",通过糅合二者,将第一种解读的内容装入第二种解读的容器中。姑且不论这样的翻译是否准确,从对外传播中国文化的角度而言,无疑是避免了缩约(reduce)中国文化的潜在学术损失;从修辞受众角度而言,也给受众提供了较为丰富的信息。假如能够在注解中对两解加以说明,在学术伦理上会更加无懈可击。"传其常情",翟里斯译文大意为"剪除

---

① "法言",根据陈鼓应的总结,学界有两个解释,一个是把它当作普通名词"格言"理解,一个是把它当作一本古书的名字。陈氏本人的现代汉语译文选择了第一种解读(下文简称"'格言'说"),但是并未给出取舍的依据。从西方修辞的基本预设而言,针对每个有争议的话题都有两个针锋相对且各自言之成理的论点/解读,在没有明确证据可以排除第二种解读之前,不妨给第二种解读(下文简称"《法言》'说")预留学术空间。

一切多余的情感表达,只陈述事实"(也就是不带感情进行客观陈述),与"不应夸大其词"尚有一定距离。华兹生译文大意为"传达既定事实,不传浮夸之词",忠实地传达了原文意思。后出的 Ziporyn 译文"Transmit their usual characteristic inclinations, not their occasional exaggerations."(传达他们平常具有稳定特征的意向,而非偶然的夸张之辞)是望文生义的翻译,与原文"唯浮辞之务去"的精神有较大偏差。"则几乎全",翟里斯理解为"风险较小",不如冯友兰的 likely to be safe(安全)来得准确。华兹生译文 come out all right(全身而退)比其他译文更加生动。

**且以巧斗力者,始乎阳,常卒乎阴,泰至则多奇巧**

翟里斯译文大意为"比拼技巧者,往往开始友好终局成敌,是因为追求技巧过头了"。关于"斗"的具体内容在翻译上有主要有两种进路,一是斗智,二是斗勇,也就是角力。翟里斯并未明确具体采纳哪一种解读,比较模糊,对整句的因果解读与原文也不尽相符。理雅各译为"As their excitement grows excessive, they display much wonderful dexterity."意为选手(参赛者)越兴奋,越能展现高超技巧(观众越有看头),明显误解了原文,把原本要反对的做法给译成值得嘉许的行为了,与预期话语修辞功能背道而驰。华兹生译文大意为"以巧斗力者,刚开始时轻松友好,终局却往往变得阴险愤怒,拉锯时间一长更是阴招叠出",逻辑上无懈可击,容易让读者接受。汪榕培译文 battles of wits begin in fair play and often end in foul play.(斗智者开始时像君子光明正大,结局时小人般偷偷摸摸)用词简约,对比鲜明且前后呼应,令人过目难忘。Ziporyn 译文"When it really gets extreme, they end up engaging in all sorts of outrageous tactics to defeat each other."(比拼白热化时,会动用各种令人不齿的手段以击败对方)修辞上虽然不如汪译,但对"奇巧"的翻译却比大部分译者都要生动。

**以礼饮酒者,始乎治,常卒乎乱,泰至则多奇乐**

翟里斯译文大意为"刚开始的时候还比较规矩,但是到了后面往往会一片混乱、大失礼仪。因为欢乐过头了",对整句的因果解读误差与前文类似,在此不赘。除了用 irregular amusements(不正常的娱乐活动)翻译"奇乐"存在偏差外,华兹生译文整体上是达意的。葛瑞汉译文"Drinkers at a formal banquet are mannerly at first, but generally end up too boisterous; when they have gone too far the fun gets more and more reckless."(参加酒宴的人,刚开始时彬彬有礼、客客气气,喝到后来,常常失态迷乱、大失礼仪;喝得过了头,就会放荡无忌了)颇得原文真趣。

凡事亦然。始乎谅①,常卒乎鄙;其作始也简,其将毕也必巨

"始谅终鄙",意思是开始时彼此讲规矩守诚信,到头来不免互相欺诈,为占上风而诡诈百出、不择手段。翟里斯译文大意为"始于真诚而终于鄙夷",对于"鄙"有些望文生义。华兹生译文大意是"始于真诚而终于欺骗",能够与前面语境整体无缝衔接,可谓文从字顺。

Hamill 等译文②也表达了相近的意思,但是措辞更有修辞考量,使用尾韵表达真诚与欺骗,对比鲜明且令人过目不忘。

关于"其作始也简,其将毕也必巨",翟里斯翻译得仿佛是在称赞事物的成就,与原文感叹事态失控的遗憾之情相去甚远。华兹生译文基本达意,但是把"巨"理解为"巨大的比例"还稍显生硬。葛瑞汉译文 sooner or later are sure to get out of hand(迟早会失控)本身要自然得多,但离原文意思还有距离,一是时间上与原文"接近尾声"有出入,二是情况复杂未必就一定失控。Mair 译文"As they approach their conclusion they become enormously complex."(快结束时变得极其复杂)忠实传达了原文意图。Palmer 对"巨"的翻译进行合理补充,使用头韵修辞将其译为 complex and confusing(复杂且令人困惑),成功再现了"令人无从下手、无法收拾"的局面。Ziporyn 的译文 end up oversized and unwieldy(尾大不掉)表达的是急于摆脱这一局面而非如何应对这一局面,与原文有出入。

九、汝不知夫螳螂乎?怒其臂以当车辙,不知其不胜任也,是其才之美者也。戒之,慎之! 积伐而美者以犯之,几矣!

——《庄子·人间世》

Do you not know (the fate of) the praying mantis? It angrily stretches out its arms, to arrest the progress of the carriage, unconscious of its inability for such a task, but showing how much it thinks of its own powers. Be on your guard; be careful. If you cherish a boastful confidence in your own excellence, and place

---

① 王叔岷认为"谅"系讹误,原本应该为"都",因为"都"与"鄙"才相对,而上文"阴"与"阳"、"治"与"乱"皆相对。依文势判断,笔者认为这一解读有很强的说服力。参见王叔岷.庄子校诠.北京:中华书局,2007:142.

② 译文为:"What begins in sincerity may end up in duplicity."。The Essential Chuang Tzu. Sam Hamill, J.P. Seaton, trans. Boston: Shambhala Publications, Inc., 1999:28.

yourself in collision with him①, you are likely to incur the fate (of the mantis).

(理雅各 译)

汝不知夫螳螂②乎

理雅各译文并未望文生义地进行字面翻译,而是在把握文本修辞意图之后通过增补 the fate of(命运;遭遇)凸显了原文的劝说或劝阻的意图。Hamill 等将原文的修辞疑问翻译为陈述句"你肯定已经听过螳螂的故事"(You've no doubt heard the story of the praying mantis),译文语气太过绝对,会让读者误以为对话中的修辞者没有受众意识,自说自话,无形中会误导读者对其修辞人格的评价。

怒其臂以当车辙

包括理雅各在内的大部分译者都把这个"怒"(奋力)误读为"愤怒",汪榕培译文注意到这个问题,翻译为"The mantis raises its fore-legs to stop an on-coming chariot.",尤其注意到"臂"在生物学意义上其实是螳螂的前足,是很科学准确的翻译。Ziporyn 也准确捕捉了"怒"的意思,同时更关注其修辞表现力,对螳螂具有标志性特征的两条前肢的钳或螯进行了凸显③。"当",理雅各翻译为 arrest(to stop or interrupt the development of something),也就是阻止,是准确且形象的。"车",Mair 的翻译增加了 onrushing(describes something such as a vehicle that is moving forward so quickly or forcefully that it would be very difficult to stop),把飞奔而至、势不可当的情形给描绘了出来。

是其才之美者也

早期的译者翟里斯译为 so admirable was its energy(其能量惊人)是因为误读了原文,既没有照顾话语逻辑也不曾考虑整个行文的修辞目的。理雅各译文大意为"只是暴露了它自视甚高这个缺点而已",把这句话作为结果,与前文逻

---

① the eldest son of duke Ling of Wei(笔者注)。
② 李时珍在《本草纲目·虫一·螳螂桑螵蛸》中对螳螂描述道:"螳螂,两臂如斧,当辙不避,故得'当郎'之名,俗呼为刀螂。兖人谓之拒斧,又呼不过也。"参见李时珍.本草纲目.北京:人民卫生出版社,1982:2243。
③ 译文为:"It flailed its pincers around to stop an oncoming chariot wheel."。参见 Zhuangzi: The Essential Writings with Selections from Traditional Commentaries. Brook Ziporyn, trans. Indianapolis: Hackett Publishing Company, Inc., 2009:29.

辑存在裂痕。而 Mair 的翻译"This is because it puts a high premium[①] on its own ability."（这是因为它高度评价自己的能力），用这句话作为原因，完美解释了前面发生的事情。

## 本章参考的英译本

庄子.理雅各,译.刘金红,王玉静,校注.郑州:中州古籍出版社,2016.

庄子.汪榕培,英译.秦旭卿,孙雍长,今译.长沙:湖南人民出版社,1999.

庄子英译.赵彦春,译.北京:高等教育出版社,2019.

Chuang Tzu: The Inner Chapters. A. C. Graham, trans. London: Unwin Paperbacks, 1986.

Chuang Tzu: Basic Writings. Burton Watson, trans. New York: Columbia University Press, 1964.

Chuang Tzu: Mystic, Moralist, and Social Reformer. Herbert A. Giles, trans. London: Bernard Quaritch, 1889.

Fung Yulan. Chuang Tzu: A New Selected Translation with an Exposition of the Philosophy of Kuo Hsiang. Heidelberg: Springer, 2016.

The Book of Chuang Tzu. Martin Palmer et al., Trans. New York: Penguin Group, 1996.

The Essential Chuang Tzu. Sam Hamill, J. P. Seaton, Trans. Boston: Shambhala Publications, Inc., 1999.

Thomas Merton. The Way of Chuang Tzu. New York: New Directions, 1965.

Wandering on the way: Early Taoist Tales and Parables of Chuang Tzu. Victor H. Mair, Trans. New York: Bantam Books, 1994.

Zhuangzi: The Essential Writings with Selections from Traditional Commentaries. Brook Ziporyn, trans. Indianapolis: Hackett Publishing Company, Inc., 2009.

---

① "put a (high) premium on something"意为"regard a treat as particularly important or valuable"。

# 第五章 《荀子》英译比较与评析

一、君子曰：学不可以已。青，取之于蓝而青于蓝；冰，水为之而寒于水。

——《荀子·劝学》①

The gentleman says: Learning should never cease. Blue comes from the indigo plant but is bluer than the plant itself. Ice is made of water but is colder than water ever is.

(华兹生 译)

The gentleman says: "Learning must never be concluded." Though blue dye comes from the indigo plant, it is bluer than indigo. Ice is made from water, but it is colder than water.

(John Knoblock 译)

"学不可以已"，华兹生译为"学习永远不该停止"，已然十分忠实。Knoblock 译为"学习从不该结束"，使用 conclude（完结）与否定词配合，形象地体现了学无止境，不可轻易宣布大功告成这一深刻意涵。"青"，Knoblock 翻译为"蓝色染液"，与原文所要表达的"青色"有偏差，华兹生译为"蓝色"，是比较准确的。

"冰，水为之"，华兹生与 Knoblock 均译为"冰是由水制成的"，不同在于华兹生使用的 is made of 是看得到原材料的，而 Knoblock 使用的 is made from 是看不到原材料的。如果一定要强调是人造的冰，那么考虑到水变成冰本质并没有变，还是可以看得出原材料的，因此华兹生译文更科学。但是考虑到原文所属的语境②，荀子讨论中提到的更大可能是因自然界温度下降而凝结的冰。就此而言，无论有无语法问题，华兹生与 Knoblock 的译文都不适

---

① 若无特别说明，本章所涉及的《荀子》引文均出自《荀子集释》，出处详见李条生.荀子集释.台北：台湾学生书局，1984.

② 人造冰块在中国古代属于奢侈品，我们现在唾手可得的冰块在荀子的时代并不常见。

切。Hutton 译文①"冰来自水,却比水更冷",最符合这一情境。

二、是故无冥冥之志者,无昭昭之明;无惛惛之事者,无赫赫之功。②行衢道者不至,事两君者不容。目不能两视而明,耳不能两听而聪。

——《荀子·劝学》

  Thus if there is no dark and dogged will, there will be no shining accomplishment; if there is no dull and determined effort, there will be no brilliant achievement. He who tries to travel two roads at once will arrive nowhere; he who serves two masters will please neither. （华兹生 译）

If you do not first have somber intention,
No brilliant understanding can there be.
If you do not first have determined effort,
No glorious achievements will you see.
One walking both forks of a road goes nowhere.
One serving two lords is not viewed welcomely.
Eyes focused on two things at once are not sharp.
Ears tuned to two things at once don't hear clearly. （Eric L. Hutton 译）

"是故无冥冥之志者",华兹生译文意为"黑暗且顽强的意志",究竟什么是"黑暗的意志",令读者困惑不已。Hutton 译为"严肃的意图"虽然不完全忠实,但至少说得通。"昭昭之明",华兹生译为卓越的成就,与原文不符,且语义与下文重复。Hutton 译为"通达的理解",与语境比较协调。"无惛惛之事者",华兹生译文意为"阴暗且坚决的努力","阴暗的努力"令读者惊愕。Hutton 译为"坚决的努力",总体达意。"行衢道者不至"③,华兹生译为"同时想走两条道的人,哪里也到不了",比较符合常理,也与原文"徘徊不定"的意思吻合。Hutton 译为"同时在走一条路的两条岔路的人,哪里都到不了",在物

---

  ① 译文为:"Ice comes from water, and yet it is colder than water."参见 Eric L. Hutton. Xunzi: The Complete Text. Princeton & Oxford: Princeton University Press, 2014:1.
  ② 原注为:"为学治事如不能精诚专一,他的智慧便不能清明通达,他的事业便不能出类拔萃。"参见李涤生.荀子集释.台北:台湾学生书局,1984:8.
  ③ 原注为:"徘徊在歧途上的人,永远不能到达目的地。"参见李涤生.荀子集释.台北:台湾学生书局,1984:8.

理上是存疑的。"事两君者不容"①,华兹生译文"服务于两个主人的人两面不讨好",除了将"君主"译为"主人"稍显宽泛之外,总体是达意的。Hutton 译文"伺候两个君主的人不受待见"并没有明确指出是谁不待见这样的人,不排除读者将其理解为事二主之臣因为修辞人格破产而被第三方排斥,这样就与原文存在较大出入。"目不能两视而明,耳不能两听而聪",华兹生没有翻译这一句。Hutton 译为"同时盯着两样事物的眼睛看不清楚,同时听着两个事情的耳朵听不清楚",虽然在这样的情况下自然是看不清、听不清的,但就实际情形而言,同时聚焦无论对视觉还是听觉在操作上都是极富挑战性的,因此这一译文尚待商榷。Knoblock 译文②"眼睛不可能同时能够看两样东西又都看得很清楚,耳朵不可能同时听两件事情又都听得很明白"则浅白又忠实地再现了原文。

### 三、君子之学也,以美其身;小人之学也,以为禽犊。

——《荀子·劝学》

The gentleman uses learning to ennoble himself; the petty man uses learning as a bribe to win attention from others.

(华兹生 译)

The learning of the gentleman is used to refine his character. The learning of the petty man is used like ceremonial offerings of birds and calves.③

(John Knoblock 译)

"君子之学也,以美其身",华兹生译为"使自己变得高贵",译文主旨依然没

---

① 原注为:"侍奉两个国君的,哪一方也容不下他。"参见李涤生.荀子集释.台北:台湾学生书局,1984:8.

② 译文为:"The eye cannot look at two objects and see either clearly; the ear cannot listen to two things and hear either distinctly."。参见 Johnn Knoblock. Xunzi: A Translation and Study of the Complete Works. Stanford: Stanford University Press, 1990:139.

③ 此处原注为:"According to *Liji*, 1'Quli,' 'in matters of ceremonial offerings, the Son of Heaven presents herbed millet wine, the feudal lords jade tablets, the ministers lamb, grand officers wild geese, knights ringed pheasants, and commoners ducks' (*Liji zhengyi* 5.14a-15b). The purpose of such offerings was to attract the attention of a superior. Scholars used their learning as a means of attracting attention to themselves. Wang Xianqian understands that the nature of the petty man remains like that of beasts. Xunzi returns to the topic below in paragraph 14.1."。参见 John Knoblock. Xunzi: A Translation and Study of the Complete Works. Stanford: Stanford University Press, 1990:272.

有超越功利性追求。Knoblock 译为"提升自己的品格",与原文主旨一致。"以为禽犊",华兹生译为"贿赂他人以赢得注意的手段",没有解释,不免让读者感到困惑。Knoblock 按字面直译为"作为像禽类与小牛犊这样的祭品使用",同时通过注解为读者介绍了《礼记》中所规定的与不同身份与级别的人(上自天子下至庶人)相适配的供品,指出这样的供品是为了引起上级的注意并解释说学者利用所学作为手段吸引别人对他们的关注。Hutton 对禽犊的解释也很到位[①],指出荀子的观点是认为小人自炫其学以取誉于人。这些注解有助于读者深入了解本句语义并为读者进一步了解中国古代文化拓宽了可能性。

四、故未可与言而言谓之傲,可与言而不言谓之隐,不观气色而言谓之瞽。

——《荀子·劝学》

To speak to someone you ought not to is called officiousness; to fail to speak to someone you ought to is called secretiveness; to speak to someone without first observing his temper and looks is called blindness[②]. (华兹生 译)

It is presumptuous to start talking with someone before he is in a mood to be addressed. It is excessively reserved [of the rhetor] to remain silent when the audience becomes addressable. And it is blind [of the rhetor] to speak out without first checking the appearance and manners of the addressee." (刘亚猛 译)[③]

"故未可与言而言谓之傲[④],可与言而不言谓之隐",华兹生译为"不该同

---

① 原注为:"In ancient China, animals were given as gifts to superiors and honored guests. Xunzi's point is that the petty man flaunts his learning to win favor with others."。参见 Eric L. Hutton. Xunzi: The Complete Text. Princeton: Princeton University Press, 2014:6.

② 原注为:"This sentence is a paraphrase of *Analects* XVI, 6, where the saying is attributed to Confucius."。参见 Basic Writings of Mo Tzu, Hsun Tzu, and Han Fei Tzu. Burton Watson, trans. New York: Columbia University Press, 1967:22.

③ Liu Yameng."Nothing Can Be Accomplished if the Speech Does Not Sound Agreeable": Rhetoric and the Invention of Classical Chinese Discourse. Rhetoric before and beyond the Greeks. Ed(s).Carol S. Lipson, Roberta A. Binkley. State University of New York Press, 2004:147-164.

④ "傲",李涤生认为是"躁"的假字。参见李涤生.荀子集释.台北:台湾学生书局, 1984:17.

对方说却去说,这叫作自以为是;有责任说却没说,这叫作有意隐瞒",关注点在于该不该说。刘亚猛译为"对方情绪不在听你说话的状态,你却开口,这叫冒昧;受众处于适合言说的状态,修辞者却保持沉默,这就属于过度矜持",关注点在于能不能说,与原文的"未可"及"可"高度契合。"不观气色",华兹生译为"不观察他的脾气与表情",表情固然可以也应该观察,"观察脾气"却并非短时间能够完成的,从逻辑上而言比较牵强。刘亚猛译为"没有事先查看对方的样貌与举止",既忠实于原文又符合事理。

五、故非我而当者,吾师也;是我而当者,吾友也;谄谀我者,吾贼也。

——《荀子·修身》

He who comes to you with censure is your teacher; he who comes with approbation is your friend; but he who flatters you is your enemy. （华兹生 译）

And so, he who rightly criticizes me acts as a teacher toward me, and he who rightly supports me acts as a friend toward me, while he who flatters and toadies to me acts as a villain toward me. （Eric L. Hutton 译）

"故非我而当者,吾师也;是我而当者,吾友也",华兹生译为"来指责你的,就是你的老师;赞同你的,就是你的朋友",逻辑不通。一方面,除了来提点我们的,来者不善的批评者也是大有人在,总是有人会无端指责他人。另一方面,出于某种难以言表的修辞目的,敌人也有可能采用"认同"的修辞策略在明面上表达赞成而在暗地里持反对态度。Hutton 译文"正确地批评我的人相当于我的老师,正确地支持我的人相当于我的朋友",在逻辑上能够自圆其说,更为可取。"谄谀我者,吾贼也",Hutton 翻译成"奉承谄媚我的人对于我而言是个恶棍",用"恶棍"表达贼害之意,显然言过其实。华兹生译为"奉承你的是你的敌人",虽然有些生硬,总体是达意的。

六、老老,而壮者归焉;不穷穷,而通者积焉;行乎冥冥而施乎无报,而贤、不肖一焉。人有此三行,虽有大过,天其不遂乎!

——《荀子·修身》

If you treat old people as they ought to be treated, then young people too will come to your side. If you do not press those who are already hard pressed, then the successful too will gather around you. If you do good in secret and seek no reward for your kindness, then sages and unworthy men alike will be with you. If a man does these three things, though he should commit a grave error, will Heaven leave him to perish?

(华兹生 译)

  If a person treats the old as befits the old, then those who are in their prime will come to him. If a person does not afflict those who are already in extreme difficulty, then those who are successful will gather by him. If a person works in obscurity and practices kindness without seeking recompense, then the worthy and the unworthy will unanimously follow him. If a person has these three kinds of conduct, then even if he were to commit some great error, Heaven would not cast him down!

(Eric L. Hutton 译)

### 壮者

华兹生译为"年轻人",不如 Hutton 译为"壮年之人"更能够传达"年富力强"的概念。

### 不穷穷

李涤生解读为"不强人以所不知不能"①。Hutton 译为"不要给已经陷入极度困难的人更多痛苦",基本达意;华兹生译为"不逼迫窘迫者",连用两个 press(迫),充满修辞意趣,令读者过目不忘。

### 行乎冥冥而施乎无报

华兹生与 Hutton 均忠实地译为"秘密地做好事,不为善行谋求回报"。Knoblock 译文②"默默行善,即便无人认可依然善良"弱化了行善者的修辞人格,因此不及其他两个译文。

### 而贤、不肖一焉

华兹生译为"圣人与无能之人都会追随你"。圣人往往是其他人追慕的对象,不会轻易屈尊去追随他人,因此用 sage(圣人)翻译"贤"是对原文的误解。Hutton 翻译为"有无才德者都一致追随他"则比较忠实。

---

  ① 李涤生.荀子集释.台北:台湾学生书局,1984:35.
  ② 译文为:"If one conducts himself in obscurity and is kind when no recognition will result." 参见 Johnn Knoblock. Xunzi: A Translation and Study of the Complete Works. Stanford: Stanford University Press, 1990:157.

### 人有此三行,虽有大过,天其不遂乎

"人有此三行",无论是华兹生翻译的"如果有人做到了这三件事",还是 Hutton 翻译的"如果一个人有这三种行为",都不如 Knoblock 译文①"拥有这三种品质的人"接近原文。"虽有大过,天其不遂乎",华兹生与 Hutton 均翻译为"即便他犯了大错误,上天也不会让他灭亡",首先是提到行为人的错误,然后才是得到宽恕。Knoblock 译文"即便对他发出了非常不祥的兆头,老天也不会毁灭他吧?"②没有提及过失,只提到惩戒与宽恕,在逻辑上不如其他两个译文严密。

### 七、君子崇人之德,扬人之美,非谄谀也;正义直指,举人之过,非毁疵也。

——《荀子·不苟》

In venerating the inner power in others or in celebrating their excellence, the gentleman does not engage in flattery or toady after others. In correcting and criticizing others in blunt terms and in pointing out their faults, he does not engage in backbiting or slander. (John Knoblock 译)

When the gentleman exalts another's virtue or praises another's excellence, it is not flattery or toadying. When he points out another's faults with straight talk and direct accusation, it is not slander or calumny. (Eric L. Hutton 译)

#### 君子崇人之德,扬人之美,非谄谀也

Knoblock 翻译为"在尊崇他人内在力量或者赞美其优点时,绅士不会去奉承讨好他人",也就是"绅士有所不为也"这个意思,在结构上与原文有很大差异。Hutton 译文"当绅士推崇别人的美德或称赞他们的优点时,并不是在奉承讨好他人",与原文的"叙述+评论"结构完全一致。

#### 正义直指,举人之过,非毁疵也

Knoblock 翻译的"用直白的语言纠正与批评他人,指出他人错误时,不会

---

① 原注为:"A person who possess these three qualities."。参见 John Knoblock. Xunzi: A Translation and Study of the Complete Works. Stanford: Stanford University Press, 1990:158.

② 译文为:"though he be sent a greatly inauspicious omen, would Heaven have wrought his ruin?"。参见 John Knoblock. Xunzi: A Translation and Study of the Complete Works. Stanford: Stanford University Press, 1990:158.

在背后说人坏话或诋毁他人",与前句在结构的处理上存在同样的问题。Hutton 译文"当他直言不讳地指出别人的错误并且进行批评时,并非是在诋毁或中伤他人"无论是内容还是结构都成功再现了原文。

八、故新浴者振其衣,新沐者弹其冠,人之情也。其谁能以己之 潐潐受人之掝掝者哉?

——《荀子·不苟》

  Accordingly, that one who has just washed his body will shake out his robes and that one who has just washed his hair will dust off his cap is because of the essential nature of humans. Who among them could bear to subject his own full understanding to the delusions of others!　　　　　　　　(John Knoblock 译)

  So, those who have just bathed shake out their clothes, and those who have just washed their hair dust off their caps. This is the natural disposition of people. Who can endure pollution from others when one's own self is pure?[①]

(Eric L. Hutton 译)

故新浴者振其衣,新沐者弹其冠

  Knoblock 翻译为"刚刚洗过身体的人,会抖一下自己的袍子;刚刚洗过头发的人,会弹一下自己的帽子"。Hutton 译文最大的差别是对"浴"的翻译,使用 bathe(沐浴),没有像 Knoblock 将洗身与洗头区分开来以再现原文这一区别;另外就是关于"衣"的翻译,译为普通意义上的"衣物",不如 Knoblock 的"袍子"更能够体现中国古代着装习俗。"人之情也",Knoblock 翻译为"是因为人性本质",未免有言过其实之嫌。Hutton 译文"这是人的自然倾向",符合人情事理,容易为读者所接受。

其谁能以己之潐潐受人之掝掝者哉

  Knoblock 翻译为"谁能够忍受让自己的全面理解受到他人的蒙蔽!",是对原文的过度解读。Hutton 译文"谁自己纯洁却能够忍受来自他人的污染?"

---

  ① 此处原注为:"The point of this last part of the paragraph may be difficult to see, but it continues the thought of the previous lines. Namely, just as someone freshly bathed does not want to get dirty, so the gentleman in ordering the state will rely on only what is orderly, and not what is chaotic."。参见 Eric L. Hutton. Xunzi: The Complete Text. Princeton: Princeton University Press, 2014:38.

忠实再现了原文,同时通过注解①对其意义做了引申。

九、凡人之患,偏伤之也,见其可欲也,则不虑其可恶也者;见其可利也,则不顾其可害也者。是以动则必陷,为则必辱,是偏伤之患也。

——《荀子·不苟》

In general, the calamities that beset mankind are the result of prejudices and the damage they cause. If, when a man sees something desirable, he does not reflect that it may come to be detestable and, something beneficial, that it could come to be harmful, then it is inevitable that his movements will ensnare him and his actions will bring disgrace. Just this constitutes the calamity of prejudice and the damages that result from it.　　　　　　　　　　　　(John Knoblock 译)

In most cases, people's problems are due to their own one-sidedness harming them. They see what may be desirable in something, but then do not consider what may be undesirable in it; they see what may be beneficial in it, but then do not look to what may be harmful in it. Thus, when they move on it they are sure to fall into trouble, and when they act on it they are sure to encounter disgrace. These are the problems that occur when one-sidedness harms a person.
(Eric L. Hutton 译)

**凡人之患,偏伤之也**

Knoblock 翻译为"困扰人类的灾难是偏见及其带来的损害",将"患"翻译为"灾难",有夸张之嫌,使用 prejudice(字面意思为"预先判断")翻译"偏"(片面性),有明显偏颇。正如李涤生所指出的那样,"偏",所见不周②,也就是说主要不在于是否带着先入之见看问题,而在于是否看到了事情的另外一面甚至是多面。"偏伤"在原句中是主谓关系而非并列关系,意思是片面性蒙蔽了人们的认知,译者误解为并列关系。Hutton 翻译为"人们的问题主要是因为他们的片面性害了他们",成功避免了 Knoblock 的误区。

---

① 大意是:这个部分的要旨可能不是那么明晰,大体上是延续了前文的思想。也就是说,正如刚刚洗完澡的人不喜欢变脏一样,绅士(译者想借此表达"君子"这个概念)要依赖秩序而非混乱治理国家。

② 李涤生.荀子集释.台北:台湾学生书局,1984:53.

见其可欲也,则不虑其可恶也者;见其可利也,则不顾其可害也者

Knoblock 译为"如果一个人看到可欲之物却没有反思它可能会变得令人憎恶,或者看到有利之物,却不曾想到它会变得有害",是说这个事物历时性的变化,与原文所要表达的共时性存在的"负面"有偏差。Hutton 译文"看到一个事物值得追求的一面,却不考虑它可能有的可厌的另外那一面;看到一个事物有利的一面,却忽略它可能有害的一面"准确再现了原文。

是以动则必陷/是偏伤之患也

"是以动则必陷",Knoblock 译为"行动不可避免地使他掉入圈套",是比较有局限性的直译,不如 Hutton 译文"一旦行动,一定会遇到麻烦"能够反映原文精神。"是偏伤之患也",Knoblock 译为"这个构成了偏见的灾难及偏见带来的损害",对原文有误读且英文句法表达方面逻辑模糊,存在歧义。Hutton 译为"这些是片面性危害一个人时产生的问题",解读到位且表达准确。

### 十、故与人善言,暖于布帛;伤人以言,深于矛戟。

——《荀子·荣辱》

Hence words of praise for another are warmer than clothing of linen and silk. The wound caused by words is deeper than that of spears and halberds.

(John Knoblock 译)

Thus, giving someone kind words is more warming than hemp-cloth and silk, while hurtful words cut people more deeply than spears and halberds.

(Eric L. Hutton 译)

"与人善言",Knoblock 翻译为"称赞他人的话语",比较狭隘,善言可以包括一般意义上体现善意的话语(如鼓励的话语、善意的问候等)。Hutton 翻译为"说带着善意的话"是比较忠实的译文。"伤人以言,深于矛戟",Knoblock 翻译为"话语造成的伤口比矛戟的创伤还要深",凸显的信息是伤口,没有与前面的中心话题保持一致。Hutton 翻译为"伤人的话语给人造成的心理切口比矛戟的创伤还要深",与前文的核心信息保持一致,容易形成对比。尤其是 while(然而)的使用,使得两种话语行为截然相反的修辞效果鲜明地呈现在读者面前,更有助于实现原文预期的劝说和劝诫功能。

十一、凡说之难：以至高遇至卑，以至治接至乱，未可直至也，远举则病缪，近世则病佣。善者于是间也，亦必远举而不缪，近世而不佣，与时迁徙，与世偃仰；缓急嬴绌，府然若渠匽檃栝之于己也，曲得所谓焉，然而不折伤。

——《荀子·非相》

All the difficulties of persuasions lie in this: that the highest must be juxtaposed with the lowest, that the most orderly must be connected with the most chaotic, and that this may never be done by the most direct route. If one adduces distant examples, they are annoyed at the exaggerations; if one cites recent examples, they are annoyed at their commonplaceness. A true expert in this pursuit is sure to avoid both difficulties by adducing only distant examples that are not exaggerated and by citing recent examples that are not commonplace. He modifies and changes them with the occasion, adapting and adjusting them to the age, sometimes indulgent, sometimes urgent, sometimes expansive, other times restrictive. Channel them like canal ditches, force them like the press-frame[①], accommodating them to the circumstances so that your audience will get hold of the idea under discussion, yet will not be given offense or be insulted.

(John Knoblock 译)

The difficulties of persuasion lie in using what is extremely lofty to encounter what is extremely base, and using what is extremely orderly to encounter what is extremely chaotic. In such cases, one cannot approach things directly. But if one raises remote parallels, then one risks being misunderstood, and if one cites closer events, then one risks being crude[②]. One who is good at it falls between

---

① 原注为："Yang Liang: canal ditches control water by determining the direction of its flow; the press-frame is the tool that controls wood by adjusting the curvature of its surface. The gentleman uses discussion to channel and direct. Xunzi uses the press-frame as an instrument of gentle pressure that the gentleman applies to others in contrast to the exactitude of the plumbline, which he applies to himself."。参见 John Knoblock. Xunzi: A Translation and Study of the Complete Works. Stanford: Stanford University Press, 1990:298.

② 原注为："I.e., the indirect means used to persuade a tyrant must neither be so vague that he misses the point, nor so close to home that he sees through it as a thinly veiled criticism. The latter fault differs little from direct confrontation and is thus crude."。参见 Eric L. Hutton. Xunzi: The Complete Text. Princeton: Princeton University Press, 2014:38.

these two; he is sure to raise remote parallels without being misunderstood, and cites closer events without being crude. He shifts with the occasions and bends with the times, slowing down or speeding up, expanding or being restrained, bending as though there were a water channel or wood-shaping frame constraining him. He achieves completely what he wants to express, but does so without causing hurt.

(Eric L. Hutton 译)

以至高遇至卑，以至治接至乱/未可直至也①

Knoblock 翻译为"将（物理上）最高的与最低的并置，将最有序的与最混乱的联结"，是典型的对原文望文生义而产生的译文。Hutton 译为"使用最高尚的去面对最卑劣的，让最有序的去面对最混乱的"，总体是对的，但是稍嫌宽泛。"未可直至也"，Knoblock 翻译为"不可以用最直接的方式去做这样的事情"，言下之意是可以用比较直接的方式进行，与原文要求婉转行事不符。Hutton 翻译为"在这样的情况下，不能直截了当去表达自己的观点"，也就是要迂回婉转地表达观点，比较符合原作精神。

远举则病缪，近世则病佣/善者于是间也

"远举则病缪，近世则病佣"，Knoblock 翻译为"如果引用遥远的例子，则他们会因为言辞夸张而感到不快；如果引用近期的例子，则他们会因为太过家常而感到不快"。原文并未提到言过其实这个问题，"常见"（commonplaceness）虽然缺乏修辞张力，但还不至于冒犯人，因此译文有偏差。Hutton 翻译为"如果举出遥远的类似例子，则要冒着被误会的风险；如果引用较近的事件，要冒着（被认为）粗鄙的风险"。Hutton 译文提到较近的事件格调不高，容易冒犯听众审美趣味，更符合情理，并且通过注解②说明为何过远过近都会得罪君主，对读者更有说服力。"善者于是间也"，Hutton 翻译为"善于说服的人属于这两者之间"，虽然达意，却不能彰显修辞者的主动性。Knoblock 翻译为"真正精于此道者避开两个困难"，提到主动去避免陷入困境，如果能够用 pitfalls（陷阱）代替 difficulties（困难）会更加文从字顺。

---

① 本句意为：用最高深的道理劝说最卑陋的人，用最理想的治国之道改变最混乱的局面。参见李波.荀子注评.上海：上海古籍出版社，2016：62.

② 大意为："间接地说服暴君的手段既不能模糊到言不及义，也不能直白切近地让他一目了然，一眼看穿这是'披着盖头/带着面纱'的批评。后者与正面冲突几乎并无二致，因此被视为粗鄙的行为。"

与时迁徙,与世偃仰

Knoblock 翻译为"根据特定场合调整改变例子,调整例子以顺应时代",虽然达意,用词未免有叠床架屋之嫌。Hutton 翻译为"根据场合与时代而调整说话内容",不拖泥带水,成功再现了原文内涵。

缓急/府然若渠匽、檃栝之于己也/曲得所谓焉,然而不折伤

Knoblock 翻译为"有时迁就,有时急迫",不如 Hutton"有时说得缓和些,有时说得急切些"契合语境。"府然若渠匽、檃栝之于己也",Knoblock 翻译为"就像运河沟渠那样引导例子,像压框那样控制例子",并增补注解①对言说与沟渠及压框的形塑与引导功能的相似性进行说明。其实原文讲的是约束自己②,而非控制话语;同时,使用"压框"翻译"檃栝"缺乏柔性与弹性,有较大偏差。Hutton 翻译为"仿佛有水渠或形塑木头的框架约束那样委屈俯就",比较接近原意。"曲得所谓焉,然而不折伤",Hutton 翻译为"他把要说的话都说给了对方听,同时又没有造成伤害",关于"伤害"的说法语焉不详,不免让读者困惑。Knoblock 翻译为"调整例子顺应情势,让受众能够明白讨论的要旨又不会被冒犯或侮辱",把前因后果交代得很清楚,因此是更容易接受的译文。

十二、言而当,知也;默而当,亦知也。故知默犹知言也。故多言而类,圣人也;少言而法,君子也;多少无法而流湎然,虽辩,小人也。③

——《荀子·非十二子》

Speaking when it is appropriate to do so is knowledge; remaining silent when appropriate is also knowledge. Hence knowing when to remain silent is as important as knowing when to speak. Therefore, a sage, though he speaks often, always observes the logical categories appropriate to what he discusses. A gentle-

---

① 大意为:运河沟渠通过决定水流方向来控制水,压框则是通过调节木头表面的曲度控制木头。绅士利用讨论引导与指引(他人)。荀子用压框作为绅士给他人施加轻微压力的手段,与之形成对比的是,他用精确的铅垂线作为对自己的严格要求。
② 原注为:"就像拦水坝控制水流、檃栝矫正曲木那样控制自己。"参见李波.荀子注评.上海:上海古籍出版社,2016:62.
③ 原注为:"以上言言论有此三等。"参见李涤生.荀子集释.台北:台湾学生书局,1984:103.

man, though he speaks but seldom, always accords with the model.① The petty man speaks frequently but in a manner that does not adhere to the model, his thoughts drowning in the verbiage of his idle chatter② even when he engages in the disciplined discourse of formal discriminations. (John Knoblock 译)

  When one speaks and it is fitting, this is wisdom. When one is silent and it is fitting, this is also wisdom. Thus, knowing when to be silent is just as good as knowing when to speak. And so, he who speaks much but whose words match the proper categories of things is a sage. He who speaks little but conforms to the proper model in everything is a gentleman. He who does not follow the proper model regardless of how much or little he speaks, and whose words are perverse and murky, even if he argues keenly, is nothing but a petty man.

(Eric L. Hutton 译)

言而当,知也;默而当,亦知也

  Knoblock 翻译为"时机恰当的时候才说话,是一种知识,时机恰当的时候保持沉默,也是一种知识"。抛开翻译不谈,从修辞话语艺术而言,把握时机才说话(时然后言)是一条颠扑不破的真理,因此译文就其本身表达的道理而言,总体是对的。从翻译角度而言,原文说的并不仅仅限于话语时机,还包括内容适切与否,因此,该译文还不够全面。Hutton 译为"说话而应景是一种智慧,沉默而应景也是一种智慧"。说话应景自然是在恰当的时间和地点,定位正确的目标受众,选择适合话语交流情境因素的语言表达自己的思想、感情、立场等,因此 Hutton 译文更立体地传达了原文思想。此外,Hutton 将"知"翻译为"智慧"而不是"知识",与语境高度契合,也与西方修辞思想中"言说能力是一种智慧"的观点相一致。

---

  ① 原注为:"Yang Liang takes this to mean that the gentleman does not presume to propound original theories on his own authority but always abides by the corpus of the model received from the sages."。参见 Johnn Knoblock. Xunzi: A Translation and Study of the Complete Works. Stanford: Stanford University Press, 1990: 304.

  ② 原注为:"The image is that of one who so overflows with talk he loses sight of what is fundamental."。参见 Johnn Knoblock. Xunzi: A Translation and Study of the Complete Works. Stanford: Stanford University Press, 1990: 304.

故多言而类,圣人也;少言而法,君子也;多少无法而流湎然,虽辩,小人也

撇开具体内容翻译是否准确这个问题,就话语结构而言,Knoblock 译文①主要是凸显三类人在言说时的相关表现并对其做出评价。这与原文使用三类人作为一种象征符号代表上中下三个等级来评价三种话语行为的修辞意图大相径庭。Hutton 译文②在结构上恰恰是先陈述行为,后用三类人作为代表加以评价,完整再现了原文的价值阶及其附带的劝说意图。

就细节词语翻译而言,Knoblock 对"法"的翻译增加了注解,大意为"不敢自造言说,所言皆守典法",有助于加深读者对这个概念的理解。对于"流湎",Knoblock 增补注解"沉湎于浮词而迷失根本的人",通过具体的形象诠释了话语实践中的小人形象。

"辩",并不是"参与讨论鉴定",而是"善于论辩",因此 Hutton 的译文对此把握得更准确。

十三、知而险,贼而神,为诈而巧,言无用而辩,辩不惠而察,治之大殃也。

——《荀子·非十二子》

Those who most threaten public order are men who are wise but engage in daring exploits, who are malefactors with diabolic cleverness, who are skillful yet given to falseness and deception, who discuss the useless but with formal discriminations, and who deal with matters of no urgency yet use precise investigations.

(John Knoblock 译)

Some men are smart but dangerous, and they can work harm with spirit-like efficacy. They are clever at artifice and deceit. Their words are useless, but they argue for them forcefully. Their arguments are not beneficial to people, but they

---

① 大意为:"圣人虽然说得多,却总是遵守与讨论话题适切的逻辑范畴。绅士,虽然说得少,却总是遵从轨范。小人则经常说话,但是其话语表达方式离经叛道。即便是进行正式讨论,其思想也往往沉溺于浮词中,表达空洞且言不及义。"
② 大意为:"话说得多但是注意让话语与事物的适切范畴相匹配者是圣人;话说得少但是中规中矩者是绅士;无论说多说少,言说罔顾轨范、任性污浊的,即便能言善辩,也不免沦为小人。"

investigate them keenly. Such men are a great calamity for good government.

(Eric L. Hutton 译)

这段话的意思是:"生性聪明而险恶,手段狠毒而高明,行为诡诈而巧妙,言论不切实际而雄辩动听,辩说不合急用而明察入微,这些是政治方面的大祸害。"

### 知而险

Knoblock 翻译为"明智却从事冒险的行为",如果真是这样,这样的人对政治并没有什么危害,充其量令观者或知情者感到遗憾罢了。Hutton 译为"精明却危险",这样的人自然是会造成巨大危害,这一译文比较符合逻辑①。

### 贼而神

Knoblock 翻译为"手段狠毒而高明的坏人",总体达意。Hutton 翻译为"胡作非为而变幻莫测",充分体现了作恶者"机警神奇"②(善变)的特征及其巨大危害,给读者带来的修辞冲击更明显可感。

### 为诈而巧,言无用而辩

Knoblock 翻译为"有技巧但是好虚假与欺骗",读起来似乎是在肯定其专业技能同时又对其品格瑕疵颇有微词,不如 Hutton 翻译为"巧与伪诈"更能够体现"伪诈而手段巧妙"③的意思。"言无用而辩",Knoblock 翻译为"讨论毫无用处的问题并且一本正经地进行细致辨析",不如 Hutton 翻译为"其话语没有用处却论证得雄辩有力"符合情境④。讨论无用的问题不一定会引发他人共鸣,但是如果雄辩滔滔地将这类话题呈现在受众面前,则受众很有可能被修辞者所影响并按其设定的议题进行讨论,甚至是开展相应行动(从而造成不良社会后果)。

### 辩不惠而察⑤

Hutton 翻译为"他们的辩说对人们没有益处,却说得很明白",不如 Kno-

---

① "王念孙曰:'知而险'与'贼而神'对文,则知其非美称。"转引自:王先谦.荀子集解.北京:中华书局,2012:97.
② 李涤生.荀子集释.台北:台湾学生书局,1984:103.
③ 李涤生.荀子集释.台北:台湾学生书局,1984:103.
④ 正符合李涤生解读:"无用之言而言之甚巧。"参见李涤生.荀子集释.台北:台湾学生书局,1984:103.
⑤ 不惠,应从王(念孙)说作"不急",也就是不急之辩而辩之甚精。参见李涤生.荀子集释.台北:台湾学生书局,1984.

block 翻译为"处理不急迫的事情却分析得很细微"更接近本土文化阐释权威的解读以及中国话语传统表达规范。

**治之大殃**

Knoblock 翻译为"危害公共秩序最为严重（的人）"，偏离了原文，因为这些人并非直接去扰乱公共秩序，而是通过其话语修辞，也就是使用象征手段颠倒黑白、混淆视听，在思想观念上对治国理政造成灾难性后果。相形之下，Hutton 的译文"这些人是善政之大灾难"更符合原意。

十四、无德不贵，无能不官，无功不赏，无罪不罚。朝无幸位，民无幸生。

——《荀子·王制》

No man of virtue shall be left unhonored; no man of ability shall be left unemployed; no man of merit shall be left unrewarded; no man of guilt shall be left unpunished. No man by luck alone shall attain a position at court; no man by luck alone shall make his way among the people.

(华兹生 译)

Those without virtue are not honored, those without ability are not given office, those without meritorious accomplishment are not rewarded, and those without criminal trespass are not punished. In the court, no one obtains their position through luck. Among the people, no one obtains a livelihood through luck.

(Eric L. Hutton 译)

**无德不贵，无能不官，无功不赏，无罪不罚**

华兹生译为"有德者不可让他没有荣耀，有才者不可让他失业，有功之人不可让他不得奖赏，有罪之人不可让他逍遥法外"，与原文有较大偏差。原文说的是要给予贵、官或执行赏、罚，就需要有德、有能、有功或无罪作为条件，译文变成讨论该如何对待有德、有能、有功或无罪之人了。Hutton 翻译为"没有美德的人不给予荣耀，没有才能的人不让他担任公职，没有功绩的人不给予奖赏，没有罪行的人不加以惩罚"，成功再现了原文设置的条件（以德、能、功、罪为开展贵、官、赏、罚的条件），实现了原文预期话语功能。

### 民无幸生

"幸生",就是虽然游手好闲却能够侥幸获得生存①,华兹生译为"不能让任何人仅仅靠运气就可以获得百姓认可的成就",偏离了原文,原文只提到生存,尚未涉及个人事业发展阶段。Hutton 翻译为"民间没有人仅仅依靠运气就可以过上好日子",与原文大体一致。

十五、凡人好敖慢小事,大事至,然后兴之务之。如是则常不胜夫敦比于小事者矣。是何也?则小事之至也数,其县日也博,其为积也大;大事之至也希,其县日也浅,其为积也小。

——《荀子·强国》

As a general rule, men prefer to neglect minor matters, which they despise. When a major matter comes along, they are roused to action and devote themselves to it, but they invariably fail to arrange minor matters. Why is this? It is that as minor matters come along, they are numerous. Only as they are strung together day by day do they become of wider significance. As they accumulate, they become of great importance. Major matters come along but rarely. As they continue on day after day, they become of narrower significance. As they accumulate, they become of less importance. (John Knoblock 译)

In general, people like to be disdainful and scorning of small matters; only when big matters arrive do they then take them up and work at them. When they are like this, they simply will never surpass those who devotedly apply themselves to small matters. Why is this? It is because the occurrence of small matters is frequent, the days over which they spread are many, and their accumulation is big, whereas the occurrence of big matters is sparse, the days over which they spread are few, and their accumulation is small. (Eric L. Hutton 译)

### 凡人好敖慢小事

Knoblock 翻译为"人们较喜欢忽视小事情,因为不看重这些事情",翻译得恰如其分。Hutton 翻译为"人们往往轻蔑、鄙视小事情",用词过于负面,把人对事情的态度由轻视翻译成鄙视乃至近乎敌视,有较大偏离。

---

① 张觉.荀子译注.上海:上海古籍出版社,1995:158.

**大事至，然后兴之务之**

Knoblock 准确地把"大事至"翻译为大事情出现，Hutton 则望文生义地翻译为"大事情到达了"。"兴之务之"，Hutton 翻译为着手解决，只翻译了"务之"。Knoblock 翻译为"行动起来，致力于解决这个问题"，比较全面。

**如是则常不胜夫敦比于小事者矣**

Knoblock 翻译为"但是他们总是处理不好小事情"，没有体现原文的比较；Hutton 译文"这样的话，他们永远不会超越那些认真做小事的人"，通过比较成功再现了原文内涵。

**则小事之至也数**

Knoblock 译为"小事情出现的数量巨大"，不如 Hutton"小事情发生的频率高"符合事理。

**其县日也博**

Knoblock 译为"只有一天一天累积起来才能够成气候"，与并未提到任何条件的原文不符；Hutton 译文"它们牵涉的时日较长"，与原文相符。

**其为积也大**

Hutton 译文"积累很大"并没有提到所产生的意义，Knoblock 译为"随着积累增大，变得越来越重要"，指明了成果越来越有影响力。

**大事之至也希**

"希"，Knoblock 译为 rarely（罕见），不如 Hutton 翻译为 sparse（稀疏的）更符合事理。

**其县日也浅**

Knoblock 译为"随着时日增加，变得越来越不重要"，与原文偏离较大，不如 Hutton 翻译为"牵涉的时间少"符合实际。

**其为积也小**

Knoblock 译为"越积累越不重要"，不仅与原文不符合，而且即便是不考虑语境，句子本身逻辑也是站不住脚的。Hutton 翻译为"其积累也小"，忠实于原文且逻辑自洽。

十六、堂上不粪，则郊草不瞻旷芸①；白刃扞乎胸，则目不见流矢；拔戟加乎首，则十指不辞断②。

——《荀子·强国》

If the trash has not been cleared from before the pavilion, then you will not notice whether the grass on the suburban altar is growing. If the naked blade strikes your chest, then your eye will not notice the fleeting arrows. If the lance is about to strike your head, then you will not notice your ten fingers' being cut off.

(John Knoblock 译)

When the area within one's hall is not cleared, then the weeds in the countryside are not expected to be removed. When a bared blade is waved before one's chest, one's eyes do not see onward-rushing arrows. When a brandished halberd is poised above one's head, then one's ten fingers will not refuse to be severed.

(Eric L. Hutton 译)

### 堂上不粪，则郊草不瞻旷芸

Knoblock 译为"如果亭子前的垃圾没有清理掉，不可能去留意郊区祭坛的杂草是不是又长长了"，逻辑上很牵强。Hutton 译文"厅堂之内的区域都没有打理清楚时，不能指望会把郊外的野草给铲除了"，与"一屋不扫，何以扫天下"的常言逻辑相近，很容易为读者所接受。

### 白刃扞乎胸，则目不见流矢

Knoblock 译为"白刃犯胸，那么眼睛就不暇去留意飞来的箭了"，形象再现了"惧白刃之甚，不暇忧流矢也"③这一修辞意象。Hutton 译为"当有人在你胸前挥舞利刃时，那么你的眼睛是看不见飞来的箭的"，有可能让读者误以为是因视线被遮挡而看不到而非"无暇他顾"的问题。

### 拔戟加乎首，则十指不辞断

李涤生认为"拔"就是"疾"的意思。这句话的意思是"戟急加于头，两手自

---

① 王念孙认为"瞻旷"是脱文阑入此句。对于这一句，王念孙认为"此言事当先其所急，后其所缓"；王先谦认为"近者未理，不暇及远"。参见王先谦.荀子集解.北京：中华书局，2012：209.

② 意为"不惜十指而救手也"。参见王先谦.荀子集解.北京：中华书局，2012：209.

③ 王先谦.荀子集解.北京：中华书局，2012：209.

然去保护,就不避十指之断了"。① Knoblock 译为"如果长矛将要刺到头上,你就不会注意到十个指头正被砍掉",只是涉及注意力分配的问题,并没有涉及本句价值排序、取舍这一核心问题。Hutton 译为"当一个戟横在头上时,(为了格挡这个戟)即便是十个指头要被切掉也在所不惜",充分体现了急迫的情形以及在此情境下"两害相权取其轻"的权宜选择。

十七、天行有常,不为尧存,不为桀亡。

——《荀子·天论》

Heaven's ways are constant. It does not prevail because of a sage like Yao; it does not cease to prevail because of a tyrant like Jie.　　(华兹生 译)

The course of Nature is constant: it does not survive because of the actions of a Yao; it does not perish because of the actions of a Jie.　(John Knoblock 译)

天行有常

华兹生译为"天堂的运行方式是恒定的",Knoblock 译为"大自然的运行方式是恒定的"。"天",华兹生译为"天堂",而 Knoblock 译为"大自然"。通观《荀子》,可以发现荀子关于"天"的认识也是在发展变化的。就这个语境中的"天"而言,与"尔曹身与名俱灭,不废江河万古流"的"江河"这种自然物有相近之处,因此,就本句而言,带有西方基督教神学色彩的"天"不如"大自然"更契合语境。

不为尧存,不为桀亡

华兹生译为"不会因为尧那样的圣人而存续,也不会因为像桀那样的暴君而消亡",为读者补充了关于尧与桀这一正一反的两个中国文化形象的背景信息;不足之处是没有指出天的运行不受他们的善政或暴政影响而调整自身不假外物的存在状态。Knoblock 译为"不会因为尧的行为而存续,也不会因为桀的行为而消亡",很清晰地指出了天"不为所动",即不会因为君主的具体行为而改变;不足之处是只翻译了两个抽象的文化符号"尧"与"桀",并未给读者具体的解释。

---

① 李涤生.荀子集释.台北:台湾学生书局,1984:359.

十八、名无固宜①,约之以命②。约定俗成谓之宜,异于约则谓之不宜。名无固实,约之以命实③,约定俗成谓之实名。名有固善,径易而不拂,谓之善名。④

——《荀子·正名》

    Names have no intrinsic appropriateness. One agrees to use a certain name and issues an order to that effect, and if the agreement is abided by and becomes a matter of custom, then the name may be said to be appropriate, but if people do not abide by the agreement, then the name ceases to be appropriate. Names have no intrinsic reality. One agrees to use a certain name and issues an order that it shall be applied to a certain reality, and if the agreement is abided by and becomes a matter of custom, then it may be said to be a real name. There are, however, names which are intrinsically good. Names which are clear, simple, and not at odds with the thing they designate may be said to be good names.(华兹生 译)

    Names have no predetermined appropriateness. One forms agreement in order to name things. Once the agreement is set and has become custom, then they are called appropriate, and what differs from the agreed usage is called inappropriate. Names have no predetermined objects. One forms agreement in order to name objects. Once the agreement is set and has become custom, then they are called names of objects. Names do have a predetermined goodness. If they are straightforward, simple, and do not conflict, then they are called good names.

(Eric L. Hutton 译)

### 名无固宜,约之以命

    李涤生认为"此就制名说。言制名之初,名实之间本来没有一定关系,故名无所谓宜与不宜。名是大家相约以命定的"⑤。"名无固宜",华兹生译为"名称没有内在的适切性",已经是忠实的翻译了,但是"内在"一词稍显抽象。

---

    ① 原注为:"名本无定"。参见王先谦.荀子集解.北京:中华书局,2012:406.
    ② 原注为:"立其约而命之"。王先谦.荀子集解.北京:中华书局,2012:406.
    ③ 王念孙认为这个"实"是衍字。参见王先谦.荀子集解.北京:中华书局,2012:407.
    ④ 原注为:"径疾平易而不违拂,谓易晓之名也。即谓呼其名遂晓其意,不待训解者。"参见王先谦.荀子集解.北京:中华书局,2012:407.
    ⑤ 关于这一句话以及下文"约定俗成谓之宜,异于约则谓之不宜"的解释,参见李涤生.荀子集释.台湾:学生书局,1984:517-518.

Hutton 翻译为"名称没有前定的适切性",更明确地否定了名与实的必然关系。"约之以命",华兹生译为"有人同意使用某一名称并颁布法令加以确定",没有说明此人同意谁的提议,又说此人颁布法令,读起来似乎是一个有政治权力的人接受了臣下的提议而确定名称规范。这与公认的名称起源说法不一致,因此该译文有待商榷。Hutton 译为"为了命名事物,大家形成共识",只是泛泛提到共识,没有提到共识的内容。Knoblock 译文①则提到了名称与事物的关联性。

约定俗成谓之宜,异于约则谓之不宜

李涤生认为"此就用名说。言名实之间的关系既然已经确定,成为习俗,用名遵守名约就是宜,不遵守就是不宜"。华兹生译为"如果约定得到遵守并成为习惯,就可以说这个特定名称是恰当的;如果人们不遵守约定,那么这个名称就是不恰当的",讨论还是停留在"定名"而非"用名"阶段,与文意有较大出入。Hutton 译文"一旦约定俗成,这些名称就被视为是恰当的;与约定的用法不同的用法就被认定为是不恰当的"很清晰地表现了"用名"的规范与操作过程。

名无固实,约之以命实,约定俗成谓之实名

李涤生认为此句"言制名之初,此名不一定命此实,但大家相约以此名命此实后,已成习俗。'命实'之'命'字是用来界定此实的,言只此一实乃所命定的"。"实",华兹生译为"现实",有偏颇,因为名称既可以指称现实存在的事物也可以指称现实中不存在的事物。Hutton 译为 object(对象)有较大包容性,既可以指抽象的也可以指具象的"实"。

名有固善,径易②而不拂,谓之善名

李涤生认为此句"言虽无固宜,却有固善。直接平易而不违拂,一听就明白的,就是善名"。③ 华兹生在译文中加入原文没有明示的逻辑衔接词"然而"(however),使得前后对比一目了然。Hutton 虽然没有这样处理,但是通过强调"有"(do have),与前面的"无"形成了鲜明反差,达到了相近的效果。"固

---

① 译文为:"They are bound to something by agreement in order to name it."。大意为:为了命名事物,大家形成共识将名称与事物联系起来。参见 Johnn Knoblock. Xunzi: A Translation and Study of the Complete Works. Stanford:Stanford University Press,1990:130-131.

② 原注为:"'易'。平易。"参见李涤生.荀子集释.台北:台湾学生书局,1984:517-518.

③ 李涤生.荀子集释.台北:台湾学生书局,1984:517-518.

善",华兹生使用"与生俱来就是妥当的",在逻辑上说得通。Hutton 译为"前定的美德",逻辑显得突兀。① "径",也就是直接的意思。② 华兹生使用 clear(清晰的)进行翻译,但是仅仅是逻辑清晰的表达未必会为目标受众降低难度,因此不如 Hutton 的 straightforward(容易理解的,不绕弯子)更能够从受众(名称的实际使用者)的角度思考问题。"不拂",华兹生译为"名与实不存在不一致的情况",忠实再现了原文。Hutton 译为"名称不冲突",语焉不详,没有为读者指明到底是什么方面不冲突才是好名称。

十九、凡人之取也,所欲未尝粹而来也;其去也,所恶未尝粹而往也。故人无动而不③可以不与权俱。

——《荀子·正名》

When men acquire something, they never get only what they desire and nothing more; when men reject something, they never rid themselves only of what they hate and nothing more. Therefore, when men act, it must be on the basis of some scale and standard. （华兹生 译）

As a general rule, when men choose, what they get is never only what they wanted; when they reject, what they lose is never only what they disliked.④ Thus, a man should weigh and balance both before he acts. （John Knoblock 译）

取

华兹生译为"获得",与后文"拒绝接受"相对;Knoblock 翻译为"选择",与后文"拒绝"无法形成强对比关系,修辞效果比原文显著弱化。

---

① Hutton 前面译文也用过这个 predetermined,比较适切,但是此处语境发生变化,因而显得突兀。华兹生所用的 intrinsic 情况类似,原来不妥当,到新语境中就变得和谐。

② 李涤生.荀子集释.台北:台湾学生书局,1984:517-518.

③ 王念孙认为这个"不"是衍字。参见王先谦.荀子集解.北京:中华书局,2012:416.

④ 此处原注为:"The point is that what we obtain from our attempts to satisfy our desires is never unalloyed, but a mixture of things we like and things we dislike. So too in our attempt to avoid the things we dislike, we surrender things we like as well."。大意为:我们为了满足自己的欲望所获得的东西从来不会是不掺任何杂质的,往往既有我们喜欢的,也掺杂着我们不喜欢的。同样地,我们想要去除某些不喜欢的东西时,也会被迫放弃某些我们喜欢的。原注参见 Johnn Knoblock. Xunzi: A Translation and Study of the Complete Works. Stanford: Stanford University Press, 1990:344.

### 所欲未尝粹而来也

Knoblock 采用直译"所得到的从来不仅仅是他们想要的",对于可能多出来的部分没有说明立场,依然存在误解空间;华兹生译为"他们永远不会只得到他们追求的(而没有多余的)",则提示读者那些多余的是他们不需要却必然附带出现的。

### 所恶未尝粹而往也

"往",Knoblock 译为"失去",体现不出事主的好恶,不如华兹生译文使用"去除"能够明确体现这是行为人的主动选择。"恶",华兹生译文使用"厌恶",语气过于强烈,不如 Knoblock 的"不喜欢"客观可信。Knoblock 译文通过加注,为读者进一步阐明了这句话的意思。

### 与权俱

华兹生使用静态的名词(scale and standard)翻译,不如 Knoblock 的"衡量与平衡"(weigh and balance)能够体现行为主体的主观能动性。

二十、心忧恐,则口衔刍豢而不知其味,耳听钟鼓而不知其声,目视黼黻而不知其状,轻暖平簟而体不知其安。故向万物之美而不能嗛也,假而得问①而嗛之,则不能离也。故向万物之美而盛忧,兼万物之利而盛害。

——《荀子·正名》

If the mind is full of anxiety and terror, then, though the mouth may be crammed with delicious food it will not recognize the flavor, though the ear listens to the music of bells and drums it will not recognize the sound, though the eye lights upon embroidered patterns it will not recognize their form, and though the body is clothed in warm, light garments and rests upon fine-woven mats, it will feel no ease. In such a case, a man may be confronted by all the loveliest things in the world and yet be unable to feel any gratification. Even if he should feel a moment's gratification, he could never completely shake off his anxieties and fears. Hence, although he confronts all the loveliest things in the world, he is

---

① 王念孙认为,"得问当为'得间'之误"。参见王先谦.荀子集解.北京:中华书局,2012:417.

overwhelmed with worry, and though he enjoys all the benefits in the world, he knows only loss. （华兹生 译）

If the mind is anxious or filled with fear, then although the mouth is filled with fine meats, it will not be aware of their taste. Although the ear hears bells and drums, it will not be aware of their sound. Although the eye beholds fine embroidered patterns, it will not be aware of their appearance. And, although the body is clothed in warm, light garments and rests on a fine bamboo mat, it will not be aware of their comfort. Thus, were such a man to have all the beautiful things of the world for his enjoyment, he would be unable to find satisfaction in them. And, even supposing he. were to feel a moment of satisfaction, he would be unable to leave his anxiety and fear behind. Thus, even with all the beautiful things of the world to enjoy, he is filled with anxiety. Combining together all the benefits of the myriad things, he is consumed by suffering. （John Knoblock 译）

口衔刍豢而不知其味

"刍豢"指牛羊猪狗等牲畜，泛指肉类食品。华兹生宽泛地译为"美食"，虽然不精确但是一目了然；Knoblock 译为"上等的肉食"，准确易懂；Hutton 翻译为 grass-fed and grain-fed meats，即"食草与食肉动物的肉"，虽然精确，但未免烦琐，容易涣散读者注意力。"衔"，华兹生译文为 be crammed，带有"填鸭式"的负面意涵，Hutton 用 stuff［(常指匆忙或胡乱地)塞］，均与美味的食物不协调；Knoblock 使用中性的"(使)充满"，比较合理。

目视黼黻而不知其状

"视"，华兹生译为"偶然发现"，与"视而不见"逻辑不冲突。Knoblock 用"注视"则与后面的"视而不见"龃龉：既然是认真去看，要否认看到的东西难免于理不合。"黼黻"，即美丽的花纹，华兹生译文未凸显"美"，只提到刺绣的纹案，Knoblock 译出"精美"这一特征，更准确全面。"状"，华兹生译文为"形式"，可以涵摄图案之美，Knoblock 使用"样子"则局限于总体外观。

簟

华兹生译为"织工精美的上等坐垫"，虽然不如 Knoblock 所译"精美竹席"精确，但从修辞角度而言并不妨碍预期话语效果的实现。Hutton 译文①

---

① 译文为"sits on sumptuous mats"。参见 Eric L. Hutton. Xunzi: The Complete Text. Princeton: Princeton University Press, 2014:246.

"坐在豪华坐垫上",强调了对坐垫、席子的社会评价而非直观生理感受,偏离了原文。

**不知其安**

华兹生译为"感受不到自在",不如 Knoblock 的"感受不到舒适",因为这里所讨论的主要是生理感受而非心理感觉。

**向/美/离**

华兹生用带负面意涵的 confront(面对)翻译"向"不如 Knoblock 直接翻译为"享受"符合原文。"美",华兹生译为 loveliest(pleasant or enjoyable),也就是令人愉悦的意思,比 Knoblock 纯粹表达视觉之美的 beautiful 更有深度。"离",华兹生译为"摆脱",Knoblock 译为"抛在身后",都很形象生动。

**故向万物之美而盛忧,兼万物之利而盛害**

"盛忧",华兹生译为"忧心忡忡"①,比 Knoblock 的"充满焦虑"更有修辞冲击力。"盛害",华兹生只译为"损失",语焉不详,不如 Knoblock 的"被痛苦所吞噬"更能够给读者留下印象。

## 二十一、多知而无亲、博学而无方、好多而无定者,君子不与。②

——《荀子·大略》

The gentleman will not associate with those who possessing much knowledge have no close companions, those who though broadly learned have no methods, and those who being fond of many things have no fixed standards.

(John Knoblock 译)

People who know many things but have no particular affections among them; people who pursue wide-ranging learning but have no direction; and people who like many things but have no fixity—these the gentleman will not take as his associates.

(Eric L. Hutton 译)

李涤生认为这句话的意思是"多知而无所专重,博学而无一定方向,多好

---

① 译文字面意思是"被忧虑所淹没、压倒"。
② 李波将本句译为:"知识很多而不亲近老师,学习广泛而没有方法,兴趣很广而没有定准,君子不赞成。"虽然在字面上似乎比较忠实,在逻辑方面则有待商榷。比如"学习广泛"与"没有方法"之间并不存在密切的逻辑关联性,将两者相提并论难免令读者感到困惑。李波译文参见李波.荀子注评.上海:上海古籍出版社,2016:425.

而不能专一,这样为学的人,君子是不嘉许的"。①

"多知而无亲",Knoblock译为"拥有很多知识但是没有亲密伙伴",既不符合上下文语境也不符合生活实际:有思想的人往往是孤独的,有没有密友并不是判断一个人品行的指标。Hutton翻译为"懂得很多但是没有特别的爱好",与下文"多与一"的讨论和谐共振,显然是更好的译文。"博学而无方",Knoblock翻译为"学得很广但是没有方法",不如Hutton译文"学得很广但是没有主攻方向"忠实于原文。"好多而无定者",Knoblock翻译为"爱好很多但是没有固定标准",逻辑上难以自圆其说。Hutton翻译为"爱好很多但是没有确定的目标",符合原文并与生活经验一致。"君子不与",Knoblock译文将这一内容放在句子开头,更符合英语句子首重原则,有利于读者获取核心信息及作者对相关事态的基本立场。Hutton的译文将这一信息放在结尾,虽然忠实于原文顺序,从修辞受众角度而言效果却并不理想。Hutton的译文受众有可能因为前面众多的信息而涣散注意力,并且因为没有提纲挈领的导语而缺乏对阅读材料的逻辑梳理与基本价值定位。

## 二十二、语曰:"流丸止于瓯、臾②,流言止于知者。"

——《荀子·大略》

There is the saying: "Balls rolling in every direction are stopped by bowls and pans. Wayward doctrines spreading in every direction are stopped by those who know."
(John Knoblock 译)

A saying goes, "A wayward ball comes to a stop when it reaches a hollow. Wayward talk comes to a stop when it reaches those with understanding."
(Eric L. Hutton 译)

"流丸止于瓯、臾",Knoblock译为"四处滚动的球被碗和平底锅截停了",难免使得读者莫名惊讶这究竟是怎样的一个场景。Hutton翻译为"一个自由滚动的圆球遇到凹陷处就停住了",合情合理,很容易为读者所认同。"流言止于知者",Knoblock翻译为"四处传播的不负责任的教义遇到懂的人就止息了",不如Hutton翻译为"不负责任的说法遇到有理解力的人就止息了"更能体现"谣言"的意思。此外,Hutton翻译两处使用wayward,恰好呼应了原文

---

① 李涤生.荀子集释.台北:台湾学生书局,1984:628.
② 原注为:"倾侧之地"。参见王先谦.荀子集解.北京:中华书局,2012:498.

"流丸"与"流言"中的两个"流",在修辞上成功再现了原文的语言特色。

## 本章参考的英译本

Basic Writings of Mo Tzu, Hsun Tzu, and Han Fei Tzu. Burton Watson, trans. New York: Columbia University Press, 1967.

Eric L. Hutton. Xunzi: The Complete Text. Princeton: Princeton University Press, 2014.

Johnn Knoblock. Xunzi: A Translation and Study of the Complete Works. Stanford: Stanford University Press, 1990.

# 第六章 《墨子》英译比较与评析

一、是故君子自难而易彼①,众人自易而难彼。

——《墨子·亲士》②

Therefore the superior man is strict with one's self but lenient with others(in matters of conduct)while the multitude are lenient with themselves but strict with others.

(梅贻宝 译)

For this reason, the superior man makes things difficult for himself but easy for others. The mass of men makes things easy for themselves but difficult for others.

(John Knoblock 等 译)

**自难而易彼**

梅贻宝(W.P. Mei)除了译出"严于律己、宽以待人"这个原文包含的内容,还增补了"在品行方面"这一点,有助于话题聚焦。Knoblock 等译为"为自己设置障碍,但是给别人便利",与人方便是美德,读者自然觉得合理,但自找苦吃、主动提高任务难度这样的行为则难免令读者觉得匪夷所思。

二、是故为其所难者,必得其所欲焉;未闻为其所欲,而免其所恶者也。

——《墨子·亲士》

Therefore, those who attempt what seems difficult to them will obtain what they desire, but few who aim at what they desire can avoid what they dislike.

(梅贻宝 译)

---

① 孙诒让解释为:"言自处于难,即躬自厚而薄责人之义。"参见孙诒让.墨子间诂.北京:中华书局,2001:2.

② 若无特别说明,本章所涉及《墨子》引文均出自《墨子间诂》。出处详见孙诒让.墨子间诂.北京:中华书局,2001.

Therefore, those who try the most difficult tasks can obtain what they want; but I never heard that those who aim for what they want can really avoid what they dislike.

(李绍昆 译)

"为其所难者",梅贻宝与 Knoblock 等均译为"尝试他们觉得困难的就(必然)会得偿所愿",虽然忠实于原文①,却未必与事理相符。李绍昆译为"凡事能够从最难处做起,就有可能实现自己的愿望",在逻辑上比较合理。"未闻为其所欲,而免其所恶者也",梅贻宝不再坚持直译,进行修辞调整后译为"老是专注于自己欲望的人很少能够避开自己不喜欢的东西",在逻辑上完全能够自圆其说。李绍昆译为"从来没有听说过追求自己想要的东西的人会真正避开他们不喜欢的东西",虽然忠实于原文,却在事理上难以圆通。

### 三、是以甘井近竭,招②木近伐,灵龟近灼,神蛇近暴。

——《墨子·亲士》

For the same reason, the sweetest well is the first to be drained, the most attractive trees are the first to be felled, the most spirit-laden tortoise shells are the first to be burnt, the snakes with the most magic are the first to be exposed to the sun.③

(John Knoblock 等 译)

In the same way, the sweetest well is the first to be used up and the tallest tree the first to be felled. [Likewise], the efficacious tortoise is the first to be burned and the magical serpent the first to be dried in the sun. (Ian Johnston 译)

"竭",Knoblock 等翻译为"汲干",符合井中取水这个场景,比 Johnston 的"用光"更具体形象。"招木",Knoblock 翻译为"吸引人的树木",不如 Johnston 的"高大的树"符合原文。"灵龟近灼",Knoblock 等翻译为"充满神性的",过犹不及。Johnston 翻译为"灵验的",最为妥帖。"神蛇近暴",Knob-

---

① 中国文化读者对于原文中这类高频出现的古代汉语夸张修辞格早已司空见惯,往往不觉得逻辑上有明显龃龉,而不熟悉中国表达习惯的读者就有可能感到言过其实。

② 吴毓江引毕沅注曰:"'招'与'乔'音相近。"参见吴毓江.墨子校注.北京:中华书局,2006:6.

③ 原注为:"Tortoise shells were used in divination; snakes were ritually exposed to the sun when rain was sought."。参见 John Knoblock, Jeffrey Riegel. Mozi: A Study and Translation of the Ethical and Political Writings. Berkeley: University of California, 2013: 402.

lock 等翻译的"有最多魔法的蛇"与 Johnston 的"有魔法的蛇"都超越了"灵验"的范畴而涉及"超自然力量",与原文有较大偏差。李绍昆译为 witch-like(像巫婆那样),也就是"有巫术的",与原文比较接近。"近暴",Johnston 翻译为"最早被晒干",稍有偏差。Knoblock 等不仅准确地翻译为"最早被拿到太阳底下暴晒",还通过加注补充说明龟壳用于占卜,蛇用于暴晒以求雨这样的习俗,为读者提供了充分的文化背景知识。

四、故虽有贤君,不爱无功之臣;虽有慈父,不爱无益之子。

——《墨子·亲士》

Therefore, even a worthy ruler does not favor ministers who accomplish nothing and even an affectionate father does not favor useless sons.

(John Knoblock 等 译)

So even a worthy ruler will not look kindly on an official without merit, and even a compassionate father will not look kindly on a son without promise.

(Ian Johnston 译)

"贤君",Knoblock 等与 Johnston 均翻译为"有德的君主",是比较准确的。"爱",Knoblock 等翻译的"偏爱"、Johnston 的"慈爱地看待"与原文"喜爱"均存在偏差;李绍昆译为 love 最为简单明了。"慈父",Knoblock 等翻译为 affectionate father(充满深情的父亲),比 Johnston"富有同情心的父亲"更接近原文。"无益之子",Knoblock 等翻译为"无用之子",虽然字面对应,却不如 Johnston 翻译为"没有前途的孩子"视野开阔且具有修辞色彩:没有前途的孩子个人生存都有困难,遑论为父亲带来助益。

五、良弓难张,然可以及高入深;良马难乘,然可以任重致远;良才难令,然可以致君见尊。

——《墨子·亲士》

Good bows may be hard to draw, but they can reach great heights and pierce deeply. Good horses may be hard to ride on, but they can carry heavy burdens and make long journeys. Real talents may be hard to command, but they can be trusted to be envoys to the court of the emperor and to meet the nobility.

(梅贻宝 译)

Though a good bow is hard to draw, arrows shot from it soar to great heights and pierce deeply. Though a good horse is difficult to drive, it is able to bear heavy loads and travel great distances. Though a man of great talent is hard to order about, he can make his lord greatly respected.　　　　　(John Knoblock 等 译)

**良弓难张,然可以及高入深/良马难乘/良才难令**

"良弓难张,然可以及高入深",梅贻宝译为"良弓可以抵达高处,穿入深处",逻辑上不如 Knoblock 等的译文"从良弓中射出的箭可以抵达高处,穿入深处"严密。"良马难乘",Knoblock 等译为"好马难以驱使",更像是赶马车。梅贻宝译为"好马难以驾驭",凸显了骑马这个动作,与原文语境比较契合。"良才难令",梅贻宝译为"真正的人才不会唯命是从",Knoblock 等译为"有大才能的人很难随意使唤",均从各自的视角再现了原文的精神。

**致君见尊**

梅贻宝译为"作为使者出使四方,与君主及贵族会面",强调其堪当大任,与 Johnston 的译文[①]一样将关注点放在优秀的人才自身获得回报上,偏离了原文考察优秀人才对君主的价值这个立足点,因此二者均不如 Knoblock 等译为"使君主处于受人尊重的地位"更加符合语境。

六、务言而缓行,虽辩必不听;多力而伐功,虽劳必不图。慧者心辩而不繁说,多力而不伐功,此以名誉扬天下。言无务多而务为智,无务为文而务为察。

———《墨子·修身》

He who devotes himself to talk but is dilatory in acting, no matter how discerning he may be, will certainly not be heeded. He who expends much energy but boasts of his achievements, no matter how hard he works, will certainly not be selected. The truly intelligent is discerning in thought but is not loquacious. He expends much energy but does not boast about accomplishments. In this way his fame and reputation are exalted in the world. In speech one should devote oneself, not to how much one says, but to the wisdom of one's remarks, not to the form

---

① 译文为:"Yet they can serve the ruler and be respected."(服务君主并使自己得到尊重。)。参见 The Mozi: A Complete Translation. Ian Johnston, trans. Hong Kong: The Chinese University Press, 2010:7.

of one's discourse, but to being discerning.　　　　　(John Knoblock 等 译)

　　One who devotes his attention to words but is tardy in conduct will certainly not be listened to even though he argues well. One who expends a lot of energy but brags about his achievement will certainly not be chosen even though he works hard. One who is wise discriminates in his mind, but does not complicate his words. He exerts his strength, but does not brag about his achievement. In this way, his reputation and praise spread through the world. In speaking, he should devote attention to wisdom and not to amount. He should devote attention to clear analysis and not to eloquence.　　　　　(Ian Johnston 译)

### 务言而缓行，虽辩必不听

"务言而缓行"，Knoblock 等与 Johnston 均译为"致力于谈说而行动迟缓"，与原文高度契合。"虽辩必不听"，Knoblock 等翻译为"即便再明辨，(其观点)也不会为他人所认可"，Johnston 翻译为"就算再能言善辩肯定也没人听"。结合上下文对"言"的整体态度，不难发现 Johnston 对"辩"的理解是符合语境的。

### 多力而伐功，虽劳必不图

Knoblock 等与 Johnston 均准确翻译为"费了很大劲但是吹嘘自己的功绩"，但是关于"虽劳必不图"，二者均翻译为"无论多卖力，都不会被选用"，有较大偏离。这里主要是对自吹自擂者的修辞人格的否定，关注的是受众对这样的修辞者的反应而不是这样的做法实际上会有多少功效。李绍昆译文①与这一预期话语功能最为切近。

### 慧者心辩而不繁说

Knoblock 等译为"真正聪明的人洞若观火却不多说"，与上下文在逻辑上无缝衔接。Johnston 翻译为"智者在心中对事物进行区分，但是不把说辞复杂化"，虽然表面上很忠实于原文字面意义，整体上却缺乏一以贯之的思想脉络，难免让读者觉得不知所云。

### 此以名誉扬天下

"名誉"，Knoblock 等与 Johnston 均翻译为"名声和赞誉"，过于烦琐，不

---

　　① 译文为："The person, who works very hard, but like to boast a great deal, in spite of his labour, will not be respected." 大意为：尽管出力很多，终究不会受人尊重。参见英译墨子全书：李绍昆，译.北京：商务印书馆，2009：6.

如梅贻宝译为 name 来得简约。

**言无务多而务为智**

Knoblock 等与 Johnston 均成功翻译为"言说不要光注重讲了多少话,而是要注意话语本身是否有智慧"。

**无务为文而务为察**

Knoblock 等翻译为"不要过于注重话语的形式,而是要关注是否有洞察力",总体是达意的,如果能够按照语境进一步将"文"表达为"口才"就更准确了。Johnston 翻译为"要致力于清晰的分析而非展示滔滔雄辩","文"的意涵已然呼之欲出,但是将"察"理解为"分析",不如 Knoblock 的"洞察力"明晰。梅贻宝将此句与上一句结合,译为"言说要注重(思想)独创性与洞察力,而非内容的多寡或是否雄辩"①可谓深得此句精义。

七、是以先王之书《术令》之道曰:"唯口出好兴戎。"则此言善用口者出好,不善用口者以为谗贼寇戎。则此岂口不善哉?用口则不善也,故遂以为谗贼寇戎。

——《墨子·尚同》

And, also, "Shu Ling", among the books of the ancient kings, says, "The same mouth can produce friendship or produce war." This is to say that he who can use the mouth well will produce friendship, and he who cannot will stir up the enemies and the besieging barbarians. Can it be that the mouth is at fault? The fault really lies in its use which stirs up the enemies and the besieging barbarians.

(梅贻宝 译)

Thus one of the *Documents* of the founding kings, the "Methods and Ordinances," teaches: "The mouth can bring about good will or lead to conflict." This means that one who uses his mouth well utters words of friendship, and one who does not use it well brings about slander, killing, brigandage, and even war. How could it be that the mouth itself is not good? It is the use to which the mouth is

---

① 译文为:"In speech, not quantity but ingenuity, not eloquence but insight, should be cultivated."。Sayings of Mo Ti. W.P. Mei, trans. New York: Columbia University Press, 1967.

put that is not good, and that is why it produces slander, killing, brigandage, and war.

(John Knoblock 等 译)

### 《术令》

《术令》，吴毓江认为是《尚书》篇名①。因年代久远，关于书名本身有不少歧解。梅贻宝使用音译，只说是古代帝王所作之书，此外没有为读者提供更多信息。Knoblock 等译为《方法与法令》，并指出是《尚书》篇名之一，至少给读者提供了一个大致方向。

### 唯口出好兴戎

梅贻宝译文"同一张嘴既能够带来友谊，也能够带来战争"虽然对"好"与"戎"的翻译谈不上全面，但是译文所用的修辞是十分明显的。译文通过使用战争与和平（友谊）这一提喻以点带面传达"好"与"戎"所涵盖的其他意义，尤其是使用"同样一张嘴"，提醒读者对于"口"（也就是话语）所能够产生的截然不同的修辞效果保持足够的警惕。Knoblock 等的译文"嘴既能带来善意，也能导致冲突"，对"好"与"戎"的翻译比较全面，但是总体话语气势不如梅贻宝译文。

### 善用口者出好

梅贻宝译文"善于用嘴（语言）的人会带来友谊"，强调的是话语带来的正面修辞效果，总体上优于 Knoblock 等的"善于用嘴（语言）的人说友善的话"。后者只关注说什么，忽略了说话之后"会怎样"的话语效果问题，而效果恰恰是原文的核心关注点。

### 不善用口者以为谗贼寇戎

梅贻宝译文只是泛泛提到敌人和围攻的野蛮人，漏译了"谗"，同时没有对话语所引发的不同修辞后果进行排序。Knoblock 等针对"谗贼寇戎"的译文（大意为"诋毁、杀戮、盗窃，甚至战争"）对每一个词都试图进行翻译（虽然有的未必妥当②），同时按照修辞后果的严重程度进行升序排列，从修辞说服角度而言，可谓深得西方修辞艺术之精髓。"口不善哉"，梅贻宝译文"是嘴有错吗？"不仅忠实，而且通过设问，让读者自行得出隐含于其中的结论，其修辞

---

① 参见吴毓江.墨子校注（上）.北京：中华书局，2006：128-129.
② 比如用 killing（杀戮）翻译"贼"（残害）就不够妥当。参见 John Knoblock, Jeffrey Riegel. Mozi: A Study and Translation of the Ethical and Political Writings. Berkeley: University of California，2013：124.

效果远甚于 Knoblock 等的"嘴自身怎么可能是不好的"。"用口则不善也",梅贻宝译文比较平淡,Knoblock 等使用强调句凸显了问题的根源。

八、兼者,处大国不攻小国,处大家不乱小家,强不劫弱,众不暴寡,诈不谋愚,贵不傲贱。

——《墨子·天志》

Because of their impartiality, those who occupied large states did not attack smaller states, those who dwelled in large hereditary houses did not disrupt small houses, the strong did not oppress the weak, the many did not tyrannize the few, swindlers did not cheat the stupid, and the noble did not treat the humble with contempt. (John Knoblock 等 译)

In promoting universality, they did not use their power to let the large states to attack the small states nor did they use their influence on large families to disturb the small families. Furthermore, the strong did not abuse the weak, the masses did not oppress the few, the clever did not deceive the stupid, and the honorable did not disdain the humble. （李绍昆 译）

兼者,处大国不攻小国,处大家不乱小家

"兼者"①,Knoblock 等将其译为 impartiality(the fact of not supporting any of the sides involved in an argument),也就是"公正,无偏见",李绍昆译为 universality(普遍),都没有能够把"包括;延及"的意涵翻译出来。Chris Fraser 译文(inclusion②)虽然体现了"包括"这一点,却与前两个存在同样的问题——没有提到"爱"。"小国",李绍昆忠实地进行直译,Knoblock 等则将其译为(与自己相比)相对小的国家,虽然与原文并不完全相符,但不违事理,从修辞角度而言是可以接受的翻译。"处大家不乱小家",李绍昆将"大家"译为"大家庭",有望文生义之嫌,读者无法从中获得政治方面的任何联想。Knoblock 等译为"世袭大家族",比较接近原意。"乱",梅贻宝译为 molest(骚扰),与原文有较大偏差,Knoblock 等的译文(扰断)与李绍昆的"打扰"都未能尽其意,

---

① "兼",即兼爱,其出处见《墨子·兼爱》章:"若使天下兼相爱,爱人若爱其身。"

② 参见 The Essential Mozi: Ethical, Political, and Dialectical Writings. Chris Frazer, trans. Oxford: Oxford University Press, 2020:98.

Johnston 的译文（制造混乱）①最为妥帖。

**强不劫弱，众不暴寡，诈不谋愚，贵不傲贱**

"劫"，Knoblock 等的译文"压迫"与李绍昆的"虐待"均不如梅贻宝的"劫夺"②妥当。"暴"，Knoblock 等译为"暴虐地对待"不如李绍昆译为"压迫"准确。"诈不谋愚"，Knoblock 等译为"骗子不骗傻子"，读起来令人疑窦丛生。如果是职业骗子，骗人就是其谋生之道，傻子是其最理想的目标受众，有什么样的力量能够让骗子克制住骗人的冲动？因此，这里对"诈"的翻译应该重新考虑。李绍昆译为"聪明的人不欺骗愚笨的人"，逻辑上说得通。"贵不傲贱"，Knoblock 等使用尾韵修辞（noble/humble），不仅忠实传达了原文意义，还在语言表达形式上给读者带来了审美愉悦。"贵"，李绍昆译为"品德高尚的、值得尊敬的"，与原文所传达的"特定社会阶层"的意思依然有较大距离。

九、**命者，暴王所作，穷人所术，非仁者之言也。今之为仁义者，将不可不察而强非者，此也。**

——《墨子·非命》

For fatalism was an invention of the wicked kings and the practice of miserable men. It was not a doctrine of the magnanimous. Therefore those who practise magnanimity and righteousness must examine it and vigorously refute it.

（梅贻宝 译）

This is to say that fatalism, having been "invented by tyrants and transmitted by the indigent," is not a doctrine held by the humane. It is for this reason that those who uphold the way of humaneness and righteousness must study this doctrine carefully and strongly condemn it. （John Knoblock 等 译）

**命**

梅贻宝与 Knoblock 译为 fatalism（the belief that people cannot change the way events will happen and that events, especially bad ones, cannot be

---

① 译文为："Those living in large houses do not bring disorder to small houses."。参见 The Mozi: A Complete Translation. Ian Johnston, trans. Hong Kong: The Chinese University Press, 2010:255.

② 原译文为："The strong did not plunder the weak."。参见 Sayings of Mo Ti. W.P.Mei, trans. New York: Columbia University Press, 1967.

avoided),也就是宿命论这样的理论体系,是很准确的。

**暴王所作,穷人所术,非仁者之言也/察而强非**

"暴王",Knoblock 等准确地译为"暴君",梅贻宝译为"邪恶的国王",过于宽泛。"穷人",梅贻宝译为"可怜的人",虽然与原文有偏离,从事理上说倒是极为可能的:越是人生境遇不如意的可怜的人,往往越容易相信这一套学说。Knoblock 等译为"十分贫困的人",与原文大体符合。"术",也就是"述",梅贻宝译为"实践",不如 Knoblock 等翻译为"传播(学说)"更加接近原文。"仁者",梅贻宝译为"大度的人",有较大偏离,不如 Knoblock 等译文接近原意。"察而强非",梅贻宝译为"考察并力斥",比 Knoblock 译为"认真研究并强烈谴责"更合事理。

### 十、辩,争彼也。辩胜,当也。

——《墨子·经》①

Bian(disputation)is contending over claims which are the converse of each other. Winning in disputation is fitting the fact.　　　　　　　　　　(梅贻宝 译)

　　Disputation is contending about "that"(the other). Winning in disputation depends on validity.　　　　　　　　　　　　　　　　　　(Ian Johnston 译)

"辩",梅贻宝与 Johnston 均译为 disputation(争论),是很准确的。梅贻宝译文大意为:"争论就是彼此相反的两个宣认/主张的竞争",读起来与普罗泰戈拉的"对言"理论②不无似曾相识之感,很容易为西方读者所认同。Johnston 虽然照原文直译("争论就是争夺那个"),却没有明确所谓"那个"究竟是什么,不免令读者困惑。"辩胜,当也",梅贻宝译为"论辩获胜就是指宣认/主张与事实相符合",这一理解是很有代表性的中国论辩观,但是对于熟悉

---

① 辛志凤等现代汉语译文为:"辩论是要争执相矛盾的命题,辩论胜利的是因为其命题恰当为真。"参见辛志凤,等.墨子译注.哈尔滨:黑龙江人民出版社,2003:265。
② 普罗泰戈拉提出"针对任何一个争议都可以提出完全相反的两个论点"("on every issue there are two arguments opposed to each other")转引自:刘亚猛.追求象征的力量:关于西方修辞思想的思考.北京:生活·读书·新知三联书店,2004:124.

西方修辞①的那部分英语读者而言,Johnston的译文("论辩能否获胜取决于论证的有效性")更符合他们的认知。

## 十一、有诸己不非诸人,无诸己不求诸人。

——《墨子·小取》

Remember, do not refuse to others what you accept for yourself. Do not propose to others what you reject for yourself. (李绍昆 译)

What one has in oneself, one does not criticise in others; what one does not have in oneself, one does not demand of others. (Ian Johnston 译)

Having it oneself, one doesn't condemn it in others. Lacking it oneself, one doesn't seek it in others. (Chris Fraser 译)

吴毓江认为这一句"言辩须自身无瑕可指"②,虽然比较偏颇,但对深入讨论这个话题却不无启发。这句话固然提到了对受众提出高要求的修辞者自身必须有近乎完美的修辞人格,或者至少在话题所涉领域拥有毋庸置疑的修辞

---

① 与中国文化中所谓"事实胜于雄辩"的提法不同,西方修辞传统认为事实需要修辞话语的加持才更能够为受众所认同。刘亚猛在《追求象征的力量》中对此有详细的论述:"在'事实胜于雄辩'的说法流行的地方,人们仍然倾向于将'事实'和'雄辩'看成是分别自成一体(discrete)、互不关联的两码事,并将前者理解为完全独立于话语和修辞的某一发生的情况或存在状态。通过不带修辞色彩的'平素语言'(plain language)的'正确'使用,我们有望准确地捕捉到或描绘出事实的'真相'。一旦'辞藻'染指,'实事求是'就可望而不可即了。在西方修辞思想的框架内,人们即便口头上不承认这一点,'事实必须被确立'也早已成了心照不宣的普遍认定。根据这一认定,任何'事实'的确立都是有关它的某一表述(representation)被广泛接受的结果。也就是说,要确认某一'事实',我们首先必须对它的'事实性'(factuality)加以宣认(claim),界定,陈述,答辩。只有在这些'事实宣认'(factual claims)或'事实表述'(factual representations)得到普遍认可,起码没有遇到公开而严肃的异议,有关事实才算确立了。有鉴于此,'事实性'的获得和事实的确立都离不开雄辩,有赖于雄辩,在对同一事实有不止一个互相冲突的宣认时尤其如此。也就是说,雄辩不可避免地将对事实认证过程进行干预并影响其结果。它既能促使某一'事实宣认'上升为被普遍接受的事实,也可以阻止它获得所声称拥有的'事实性'。顺着这一思路再进一步,我们不难想象人们还完全有可能通过雄辩撤回原来已'颁发'的事实'认证',从而推翻某些一度被普遍接受的'事实'。"参见刘亚猛.追求象征的力量:关于西方修辞思想的思考.北京:生活·读书·新知三联书店,2004:59-60.

② 吴毓江.墨子校注(上).北京:中华书局,2006:632.

素养和威望,还着重强调了"己所欲,勿轻施于人"①的"恕"道,强调从对方的角度去思考问题,不强人所难,不轻易提要求。李绍昆译文②虽然也翻译出了"己所不欲,勿施于人"的意涵,但其焦点是爱好、习惯这类一般性的话题,没有明确反映出与原文提到的品德这类修辞人格话题的关联性。Johnston 译文大意为"自己有这样的问题,就不要批评别人也有这样的毛病;自己没有的优点,就不要强求别人具备这些优点",是比较忠实的翻译。Fraser 译文使用"谴责"翻译"非",过于严厉,与语境不协调。

十二、巫马子谓子墨子曰:"子兼爱天下,未云利也;我不爱天下,未云贼也。功皆未至,子何独自是而非我哉?"子墨子曰:"今有燎者于此,一人奉水将灌之,一人掺火将益之,功皆未至,子何贵于二人?"巫马子曰:"我是彼奉水者之意,而非夫掺火者之意。"③子墨子曰:"吾亦是吾意,而非子之意也。"④

——《墨子·耕柱》

Wu Mazi said to Mozi: "Though you love universally the world cannot be said to be benefited; though I do not love(universally)the world cannot be said to be injured. Since neither of us has accomplished anything, what makes you then praise yourself and blame me?" Mozi answered: Suppose a conflagration is on. One person is fetching water to extinguish it, and another is holding some fuel to reinforce it. Neither of them has yet accomplished anything, but which one do you value? Wu Mazi answered that he approved of the intention of the person who fetches water and disapproved of the intention of the person who holds fuel. Mozi said:(In

---

① 与传统上对"恕"道做"己所不欲,勿施于人"这样的解读略有不同,这个语境中的"恕"道主要是指"己所欲,勿轻施于人"(自己觉得好的,不考虑对方需不需要、喜不喜欢,一厢情愿地要给对方;自己觉得理想的状态,不考虑对方的能力与意愿,随意地要求对方做到)。

② 大意为"你自己已经接受的就不要拒绝别人也接受这样的事物;你自己都排斥的事物,就不要劝别人去接受"。

③ 本句意为"我认为那个捧水的人的心意是正确的,而那个拿火苗的人的心意是错误的"。参见王焕镳.墨子校释.杭州:浙江古籍出版社,1987:333。

④ 本句意为"我也认为我兼爱天下的心意是正确的,而你不爱天下的心意是错误的"。参见王焕镳.墨子校释.杭州:浙江古籍出版社,1987:333。

the same manner)do I approve of my intention and disapprove of yours.

(梅贻宝 译)

Master Wuma spoke to our Master Mozi, saying: "You love the whole world impartially, but it has not yet produced any benefit. I do not love the whole world, but it has not done any harm. Since neither of us has accomplished anything, why then do you consider yourself right and condemn me as wrong?" Our Master Mozi responded: "Suppose there were a fire here. One man is holding up a bucket of water to extinguish it, and another is grasping firewood to add to the flames. Though neither has as yet accomplished anything, which of the two would you esteem?" Master Wuma replied, "I would consider correct the intention of the one who held the water and would condemn the intention of the one who grasped the firewood." Mozi concluded: "I likewise consider my intention to be correct and condemn yours."

(John Knoblock 等 译)

### 子兼爱天下,未云利也;我不爱天下,未云贼也

"兼爱",梅贻宝与 Knoblock 等都没能把"包括;延及"的意涵翻译出来。Fraser 译文[①]就体现了这一点。"未云利也",梅贻宝译为"天下谈不上获益",是很到位的翻译。Knoblock 等译为"没有带来好处",逻辑衔接不如梅译紧密。"贼",梅贻宝译为 injure(physical harm to person or animal)"对人或动物身体上的伤害",过于具体,不如 Knoblock 译为 harm(physical or other injury or damage)"身体或其他方面的伤害/危害/损害"适切。

### 功皆未至,子何独自是而非我哉

"功皆未至",两个译本均准确地翻译为"彼此均无甚成就"。"自是",梅贻宝译为"称赞自己",不如 Knoblock 等译为"觉得自己是对的"准确。"非我",梅贻宝译为"责备我",Knoblock 等译为"谴责我",均超出"否定"的中性情感色彩。

### 燎/奉水将灌之/掺火将益之

"燎",梅贻宝译为"大火",有助于营造迫在眉睫的紧张氛围,Knoblock 等翻译为"火"则很难体现明显的危机感。"奉水将灌之",Knoblock 等忠实直译

---

① 译文为:"You inclusively care about all the world."。参见 The Essential Mozi: Ethical, Political, and Dialectical Writings. Chris Frazer, trans. Oxford: Oxford University Press,2020:183.

为"举着一桶水准备倒下去灭火",梅贻宝则译为"取水灭火",多了取水环节,虽然没有忠实地译出"水已在手上"这一点,但是在凸显这是一种行为意向方面与原文话语功能高度一致。"掺火将益之",两位译者都成功译出了"火"的含义,Knoblock等尤其细致,用木柴(firewood)这一中国古代生活中最常见的燃料使得场景更加具体可感。

**我是彼奉水者之意,而非夫掺火者之意**

两个译本均进行了直译,李绍昆译文[①]则修辞性地对两类行为进行概括评价,表达清晰且逻辑严密,为读者阅读提供了极大便利。

十三、后生有反子墨子而反者,"我岂有罪哉？吾反后。"子墨子曰:"是犹三军北,失后之人求赏也。"

——《墨子·耕柱》

Some pupils deserted Mozi and then returned. (They said:) "How are we to blame? We deserted late." Mozi said: This is like asking for reward for late desertion in a defeated army."

(梅贻宝 译)

Among the disciples there was one who forsook Master Mo Zi but later returned, saying: "How am I at fault? I did later return." Master Mo Zi said: "This is like the three armies being defeated and those who have lagged behind or lost their way seeking reward."

(Ian Johnston 译)

**后生有反子墨子而反者**

梅贻宝译为"有一些弟子背弃了墨子,然后又回来了",生动地再现了弟子可疑的修辞人格,不足之处是译文使用复数将个例变成了群体行为。Johnston译文"弟子中有一个遗弃墨子的人后来又回来了",在弟子数量的理解与呈现方面是准确传神的,但是使用forsake(to leave someone for ever, especially when they need you),读起来像是墨子有求于弟子而弟子却弃他而去,使得墨子的修辞人格无形中被矮化了。根据下文墨子对学生的批评、嘲讽来看,实际情况显然并非如此,弟子与老师的话语权力关系并没发生过反转,

---

① 译文为:"I value the one who takes water with his good intentions and disapprove the one who holds fuel with his bad intentions."。参见英译墨子全书.李绍昆,译.北京:商务印书馆,2009:242-243.

弟子只是因为自身原因离开了老师,因此这一措辞有待斟酌。汪榕培的译文①使用不带情感色彩的"离开"虽然能够包容各种可能的场景,但广度难免影响强度,无法与"回来"形成较强的修辞张力。

**吾反后**

梅贻宝翻译为"我们比别人迟离开",符合语境以及事情发展的逻辑;Johnston翻译为"我后来确实回来了",是对原文的误解,逻辑上无法与上下文兼容。

**是犹三军北,失后之人求赏也**

"三军",梅贻宝翻译为一般意义上的"军队",是很恰当的;Johnston翻译为"三个军队"反而有过犹不及之嫌。"失后之人",主流解读②多为失道后还之人,Johnston翻译为"落后或迷路的败兵",即是按照这一思路翻译的。也有学者对此有不同解读,如张永祥等就认为这个"失"通"佚"(逃跑)③,梅贻宝翻译为"败军之中后面当逃兵的"即是按这一思路翻译的。二者最大的区别在于是否具备主观故意,显然,落伍或迷路是不可抗力造成的,而逃兵是自主行为,二者虽然都不光彩(前者体现当事人不专业,后者暴露当事人不勇敢),却不可相提并论,因为主观故意而犯的错误是要被谴责或处罚,客观原因造成的失误却往往容易被原谅,甚至会收获一丝同情。考虑到这个故事的修辞情境,墨子显然是在做类比,为了让其话语产生最大的修辞效果和杀伤力,梅贻宝的译法更为可取。Knoblock等这一处译文④大意为"撤退时最后走的",没有明确是因为客观原因还是主观选择,比较模糊,修辞效果不如梅贻宝译文。

---

① 译文为:"After leaving Master Mozi for quite some time, one of his pupils returned."。参见墨子.汪榕培,王宏,英译.周才珠,齐瑞端,今译.长沙:湖南人民出版社,2006:425.

② 主流解读有两种。孙诒让曰:"谓战败失道而后归,不得与殿者同赏。"吴毓江曰:"言三军败北,失道后还之人不得求赏。"孙诒让解读参见孙诒让.墨子间诂.北京:中华书局,2001:434.吴毓江解读参见吴毓江.墨子校注.北京:中华书局,2006:664.

③ 墨子译注.张永祥,肖霞,译注.上海:上海古籍出版社,2016:420.

④ 译文为:"The situation is like that of the three armies in retreat, with those who are the last to leave asking for rewards."。参见John Knoblock, Jeffrey Riegel. Mozi: A Study and Translation of the Ethical and Political Writings. Berkeley: University of California, 2013:334.

## 第六章 《墨子》英译比较与评析

十四、子墨子自鲁即齐,过故人,谓子墨子曰:"今天下莫为义,子独自苦而为义,子不若已。"子墨子曰:"今有人于此,有子十人,一人耕而九人处,则耕者不可以不益急矣。何故?则食者众而耕者寡也。今天下莫为义,则子如劝我者也,何故止我?"

——《墨子·贵义》

On his way from Lu to Qi, Mozi met an old friend who said to him: "Nowadays none in the world practises any righteousness. You are merely inflicting pain on yourself by trying to practise righteousness. You had better give it up." Mozi replied: Suppose a man has ten sons. Only one attends to the farm while the other nine stay at home. Then the farmer must work all the more vigorously. Why? Because many eat while few work. Now, none in the world practises righteousness. Then you should all the more encourage me. Why do you stop me? (梅贻宝 译)

When our Master Mozi was traveling from Lu to Qi, he passed by an old friend, who told our Master Mozi: "Nowadays no one in the world does what is right. Only you inflict bitter toils on yourself to do what is right. It would be best for you to stop doing this." Our Master Mozi said: "Suppose there were a man who had ten sons, of whom one farmed while the other nine stayed at home. If this were the case, then the one who did the farming must have been even more anxious. Why is this? Because those he must feed are many, and he alone is doing the farming. Now if no one in the world does the right thing, then you should encourage me. Why are you trying to stop me?" (John Knoblock 等 译)

今天下莫为义,子独自苦而为义,子不若已

"天下莫为义",梅贻宝翻译为"无人行义",勉强还说得过去,Knoblock 等翻译为"没有人做正确的事情",在逻辑上说不通。"自苦",梅贻宝翻译为"给自己施加生理上的痛苦",于理不合。Knoblock 等翻译为"让自己极度辛劳",对于心怀天下者而言,这个可能性是存在的。"不若已",梅贻宝译文语气有强制之嫌,Knoblock 等翻译为"最佳选择"也嫌"过",Fraser 译文"It'd be better if you quit."(不如放手不管)最为适切。

有人于此,有子十人,一人耕而九人处

梅贻宝翻译成"有这么一个人,假设他有十个儿子",关注的重点是这个人有十个孩子;Knoblock 等翻译为"假如有个拥有十个儿子的人",重心是这个人自身,符合原文精神。"一人耕而九人处",梅贻宝翻译为"只有一人打理田园,而其他九人待在家里",是很恰当的,暗含了 Knoblock 等译文所缺乏的对袖手旁观的其他九人的谴责。汪榕培译文①读起来好像是其余九个孩子想参与,却被排除在劳动俱乐部之外,与原文"袖手旁观"的意象差距较大。Fraser 译"One ploughs the fields while nine sit around."(一人耕地,九人闲坐)用词简约且形象生动,有如白描,所有的评论与谴责均由读者自发生成。译者好像什么都没有说,又好像说了不少,一切尽在不言中。这一译文可谓深得艺术留白之妙。

益急

梅贻宝翻译为"更加卖力",是合理的。Knoblock 等翻译为"更加焦虑",偏离了原文。Johnston 译文②"耕地的那个儿子不免会有一种紧迫感",更是富有修辞张力,把那种义不容辞、时不我待的情形给凸显了出来。③

食者众而耕者寡也

梅贻宝的翻译是忠实的,Knoblock 等的翻译则修辞性地进行了呈现,先说消费者数量多,再提严重失衡的生产者人数,从而通过倒金字塔的结构将这一岌岌可危的情形鲜活地呈现在读者面前。

劝我

"劝我",梅贻宝用 all the more encourage me(进一步鼓励我),对原文字里行间隐含的语气把握得比 Knoblock 等要准确,细节也呈现得更好。

---

① 汪榕培将这句话翻译为"But only one son is still cultivating the field while the other nine sons are left idle with noting to do."(只有一个儿子还在耕地,其他九人却被撂在一旁无所事事。)。参见墨子.汪榕培,王宏,英译.周才珠,齐瑞端,今译.长沙:湖南人民出版社,2006:431.

② 译文为:"The one who ploughed could not help but work with increased urgency."。参见 The Mozi: A Complete Translation. Ian Johnston, trans. Hong Kong: The Chinese University Press, 2010:661.

③ 墨子的论辩理路并非无懈可击:照理,遇到这样的情况,最紧要的事情是去动员其他九人一起劳作,墨子却默认这些人是无法争取的,因而将所有的担子都放在一个人身上。

十五、子墨子有疾,跌鼻进而问曰:"先生以鬼神为明,能为祸福,为善者赏之,为不善者罚之。今先生圣人也,何故有疾?意者,先生之言有不善乎?鬼神不明知乎?"子墨子曰:"虽使我有病①,何遽不明?人之所得于病者多方,有得之寒暑,有得之劳苦。百门而闭一门焉,则盗何遽无从入?"

——《墨子·公孟》

Mozi was sick. Die Bi came and inquired: "Sir, you have taught the ghosts and spirits are intelligent and are in control of calamity and blessing. They will reward the good and punish the evil. Now you are a sage. How can you become sick? Can it be that your teaching was not entirely correct, that the ghosts and spirits are after all unintelligent?" Mozi said: "Though I am sick how (does it follow that the ghosts and spirits) should be unintelligent? There are many ways by which a man can contract diseases. Some are affected by climate, some by fatigue. If there are a hundred gates and only one of them is closed, how is it that the burglar should not be able to get in?" (梅贻宝 译)

Our Master Mozi had an illness. Die Bi came forward and said:② "You, sir, consider that ghosts and spirits are perceptive and able to cause fortune or misfortune: they reward those who are good and punish those who are not. Now as you are a sage, why have you become ill? Could it possibly be that your doctrine is in some way flawed, or that the ghosts and spirits are not percipient and wise?" Our Master Mozi replied: "Even though I am sick, why should you conclude that they are not percipient? There are numerous ways in which a man acquires an illness. Some are acquired as a result of heat, others of cold, still others of fatigue and exhaustion. If there are a hundred gates and only one of them has been closed, then why should robbers not find a way to enter?" (John Knoblock 等 译)

跌鼻进而问曰

跌鼻的身份,梅贻宝没有过多介绍,模糊了人物形象,同时还减弱了门徒

---

① 吴汝纶认为"虽使我有病"下应当补上"吾言何遽不善,而鬼神"。参见王焕镳.墨子校释.杭州:浙江古籍出版社,1987:377.

② 原注为:"Die Bi is apparently one of Mozi's disciples. This is the only appearance of his name in the transmitted literature."。参见 John Knoblock, Jeffrey Riegel. Mozi: A Study and Translation of the Ethical and Political Writings. Berkeley: University of California, 2013:470.

挑战老师的修辞张力。Knoblock 等通过注解为读者补充说明了师徒关系。根据下文情节,不难看出跌鼻是有备而来,并非为了求教,而是前来质疑的。梅贻宝使用"询问",Knoblock 等翻译为"说",均不如 Johnston 的"质问"①更能够营造"来者不善"的气氛。

以鬼神为明,能为祸福,为善者赏之,为不善者罚之

"明",梅贻宝翻译为"高智商的;有才智的"固然不错,Knoblock 等翻译为"有洞察力的",能够体现透过表象明辨是非的识别力,显然更胜一筹。"为祸福",梅贻宝翻译为"控制施福降祸"的话语权,Knoblock 等则翻译为"可以带来祸福";Knoblock 等译文比较忠实,梅贻宝译文不拘泥于字面,属于视野更广的意译。"不善者",梅贻宝翻译为 the evil(邪恶的人),是比较准确的。Knoblock 等翻译为"不是善良的人",未必就是坏人,有可能是像孔子提到的那种乡愿式的既不好也不坏的人,这种人虽然在是非方面没有明确立场,倒也不至于要被鬼神惩罚,因此这一译法过于模糊。

言有不善乎

梅贻宝翻译为"讲授的观点不完全正确",比较婉转,"杀伤力"不如 Knoblock 等直言"教义有某种缺陷"。

不明知

梅贻宝翻译为 after all unintelligent,虽然关于"明"的措辞未见改进,但是使用"毕竟"则很清晰地表达了原来的怀疑现在得到了某种强化,有助于建构紧张的修辞氛围。Knoblock 等译文的优势则在于对"明知"译文措辞的准确选择。

何遽不明

Knoblock 等译文使用 why(为什么)不免让读者有明知故问之感,梅贻宝翻译使用 follow 则显得客观理性,同时凸显逻辑严密性。

人之所得于病者多方,有得之寒暑,有得之劳苦

"得于病",梅贻宝翻译使用 contract[患(病)]是很地道的,Knoblock 等译文过于强调"得",使用意义过于正面的 acquire(习得;获得)反而适得其反。梅贻宝翻译使用 affected by(受影响)翻译另外这个"得",不仅准确再现了原文语义,也使得行文措辞多样化。"劳苦",梅贻宝与 Knoblock 等翻译为"疲

---

① 完整译文为:"Die Bi approached and questioned him."。参见 The Mozi: A Complete Translation. Ian Johnston, trans. Hong Kong: The Chinese University Press, 2010: 695。

劳",甚至"筋疲力尽",不如汪榕培的 overwork(过度劳累)合情合理。"寒暑",Knoblock 等译文按照字面翻译,固然忠实,但不如梅贻宝译文"气候"来得有概括力。

门/盗

"门",梅贻宝译为 gate(大门),与原文"百门"情理不合,Knoblock 等译文使用通用意义上的 door("门"),比较可信。"盗",梅贻宝译文用入室的"窃贼"比 Knoblock 所译的使用暴力的"强盗"更有逻辑。

十六、钓者之恭,非为鱼赐也;饵鼠以虫①,非爱之也。②

——《墨子·鲁问》

The fisherman's bait is not intended to feed the fish. Trapping a mouse with worms is not for the love of the mouse.

(梅贻宝 译)

The arched posture of the fisherman appears reverent, but it is not due to his offering thanks to the fish. Using worms to entice rats is not from a love for rats.

(John Knoblock 等 译)

本句的修辞意图是通过个例说明应该透过表象洞察被表象掩盖的真实意图。撇开翻译忠实与否的问题,梅贻宝译文("鱼人的饵不是为了喂鱼而投下去的,用虫诱捕老鼠不是出于对老鼠的爱")本身是人所共知的生活常识,就语言表达而言无可非议;从整个话语的修辞意图而言,则不是这么回事。Knoblock 等译文("鱼人弓着身子的样子看起来好像很尊敬的样子,但他这样做其实不是为了向鱼表示感谢。用虫子去诱骗老鼠,并不是出于对老鼠的爱")凸显了不能将表面现象照单全收这一点。整个句子虽然没有直接号召读者采取某种行动,但其劝导的意图已然是呼之欲出了。

---

① 此句有多种解读。孙诒让曰:"虫非所以饵鼠,疑当为'蛊'字之误。饵鼠以蛊,即谓毒鼠,故云'非爱之也'。"参见孙诒让.墨子间诂.北京:中华书局,2001:472.吴毓江曰:"原文之意为似爱而非爱者,若饵鼠以毒,则根本已不似爱,不得与爱之混淆矣。艺文类聚六十六引'虫'作'肉',于义为长。"参见吴毓江.墨子校注.北京:中华书局,2006:734.

② 王焕镳的现代汉语译文为:"钓鱼人躬着身子,并不是对鱼表示恭敬;用虫子作为捕鼠的诱饵,并不是喜爱老鼠。"参见王焕镳.墨子校释.杭州:浙江古籍出版社,1987:388.

## 本章参考的英译本

英译墨子全书:李绍昆,译. 北京:商务印书馆,2009.

墨子. 汪榕培,王宏,英译. 周才珠,齐瑞端,今译. 长沙:湖南人民出版社,2006.

Ian Johnston. The Mozi：A Complete Translation. Hong Kong：The Chinese University Press,2010.

John Knoblock,Jeffrey Riegel.Mozi：A Study and Translation of the Ethical and Political Writings.Berkeley：University of California,2013.

Mo Tzu. Burton Watson, trans. New York：Columbia University Press,1967.

Sayings of Mo Ti. W. P. Mei, trans. New York：Columbia University Press,1967.

The Essential Mozi：Ethical,Political,and Dialectical Writings. Chris Fraser, trans. Oxford：Oxford University Press,2020.

# 第七章 《韩非子》英译比较与评析

一、凡说之难,非吾知之有以说之之难也;又非吾辩之能明吾意之难也;又非吾敢横失而能尽之难也。凡说之难:在知所说之心,可以吾说当之。所说出于为名高者也,而说之以厚利,则见下节而遇卑贱,必弃远矣。所说出于厚利者也,而说之以名高,则见无心而远事情,必不收矣。所说阴为厚利而显为名高者也,而说之以名高,则阳收其身而实疏之;说之以厚利,则阴用其言显弃其身矣。此不可不察也。

——《韩非子·说难》①

On the whole, the difficult thing about persuading others is not that one lacks the knowledge needed to state his case nor the audacity to exercise his abilities to the full. On the whole, the difficult thing about persuasion is to know the mind of the person one is trying to persuade and to be able to fit one's words to it. If the person you are trying to persuade is out to establish a reputation for virtue, and you talk to him about making a fat profit, then he will regard you as low-bred, accord you a shabby and contemptuous reception, and undoubtedly send you packing. If the person you are trying to persuade is on the contrary interested in a fat profit, and you talk to him about a virtuous reputation, he will regard you as witless and out of touch with reality, and will never heed your arguments. If the person you are trying to persuade is secrely out for big gain but ostensibly claims to be interested in a virtuous name alone, and you talk to him about a reputation for virtue, then he will pretend to welcome and heed you, but in fact will shun

---

① 若无特别说明,本书所涉及《韩非子》引文均出自《韩非子集解》。出处详见王先慎.韩非子集解.钟哲,点校.北京:中华书局,1998.

you aside; if you talk to him about making a big gain, he will secretly follow your advice but ostensibly reject you. These are facts that you must not fail to consider carefully.

(华兹生 译)

The difficulty in speaking to a person is not that of knowing what to say, nor that of method of argument to make one's meaning clear. Nor does it consist in the difficulty of having the courage to speak one's mind fully and frankly. The difficulty lies in knowing the mind of the person spoken to and fitting one's proper approach to it. If the person spoken to likes to have a name for altruism and idealism and you speak to him about utilitarian profits, he will think you vulgar-minded and keep away from you. On the other hand, if the person spoken to has a good mind for commercial profits and you speak to him about idealism, he will think you an impractical sort of person with whom he will have nothing to do. If the person spoken to likes to appear as a man of principles and is at heart after the profits and you speak to him about principles, he will make a pretense of being close to you but will not take you into his confidence. If you speak to the same person about big profits, he will secretly take your advice but outwardly keep you at a distance. These things one must know.

(林语堂 译)[①]

### 凡说之难,非吾知之有以说之之难也

对于"凡说之难"中暗含的"说服所要面对的受众",华兹生与林语堂分别用"others"(其他人)与 a person(某人)这类模糊的泛指加以翻译。关于韩非致辞的对象,王先慎在其《韩非子集解·序》中定位为"操权柄者"[②],本章案语中也提到言说的潜在回报与风险[③],尤其是"祸"这一灾难性后果,比较符合修辞者与身居高位的受众话语权力严重不对等的情境。梁启雄也认为《说难》"是一篇反映出人情世故和君主心理的作品"。[④] 基于这些讨论,把这里隐含的"受众"翻译为"the ruler"(君主)更为精准。"有以说之",华兹生翻译为"需要用来陈述观点的知识",相当于知识储备,林语堂译为"知道要说什么",Joel

---

① 林语堂.诸子百家:英、汉.北京:外语教学与研究出版社,2015:138.

② 王先慎指出韩非写作总体上是因为"疾夫操权柄者,不能伸其自有之权利,斩割禁断,肃朝野而谋治安"。参见王先慎.韩非子集解.钟哲,点校.北京:中华书局,1998:2.

③ 原注为:"夫说者有逆顺之机,顺以招福,逆而致祸。失之毫厘,差之千里,以此说之,所以难也。"参见王先慎.韩非子集解.钟哲,点校.北京:中华书局,1998:85.

④ 梁启雄.韩子浅解.2 版.北京:中华书局,2009:89.

Sahleen 译文①大意为"从知识储备中寻找可以用于说服听者的论点"。林语堂与 Sahleen 译文都涉及了说服话语的修辞发明(invention)。林语堂译文简单直白,忠实再现了原文。但是从修辞效果而言,林语堂只提到需要拥有适切的修辞素材,没有强调修辞发明的过程,Sahleen 译文则凸显了修辞觅材的动态过程,更能够体现修辞者的主动性。

**又非吾辩之能明吾意之难也**

华兹生漏译了本句。林语堂将"辩"理解为论证方法,比较局限,不如 Sahleen 理解为表达能力②来得妥当。

**又非吾敢横失而能尽之难也**

华兹生将"敢"翻译为 audacity(courage or confidence of a kind that other people find shocking or rude),也就是胆识,比林语堂的 courage 更有"明知山有虎,偏向虎山行"的修辞色彩。"横失而能尽之",华兹生译文没有提到本句讨论的中心词——"发言",只泛泛提到"充分发挥才干"。林语堂使用 speak one's mind fully and frankly(毫无保留地说出心里话),把进言者对有强烈感受的话题想一吐为快的那种情形形象地描绘出来。同时,通过辅以头韵修辞,译文构筑了侃侃而谈、知无不言且言无不尽的理想进言者修辞人格。

**凡说之难:在知所说之心,可以吾说当之**

"所说",华兹生翻译为修辞者所要说服的对象,林语堂翻译为被致辞者,措辞均欠简约;刘亚猛把它翻译为 addressee(致辞对象),最为简约明了。"心",华兹生与林语堂均翻译为 mind(所思所想),是比较准确的。

**所说出于为名高者也,而说之以厚利,则见下节而遇卑贱,必弃远矣**

华兹生将"名高"理解为"有美德之名声",比较切近人情,容易得到读者认同。林语堂使用哲学术语③,译为"利他主义与理想主义的名声",容易因此而

---

① 译文为:"As for the true difficulty of persuasion, it is not the difficulty of finding something in my knowledge that can be used to persuade the listener."。参见 P. J. Ivanhoe, Bryan W. Van Norden. Readings in Classical Chinese Philosophy. New York: Seven Bridges Press, 2001:316.

② 完整译文为:"nor is it the difficulty of being able to express myself in a way that elucidates my meaning"。参见 P. J. Ivanhoe, Bryan W. Van Norden. Readings in Classical Chinese Philosophy. New York: Seven Bridges Press, 2001:316.

③ 林语堂同样使用"功利主义利益"(utilitarian profits)这样的术语翻译"厚利"。

疏离读者。"下节",华兹生理解为缺乏教养,不如林语堂所用"vulgar-minded"(念头庸俗)切近原文。"必弃远矣",林语堂忠实地翻译为疏远,华兹生则修辞性地翻译为 send you packing(以粗暴或突兀方式驱离),该译文字面是让人马上卷铺盖离开,颇有勒令劝退的画面感。

所说出于厚利者也,而说之以名高,则见无心①而远事情,必不收矣

"无心",林语堂没有翻译,华兹生将其译为 witless [(of especially persons)lacking sense or understanding or judgment],也就是不善于观察且缺乏判断力,是很适切的。"远事情",华兹生将其理解为 out of touch with reality(脱离现实),与林语堂的译文 impractical(不切实际)可谓殊途同归,都体现了不通达人情世故这个特征。

所说阴为厚利而显为名高者也,而说之以名高,则阳收其身而实疏之

对再次出现的"名高",华兹生译文并无太大变化,林语堂显然考虑到了行文多样性,将其翻译为"有操守或原则",比较切合语境。"阳收其身",华兹生译为"假装欢迎并听从你的建议",不仅比林语堂译文"假装亲近你"更有修辞内涵,而且紧扣本节论述主题。

说之以厚利,则阴用其言显弃其身矣

"显弃其身",华兹生译文很忠实,林语堂的翻译则比较形象地体现了君主假装拒人于千里之外的样子。Sahleen 译文 outwardly rejecting you for the sake of appearances(为了装点门面而拒斥你的提议)更是直接点明君主这样做的修辞目的不过是掩人耳目罢了。

不可不察

林语堂并未使用双重否定进行翻译,语气因而减弱。华兹生译文成功再现了原文的双重否定结构,实现了提醒读者的预期话语功能。

---

① 原注为:"此则为己无相时之心而阔远事情矣。"参见王先慎.韩非子集解.钟哲,点校.北京:中华书局,1998:86.

二、凡说之务，在知饰所说之所矜而灭其所耻。彼有私急也，必以公义示而强之。其意有下也，然而不能已，说者因为之饰其美而少其不为也。其心有高也，而实不能及，说者为之举其过而见其恶而多其不行也。有欲矜以智能，则为之举异事之同类者，多为之地；使之资说于我，而佯不知也以资其智。欲内相存之言，则必以美名明之，而微见其合于私利也。欲陈危害之事，则显其毁诽，而微见其合于私患也。誉异人与同行者，规异事与同计者。有与同污者，则必以大饰其无伤也；有与同败者，则必以明饰其无失也。彼自多其力，则毋以其难概之也；自勇其断，则无以其谪怒之；自智其计，则毋以其败穷之。大意无所拂悟，辞言无所系縻，然后极骋智辩焉。此道所得亲近不疑而得尽辞也。

——《韩非子·说难》

The important thing in persuasion is to learn how to play up the aspects that the person you are talking to is proud of, and play down the aspects he is ashamed of. Thus, if the person has some urgent personal desire, you should show him that it is his public duty to carry it out and urge him not to delay. If he has some mean objective in mind and yet cannot restrain himself, you should do your best to point out to him whatever admirable aspects it may have and to minimize the reprehensible ones. If he has some lofty objective in mind and yet does not have the ability needed to realize it, you should do your best to point out to him the faults and bad aspects of such an objective and make it seem a virtue not to pursue it. If he is anxious to make a show of wisdom and ability, mention several proposals which are different from the one you have in mind but of the same general nature in order to supply him with ideas; then let him build on your words, but pretend that you are unaware that he is doing so, and in this way abet his wisdom.

If you wish to urge a policy of peaceful coexistence, then be sure to expound it in terms of lofty ideals, but also hint that it is commensurate with the ruler's personal interests. If you wish to warn the ruler against dangerous and injurious policies, then make a show of the fact that they invite reproach and moral censure, but also hint that they are inimical to his personal interests.

Praise other men whose deeds are like those of the person you are talking to; commend other actions which are based upon the same policies as his. If there is someone else who is guilty of the same vice he is, be sure to gloss it over by showing that it really does no great harm; if there is someone else who has suffered the same failure he has, be sure to defend it by demonstrating that it is not a loss after all. If he prides himself on his physical prowess, do not antagonize him by mentioning the difficulties he has encountered in the past; if he considers himself an expert at making decisions, do not anger him by pointing out his past errors; if he pictures himself a sagacious planner, do not tax him with his failures. Make sure that there is nothing in your ideas as a whole that will vex your listener, and nothing about your words that will rub him the wrong way, and then you may exercise your powers of rhetoric to the fullest. This is the way to gain the confidence and intimacy of the person you are addressing and to make sure that you are able to say all you have to say without incurring his suspicion.　（华兹生 译）

凡说之务,在知饰所说之所矜而灭其所耻

"饰"与"灭",华兹生译为 play up/down(突出/淡化)不仅忠实再现原文意思,而且通过反义词组形成强烈对照(contrast)。

彼有私急也,必以公义示而强之①

华兹生将"急"译为 personal desire,即个人欲望,很明确地让君主不得不扛起证明这些欲望合理性的举证责任(the burden of proof),下文提到为其寻找或发明正当的理由(justification)也就顺理成章了。"公义",华兹生译文(大意为做这样的事情是他的公共责任)不仅为一己的欲望找到了合适理由,甚至将其升华为一种美德,隐隐含有一种舍我其谁、义不容辞的悲壮之感。译文虽然没有挑明,读者却不难体会其中的反讽之意。"强",华兹生并未从正面翻译其"鼓励"之意,而是从反面着笔,译为催促他"事不宜迟",给读者的修辞冲击更强。

其意有下也,然而不能已,说者因为之饰其美而少其不为也②

华兹生译文将"少其不为"理解为淡化这一行为对公众的危害,是个误读。

---

① 本句王先慎解读为"或有私事,将欲急为,则示以公义而勉强之"。参见王先慎.韩非子集解.钟哲,点校.北京:中华书局,1998:89.

② 原译为:"当他的意图有某种卑下的倾向,然而不能自止时,说话者就给那个意图夸饰成是美好的,反而不满他不去干。"参见梁启雄.韩子浅解.2 版.北京:中华书局,2009:93.

Sahleen 译文①大意为责备君主不早行此事,虽然方向正确,但是使用"责备"严重扭曲了该场景中修辞者与受众的权力关系,将原本处于弱势的修辞者与占据强势话语地位的君主的关系不恰当地进行翻转,读者无法理解为什么说客可以像尊长训斥顽童一样去批评高高在上的君主。

其心有高也,而实不能及,说者为之举其过而见其恶而多其不行也②

"高",华兹生译为 lofty(高尚),与前文"下"(不那么上得了台面的)刚好相对。"举",华兹生译为 point out(指出)固然忠实,如能译为 enumerate(罗列),则更能通过凸显这一行动面临的问题从而实现劝阻目标受众(君主)的预期修辞目的。"过",华兹生译文 faults(缺陷)以及 Sahleen 译文③ problems(问题)都很妥帖。"多其不行",华兹生译文提到"让主动不做这个事情显得行为人颇有美德",与西方古典修辞策略 make virtue of necessity(化必需为美德)遥相呼应,浸淫在西方修辞传统中的受众很容易对此产生认同感。

有欲矜以智能,则为之举异事之同类者,多为之地,使之资说于我,而佯不知也以资其智④

"矜",华兹生译文十分形象生动,将君主迫不及待地要在人前显摆其才智的样态活灵活现地呈现在读者面前。

"举异事之同类者",华兹生译文为读者重构了一个具体修辞语境,就是(针对特定话题)摆出若干与进言者(修辞者)心中已有方案大同小异的选项供君主进行修辞觅材之用,既符合实际话语互动场景又具有可操作性。

---

① 译文为:"The persuader should highlight the good points of the plan and scold the ruler for not carrying it out."。参见 P. J. Ivanhoe, Bryan W. Van Norden. Readings in Classical Chinese Philosophy. New York: Seven Bridges Press, 2001:318.

② 王先慎引俞樾曰:"此两文(即本句与"其意有下也,然而不能已,说者因为之饰其美而少其不为也"两文)相对。其意虽甚卑下,而有所不能已,则说者必为之饰其美,反若以其不行而少之;如此,乃见不能已之不足为病矣。其意虽甚胜高尚,而有所不能及,则说者必为之举其过而见其恶,反若以其不行而多之;如此,乃见不能及之不足为耻矣。"转引自王先慎.韩非子集解.钟哲,点校.北京:中华书局,1998:90.

③ 译文为:"the persuader should point out the problems with the plan, expose its bad points."。参见 P. J. Ivanhoe, Bryan W. Van Norden. Readings in Classical Chinese Philosophy. New York: Seven Bridges Press, 2001:318.

④ 原注为:"所说或矜于广智,则多与举彼同类之异事,以宽所取之地;令其取说于我而我佯若不知,如此者所以助其智也。"参见梁启雄.韩子浅解.2版.北京:中华书局,2009:90.

"以资其智"这一修辞行为的最终目的,是让君主觉得有人为其修辞发明提供语料与其他必要的智力支持,从而相应地形成对进言者的好感。基于这一理解,华兹生巧用"abet"(助长)这个充满修辞张力的词①暗示进言者是这个修辞情境中的话语操盘手,为推进自己既定目标的实现而操控包括听话人(君主)在内的一切修辞资源。换言之,abet 的使用很有助于提醒读者注意进言者"反客为主"的特殊话语地位:表面上是在为君主服务,归根结底是在通过收割预期的话语红利以推进自己设置好的议程。基于这一参照点,Sahleen 译文 and increase his own wisdom without even knowing it(让君主在不知不觉中增长智慧)这一完全利他的解读就不免显得过于理想主义了。

欲内②相存之言,则必以美名明之,而微见其合于私利也

"相存",华兹生译为"和平共处",更有包容性,可以兼容多种场景。"以美名明之",华兹生译文成功传达了原文"高尚其事"的意思。Sahleen 译文 use beautiful words to explain the proposal(使用漂亮的词语解释这个提议)则不免流于表面,有隔靴搔痒之嫌。

欲陈危害之事,则显其毁诽,而微见其合于私患也

"陈",华兹生译文使用 warn…against(警告),有效传达了劝阻这一修辞意图。"显",华兹生译文 make a show of(卖弄/显摆)偏离了原文的情感色彩,如能译为 enumerate(列举),则比较客观忠实。"毁诽",在这里并非毫无根据的批评,而是有根有据的批判。华兹生译为"批评与道德谴责",比较准确。Sahleen 的译文"You must make the potential for destruction or defamation clear."(毁灭与诋毁)则与原文相去甚远。

誉异人与同行者,规异事与同计者③

"誉异人与同行者",华兹生译文"称赞其他与君主有相同事迹者"的话语重心在于"其他人",后文又缺乏必要的交代,容易让读者感到困惑。如能将话语重点调整到"相似性",比如译为 Praise those men doing the same things as

---

① abet(to help or encourage someone to do something wrong or illegal)通常带有贬义,如教唆、唆使、怂恿、伙同……作案等。"教唆"者对局势自然是洞若观火,清楚地知道自己需要获得的利益,更懂得如何使用手头已有修辞资源达成这一目的,在这里主要是取其"控局"这一意涵加以讨论。

② 意为"进献"。

③ 原注为:"说者或延誉异人与彼同行,或规谋异事与彼同计。"参见梁启雄.韩子浅解.2 版.北京:中华书局,2009:90.

he does(称赞那些与君主做同样事情的人),则读者不难读出"这些事情是值得肯定的"这一层意思,从而顺理成章得出"君主的行为是值得肯定的"这个结论。"规异事与同计者",华兹生误解"规"并将其翻译为"赞扬",与前文"誉"语义重复,削弱了文本的思想性。Sahleen 译文 give examples of other affairs where plans like those of the ruler you are talking to have been used(征引与君主所做的事情思路相同的其他事情),容易让读者联想到这一做法的修辞目的是间接帮助君主进行修辞发明或为君主的行动增加底气。

有与同污者,则必以大饰其无伤也;有与同败者,则必以明饰其无失也①

"污",华兹生译文 vice(邪恶)能够清晰表明道德评价,暗示这些不良行为原本可以通过主观努力加以回避或克制,只是由于君主本人意志薄弱而放任自己做这些卑污之事。"必以大饰其无伤",华兹生译文凸显"务必费力文过饰非,对此进行'无害化'处理",十分形象生动。"必以明饰其无失"的"饰",华兹生使用 defend(捍卫),表明了这一行为的修辞目的,让读者不仅能够知其然更能够知其所以然。

彼自多其力,则毋以其难概之也;自勇其断,则无以其谪怒之;自智其计,则毋以其败穷之②

"则毋以其难概之也",华兹生译文将焦点放在君主过往遇到的困境与现在的自信的对冲上,与这一思路相近的是 Sahleen 译文 do not use his past difficulties to correct him(不要用君主过去遇到的困难去纠正他的观点)。撇开翻译不谈,仅仅就文势而言,由于后文提到的两个例子都是以君主过去的"战果/业绩"来"以子之矛攻子之盾",华兹生与 Sahleen 的译文在修辞上不仅完全可以接受,而且逻辑更是天衣无缝。

"自勇其断",华兹生译为"君主自认为善断时,不要提起过去误判的事例

---

① 原注为:"其异人之行若与彼同污,则大文饰之,言此污何所伤;其异事之计若与彼同败者,则明为文饰,言此败何所失。如此必以己为善补过而崇重之也。"参见梁启雄.韩子浅解.2版.北京:中华书局,2009:90-91.

② 梁启雄译文为:"当君主夸张他自己的力量时,说者就不要拿事实的困难来纠正他。当君主勇于武断时,说话者就不要指出他的过错来招他生气。当君主自以为计事明智时,就不要指出他曾经失败过的往事来使他窘迫。"参见梁启雄.韩子浅解.2版.北京:中华书局,2009:94.王先慎一语中的地指出这些行为的修辞目的:"凡此皆所以护其短而养其锐者,说者可以无伤也。"参见王先慎.韩非子集解.钟哲,点校.北京:中华书局,1998:91.

去触怒他"。这一译文由于和日常经验高度吻合,从修辞角度而言,很容易获得读者认同。"穷",华兹生译为 tax(使大伤脑筋),虽然在大方向上并无不妥,但就具体语境而言,还不够细致适切。如能译为 embarrass(使……尴尬),则能够与整个文本意在保留君主颜面的修辞基调相契合。

*辞言无所系縻,然后极骋智辩焉*

"辞言无所系縻",华兹生译文 rub him the wrong way(无意间触犯君主),形象地把进言者与君主那种不平等的话语权力关系以及进言者战战兢兢、如履薄冰的样态呈现在读者面前。"智辩",华兹生译为 powers of rhetoric (修辞能力),将智慧与雄辩统一在修辞名下,与西方古典修辞观不谋而合,是很精彩的翻译。就中西修辞传统视域融合而言,华兹生译文比较容易为英语读者所接受。

*亲近不疑而得尽辞也*

"亲近不疑而得尽辞",华兹生译文先提到"尽其辞"而后论及"不见疑"。基于西方修辞理论,修辞人格是说服的决定性因素,很难想象一个不被君主信任的进言者会有机会发表观点或者充分表达自己的意见。因此,从逻辑角度而言,如能调整为 you can become near and dear to him, avoid all suspicion, and exert your speech to the utmost(先"不见疑"而后"尽其辞"),则会更容易为读者所接受。


三、昔者弥子瑕有宠于卫君。卫国之法,窃驾君车者罪刖。弥子瑕母病,人闻,有夜告弥子,弥子矫驾君车以出。君闻而贤之,曰:"孝哉!为母之故,忘其犯刖罪。"异日,与君游于果园,食桃而甘,不尽,以其半啖君。君曰:"爱我哉!忘其口味,以啖寡人。"及弥子色衰爱弛,得罪于君,君曰:"是固尝矫驾吾车,又尝啖我以余桃。"故弥子之行未变于初也,而以前之所以见贤而后获罪者,爱憎之变也。故有爱于主,则智当而加亲;有憎于主,则智不当见罪而加疏。故谏说谈论之士,不可不察爱憎之主而后说焉。

——《韩非子·说难》

In ancient days, Mitseshia [a man] was a favorite of the duke of Wei. There was a law in Wei that whoever made use of the duke's carriage without permission should have his feet amputated. One day Mitse learned that his mother was ill, but it was night and Mitse took the ducal carriage to go and see his mother. The duke heard of this and remarked, "What a good son. He risked having his feet chopped off for the sake of his sick mother." One day Mitse was taking a stroll with the duke in his garden. Mitse tasted a peach which he had plucked from the tree, and finding it very good, offered the uneaten half to the duke. "How he loves me!" remarked the duke. Later when the boy was not so handsome any more and had lost the duke's favor, he said, "He is the one who made unauthorized use of my carriage and who insulted me by giving me the uneaten half of a peach." What the duke now condemned in Mitse's conduct was the same as what he had praised before; the change was in the duke's own love and hatred. Therefore, when a ruler likes a man, his words seem wise and he shows confidence in him; when he dislikes a man, his misdemeanors seem to increase and their relations seem increasingly strained. Therefore, one who wants to speak to a ruler must first abide his time and ascertain whether he is liked or disliked. （林语堂 译）

In ancient times Mi Zixia won favor with the ruler of Wei.[①] According to the laws of the state of Wei, anyone who secretly made use of the ruler's carriage was punished by having his feet amputated. When Mi Zixia's mother fell ill, someone slipped into the palace at night to report this to Mi Zixia. Mi Zixia forged an order from the ruler, got into the ruler's carriage, and went off to see her, but when the ruler heard of it, he only praised him, saying, "How filial! For the sake of his mother he forgot all about the danger of having his feet cut off!" Another day Mi Zixia was strolling with the ruler in an orchard and, biting into a peach and finding it sweet, he stopped eating and gave the remaining half to the ruler to enjoy. "How sincere is your love for me!" exclaimed the ruler. "You forget your own appetite and think only of giving me good things to eat!" Later, however, when Mi Zixia's looks had faded and the ruler's passion for him had cooled, he was accused of committing some crime against his lord. "After all," said the ruler, "he once stole my carriage, and another time he gave me a half-eaten peach to eat!" Mi Zixia was actually acting no differently from the way he always had; the fact that he was praised in the early days, and accused of a crime later on, was be-

---

① 原注为："Duke Ling of Wei ( r. 534-493 B. C.)"。参见 Han Fei Tzu: Basic Writings. Burton Watson, trans. New York: Columbia University Press, 1964:78.

cause the ruler's love had turned to hate. If you gain the ruler's love, your wisdom will be appreciated and you will enjoy his favor as well; but if he hates you, not only will your wisdom be rejected, but you will be regarded as a criminal and thrust aside. Hence men who wish to present their remonstrances and expound their ideas must not fail to ascertain the ruler's loves and hates before launching into their speeches.

(华兹生 译)

### 昔者弥子瑕有宠于卫君

华兹生译文没有对弥子瑕做进一步介绍,林语堂译文有提到弥子瑕是个男性(a man),但是依然语焉不详。潘智丹译文①为读者增补了很多背景信息,如卫灵公有龙阳之兴,俊美的弥子瑕年轻时为其男宠等。

### 窃驾君车者罪刖

华兹生把这一句翻译成"秘密地使用国君车驾会被砍掉双脚",逻辑上不免令人生疑:既然是偷偷使用,是如何被发现的?林语堂译文明确指出是未经许可使用国君车驾会被处罚,逻辑清晰严密,容易为读者所接受。

### 弥子瑕母病,人闻②,有夜告弥子,弥子矫驾君车以出

"夜告弥子",林语堂译文忽略了这个重要细节,淡化了事情的紧迫性与特殊性,没能够为下文弥子瑕的权宜行为做铺垫。华译将报信者形容为"潜入宫中",会让读者误以为这是不可告人的事情,同时也与中国古代社会"百善孝为先"的主流价值相悖。在子女不在场的情况下,周边的人连夜去告知其父母生病的消息,这是天经地义的事情,完全不必遮遮掩掩。或许是因为华兹生所参照的版本用词不同,但是从西方修辞的受众角度而言,译文首先需要在逻辑上能够自圆其说,才能够被读者所接受并流传久远。

"矫驾君车",林语堂译文提到驾车就走,并未提到"矫诏"这个核心情节。华兹生不折不扣地翻译了原文内容,有利于推动故事发展。

---

① 译文为:"Duke Ling of Wei had a gay pal named Mi Zixia. The boy was handsome when he was young, so Duke Ling of Wei was very fond of him."。参见姚萱.韩非子智慧故事.潘智丹,译.上海:上海外语教育出版社,2010:208.

② 这一处文字究竟是"间"还是"闻",有不同版本以及相应的不同断句方式,笔者赞同王先慎的改动与解读:"此谓人闻其母病,有夜来告者,形容弥子瑕得传闻之言而归。已显卫君之称为孝,文相照应,今据二唐本改。"参见王先慎.韩非子集解.钟哲,点校.北京:中华书局,1998:93.

为母之故,忘其犯①刖罪

两个版本都体现了"孝不顾身"这一点,但是二者均未能译出"犯罪"这一层意思,如能译为 he even forgot that he was committing a crime making him liable to lose his feet(他甚至没有意识到自己正犯下有可能遭致刖刑的罪行),则有助于通过"liable"(负有法律责任的)建构的法律辞屏引导读者思考本故事所涉及的情与法的冲突。

食桃而甘,不尽,以其半啖②君

"食桃而甘",林语堂译文对部分情节(诸如亲自摘桃)进行了合理想象与补充,与后文的品尝、评价与分享环环相扣,让故事既连贯又真实,容易为读者所接受。

"以其半啖君"之"啖君",林语堂翻译为 offered…to the duke[递给君主(吃)],显得比较简慢。华兹生译文使用 gave…to the ruler to enjoy(给君主享用),有助于揭示这一行为的动机,并能够为下文(卫灵公态度转变,对这一行为做出截然相反的评价)的修辞冲突做好充分铺垫。

君曰:"爱我哉! 忘其口味③,以啖寡人。"

对于"忘其口味"这一细节林语堂译文并未触及。华兹生译文大意为"忘记了自己也喜欢吃这个,光想着把好吃的给我了",不仅文从字顺,而且贴近人情;从修辞角度而言,这样的译文不仅受众更加乐于接受,也比较适合译出文化推广。潘智丹译文④的大意为"舍不得吃,留下来给我",也是很适切的。

及弥子色衰爱弛,得罪于君

林语堂与华兹生都从各自角度成功翻译出了原文的意思。尤其是关于"爱弛"的翻译,林语堂译文 had lost the duke's favor(失宠)与华兹生译文 the ruler's passion for him had cooled(激情冷却)都很形象生动。潘智丹译文⑤

---

① 虽然很多版本都没有这个"犯"字,但基于文本逻辑角度考量,笔者赞同王先慎的增补。参见王先慎.韩非子集解.钟哲,点校.北京:中华书局,1998:94.

② "啖"与"哈"的区别,王先慎指出:"自食为啖,食人为哈,二字义别。"参见王先慎.韩非子集解.钟哲,点校.北京:中华书局,1998:94.

③ "口味",不宜望文生义地理解,其实指的是"喜欢吃的东西"。

④ 译文为:"When he has delicious food, he begrudges eating it himself and saves it for me."。参见姚萱.韩非子智慧故事.潘智丹,译.上海:上海外语教育出版社,2010:209.

⑤ 译文为:"Later Mi Zixia lost his beauty when gaining in age, and Duke Ling had a new gay pal."。参见姚萱.韩非子智慧故事.潘智丹,译.上海:上海外语教育出版社,2010:209.

(大意为"后来弥子瑕年老色衰之时,卫灵公有了新欢")不仅提到了弥子瑕遭遇的生理变化,还进一步补充了他所遭遇的人生变故(即国君另结新欢),虽然不是原文明示的,从修辞角度而言倒也合情合理,有助于增加故事的可读性。

君曰:"是固尝矫驾吾车,又尝啖我以余桃。"

"尝矫驾吾车",林语堂译文(大意为未经授权擅自使用我的车驾)用词庄重,谴责的意味更浓厚。华兹生的译文(大意为他曾经偷了我的车驾)则与原文有较大偏差:弥子瑕用车固然涉及欺骗,却只涉及该车的使用权而不涉及其所有权,其最终目的是借用而非占有。

"又尝啖我以余桃",华兹生译文只是如实对字面进行翻译,并没有明确传达谴责的话语意图。林语堂译文明确将"余桃啖君"的行为定性为对卫灵公的人格侮辱。

故弥子之行未变于初也,而以前之所以见贤而后获罪者,爱憎之变也

华兹生译文依照原文顺序进行了忠实翻译,林语堂译文对这些内容进行整合提取,形成了一个"变"与"不变"的强烈对照,使得一个喜怒无常、善变的"君主"形象跃然纸上。同时,其译文也让读者直观感受到修辞者的修辞人格对说服效果乃至于修辞者本人命运的巨大影响。

故有爱于主,则智当而加亲;有憎于主,则智不当见罪而加疏

关于"智当",华兹生译文有提到修辞者的智慧得到受众(君主)赏识,但是没有体现整个讨论的核心话题,也就是话语在不同情况下所能够产生的修辞效果。林语堂译文紧扣主题,将"智当"翻译为 his words seem wise(他的话语在这种情况下就显得充满智慧),与原文话语意图高度契合。

"智不当见罪",华兹生译文望文生义地翻译为"被当作罪犯",偏离了原文。林语堂译文大意为"他的行为会越看越不像话",也就是将其理解为责怪的意思,是符合原文精神的灵活处理。

故谏说谈论之士,不可不察爱憎之主而后说焉

"谏说谈论",林语堂译文译将其概括为"言说",稍显空泛,华兹生译为"劝谏与论述",详略得当、恰到好处。"察爱憎之主而后说",林语堂译文将"察"理解为等待时机与确认自己是否被受众所认可,增补了原文没有提到但是在西方经典修辞理论中不可或缺的一个关于修辞发明的要素——时机(kairos)。

华兹生译文则强调务必先确认君主的好恶而后才发言,其中使用 launching into(启动)尤其能够凸显修辞者对待"言"的慎重态度乃至对"言"的后果的敬畏之心。

四、子独不闻涸泽之蛇乎?泽涸,蛇将徙。有小蛇谓大蛇曰:"子行而我随之,人以为蛇之行者耳,必有杀子者。子不如相衔负我以行,人必以我为神君也。"乃相衔负以越公道而行。人皆避之,曰:"神君也。"

——《韩非子·说林》

How Two Water Snakes Moved House
The snakes wanted to move away from a marsh which was drying up.

"If you lead the way and I follow," said a small to a large snake, "men will know we are moving away and someone will kill you. You had better carry me on your back, each holding the other's tail in his mouth. Then men will think I am a god."

So, each holding the other, they crossed the high way. And everybody made way for them, crying out: "This is a god!"

(杨宪益等 译)

**泽涸,蛇将徙**

"泽涸",是不可控的自然环境变数,因此蛇的迁徙很可能是被迫的。杨宪益译文 wanted to(想这么做)固然不错,但是凸显的是蛇主观层面的打算,如果能够译为 had to(不得不),会更加符合客观实际。

**人以为蛇之行者耳**

杨宪益译文并未强调"蛇之行者不足为奇"这一对故事发展至关重要的信息,如能译为 men will think it is nothing but the migration of snakes(人们会觉得不过是蛇类寻常之迁徙行为),则有助于忠实传达这一要点。潘智丹译文[①]最有修辞考量,凸显了这种行走方式乃是最寻常的生物本能,为后文的"行为'修辞'"组合做了充分铺垫。

---

[①] 译文为:"If we go as usual, with you walking ahead and me following you behind, people will think we are just ordinary snakes, so someone may want to kill us."。参见姚萱.韩非子智慧故事.潘智丹,译.上海:上海外语教育出版社,2010:103.

### 子不如相衔负我以行，人必以我为神君也

"子不如相衔负我以行"，是一个提议，杨宪益译文 You had better 表面上是"你最好（这么做）"，在真实语用中多为一种强制要求，难免给人一种不由分说、别无选择的话语压迫感，与原文语境不符。小蛇虽然机灵，也要明白自己在所属社群中的话语地位，在提议时要给予大蛇充分的决定权。这样的译文容易投射出小蛇狂妄自大、目中无"人"的修辞人格，与文本的总体修辞目的相悖。如能译为 How about your carrying me on your back while moving onward?（你背着我往前走如何？），则有助于投射出一个思维缜密又彬彬有礼的修辞人格，比较容易引起读者认同。"神君"，就是"神灵"的意思，杨宪益翻译为"（主宰某个领域的）神"，是比较接近的；如果能够撇开身份，而专注于翻译拥有超自然力量（possessing supernatural power），会更契合原文精神。

### 乃相衔负以越公道而行/人皆避之/神君也

"乃相衔负以越公道而行"，杨宪益等理解为"两蛇相互衔着，大蛇背小蛇前行"，是比较准确的。潘智丹译文[①]使用 in tandem（协同）表现两蛇高度协调、意在影响他人认知与判断的动作，尤其精彩。"人皆避之"，杨宪益等的译文不仅忠实，还进一步指出人们主动给蛇让路（这恰恰是蛇的真正"修辞目的"，即安全过大路）。"神君也"，杨宪益等只是按字面直译，泛泛地提到"它是有神性的"，并没有指出哪一条蛇天赋异禀，语法上也与前面的"它们"龃龉。潘智丹译文[②]则明确指出小蛇并非等闲之辈，在语法上十分严密，同时将完整的推理过程呈现给读者，让译文整体能够自圆其说，更容易获得读者认可。

---

## 本章参考的英译本

林语堂.诸子百家:英、汉.北京:外语教学与研究出版社,2015.
中国古代寓言选.杨宪益,戴乃迭,译.北京:外文出版社,2001.

---

① 译文为:"Then they went onto the road in tandem, and the big snake carried the small one on its back."。参见姚萱.韩非子智慧故事.潘智丹,译.上海:上海外语教育出版社,2010:104.

② 译文为:"The small snake must be a god, as a big snake serves it."。参见姚萱.韩非子智慧故事.潘智丹,译.上海:上海外语教育出版社,2010:105.

姚萱.韩非子智慧故事.潘智丹,译. 上海:上海外语教育出版社,2010.

Han Fei Tzu: Basic Writings. Burton Watson, trans. New York: Columbia University Press, 1964.

P. J. Ivanhoe, Bryan W. Van Norden. Readings in Classical Chinese Philosophy. New York: Seven Bridges Press, 2001.

# 第八章 《孙子兵法》英译比较与评析

一、兵者,诡道也。

——《孙子兵法·始计》[①]

All warfare is based on deception. （翟林奈 译）
A military operation involves deception. (Thomas Cleary 译)
War is a game of deception. （林戊荪 译）

翟林奈(Lionel Giles)译文说欺骗是战争的基础,有言过其实之嫌。欺骗固然是战争很突出的一个维度,却不能说是其基础。Cleary译文提到军事活动难免涉及欺骗,这样的译法虽然在逻辑上比较站得住脚,却因使用欺骗一词而不免有损军事行动这一高度复杂的人类协同行为的参与者的修辞人格;Cleary同时还翻译了王晢[②]对欺骗的辩证分析的注解,即之所以使诈是为了制敌,要指挥部队则统帅必须真诚。林戊荪译文使用隐喻的修辞手法,将战争比作欺骗竞赛,双方斗智斗勇,为了获胜穷尽各种军事修辞手段与策略;通过使用"竞赛"为"欺骗"这个充满负面语义的词设置了修辞缓冲区,使得整个句子更容易被公众所接受并得以进入话语流通领域。索耶尔(Ralph D.Sawyer)注意到了单独使用"欺骗"翻译"诡道"可能失之片面的问题,倾向于使用deception and artifice(诈谋奇计)进行翻译。索耶尔指出欺骗既有消极地隐藏(最简单的欺骗形式),也有积极主动地制造假象以迷惑敌人。同时,索耶尔还向读者介绍了孙子这句话在军事哲学上的独特地位,指出虽然所有的军事著作都探究欺诈的使用,孙子的论断却是该原则最为明晰的总结。此句下文的

---

① 若无特别说明,本章所涉及《孙子兵法》引文均出自《孙子十家注》。出处详见孙武.孙子十家注.曹操,等,注.天津:天津市古籍书店,1991.
② 原注为:"诡者所以求胜敌,御众必以信也。"参见孙武.孙子十家注.曹操,等,注.天津:天津市古籍书店,1991:27. Cleary对该注解的译文为:"Deception is for the purpose of seeking victory over an enemy; to command a group requires truthfulness."参见 The Art of War. Thomas Cleary, trans. Boston: Shambhala Publications, Inc., 1988:10.

十四句都是这一战略原则的具体战术体现。①

二、孙子曰：凡用兵之法：全国为上，破国次之；全军为上，破军次之；全旅为上，破旅次之；全卒为上，破卒次之；全伍为上，破伍次之。是故百战百胜，非善之善者也；不战而屈人之兵，善之善者也。

——《孙子兵法·谋攻》

Hence to fight and conquer in all your battles is not supreme excellence; supreme excellence consists in breaking the enemy's resistance without fighting.

(翟林奈 译)

For this reason attaining one hundred victories in one hundred battles is not the pinnacle of excellence. Subjugating the enemy's army without fighting is the true pinnacle of excellence. (Ralph D. Sawyer 译)

"不战而屈人"，翟林奈的译文"不通过战斗就突破敌人的防线"更多的是指物理层面的胜利成果，离"不战而屈人之兵"还有相当距离。索耶尔使用 subjugating 更有征服的意涵。Cleary 翻译了梅尧臣的注解②，提到为什么不可轻易卷入战斗：因为战斗往往意味着人员伤亡，攻城难免毁坏物件。Cleary 翻译的李筌注解③为读者指明了如何可以"不战而屈人"，即使用特定战术瓦解

---

① 原注为："The term 'deception' here inadequately conveys both the positive and negative aspects of the matter. We prefer to translate as 'deception and artifice' because much craft is involved in not only concealing appearance, which is the simplest form of deception, but also in creating false impressions. Although all the military writings exploit deceit and deception, Sun-tzu's statement is the most explicit formulation of the principle. The fourteen sentences that follow should be understood as tactical principles flowing from this realization."《孙子兵法》中体现上述战略原则的具体战术为："故能而示之不能，用而示之不用，近而示之远，远而示之近。利而诱之，乱而取之，实而备之，强而避之，怒而挠之，卑而骄之，佚而劳之，亲而离之。攻其无备，出其不意。"索耶尔原注参见 Sun Tzu. Sawyer. The Art of War. Ralph D, Sawyer, trans. Boulder: Westview Press, 1994:305.

② 译文为："MEI YAOCHEN: Battle means hurting people, siege means destroying things." 参见 Sun Tzu. The Art of War. Thomas Cleary, trans. Boston: Shambhala Publications, Inc., 1988.

③ 译文为："LI QUAN: Use tactics to overcome opponents by dispiriting them rather than by battling with them; take their cities by strategy. Destroy their countries artfully, do not die in protracted warfare." 参见 Sun Tzu. The Art of War. Thomas Cleary, trans. Boston: Shambhala Publications, Inc., 1988.

敌军斗志,使用谋略夺取敌人城池。Cleary 翻译的张预注解①还提到"不战而屈人"的其他各种方法,使得文本具有坚实的逻辑基础,并进一步增强了说服力。

三、故形兵之极,至于无形,无形,则深间不能窥,智者不能谋。因形而错胜于众,众不能知。人皆知我所以胜之形,而莫知吾所以制胜之形。故其战胜不复,而应形于无穷。

——《孙子兵法·虚实》

In making tactical dispositions, the highest pitch you can attain is to conceal them; conceal your dispositions, and you will be safe from the prying of the subtlest spies, from the machinations of the wisest brains. How victory may be produced for them out of the enemy's own tactics—that is what the multitude cannot comprehend. All men can see the tactics whereby I conquer, but what none can see is the strategy out of which victory is evolved. Do not repeat the tactics which have gained you one victory, but let your methods be regulated by the infinite variety of circumstances.

(翟林奈 译)

The ultimate skill in taking up a strategic position (hsing) is to have no form (hsing).② If your position is formless(hsing), the most carefully concealed spies will not be able to get a look at it, and the wisest counsellors will not be able to lay plans against it. I present the rank and file with victories gained through(yin)strategic positioning(hsing), yet they are not able to understand them. Everyone knows the position(hsing)that has won me victory, yet none fathom how I came to settle on this winning position(hsing). Thus one's victories in battle cannot be repeated—they take their form(hsing)in response to inexhaustibly changing circumstances.

(安乐哲 译)

---

① 译文为:"ZHANG YU: A skillful martialist ruins plans, spoils relations, cuts off supplies, or blocks the way, and hence can overcome people without fighting. One way that a city can be taken is to attack a place they will be sure to want to save, so as to draw the enemy out of the city stronghold to come to the rescue, and then take the city by sneak attack."。参见 Sun Tzu. The Art of War. Thomas Cleary, trans. Boston: Shambhala Publications, Inc., 1988.

② 原注为:"The Han strips does not have ku here—commonly translated as 'therefore'. Even if we retain it, it only functions as a passage marker."。参见 The Art of Warfare: The First English Translation Incorporating the Recently Discovered Yin Ch'Ueh Shan Texts. Roger T. Ames, trans. New York: Ballantine Books, 1993:216.

### 无形/深间

"无形",安乐哲翻译为"没有形状",过于抽象,让读者不明所以,翟林奈翻译为"藏形"是比较明晰的。Cleary 翻译张预注解①,试图为读者解释如何做到"无形"及"无形"的功用,但是将"虚实"机械地翻译为"空与满",未能传达原文"掩人耳目"这一层意涵。"深间",翟林奈译文用语义比较模糊的 subtle 翻译"深",既可以形容专业素养过硬、老成练达的间谍,也可以形容善于伪装、隐藏深密的间谍。安乐哲与戴梅可(Michael Nylan)②选择性地翻译了"藏得深"这一面,忽略了"城府深"的那一面。格里菲斯翻译为 the most penetrating spies(眼光最"毒"的间谍),则忽略了隐蔽性那一面。Chen Song 译文 even the most well-placed and observant spy 则非常明确地将这两个方面同时翻译了出来。

### 智者不能谋

翟林奈译文(you will be safe)from the machinations of the wisest brains 大意为"最聪明的大脑也无法谋算你",安乐哲译文"The wisest counsellors will not be able to lay plans against it."大意为"最聪明的军事顾问也无从下手",二者都比较关注对手如何主动出击。Chen Song 译文对"谋"的理解则别具一格:"The wisest strategist will not be able to uncover your plans or plot against you."(最聪明的战略家也无法拆穿你的计划或算计你)。军事斗争,保密第一,如果计划在敌人面前一览无余,必定会极大挫伤指挥官的自信。因此,识破对手的排兵布阵基本理路,虽然表面上不算进攻,其实是一种更能震撼对手的柔性进攻。Chen Song 对"谋"这一维度的补充是很有见地的。

### 因形而错胜于众,众不能知

翟林奈译文为:"How victory may be produced for them out of the

---

① Thomas Cleary 译文为:"First you use emptiness and fullness to induce the enemy to adopt a specific formation while remaining unfathomable to the enemy, so that ultimately you reach formlessness. Once you have no perceptible form, you leave no traces to follow, so spies cannot find any chinks to see through and those in charge of intelligence cannot put any plans into operation."。张预注解为:"始以虚实形敌,敌不能测,故其极致卒归于无形。既有形可观,无形可求,则间者不能窥其隙,智者无以运计。"Thomas Cleary 译文参见 The Art of War. Thomas Cleary, trans. Boston:Shambhala Publications, Inc., 1988.张预注解参见孙武.孙子十家注.曹操,等,注.天津:天津市古籍书店,1991:222.

② 译文为:"spies embedded in your camp"(安插在阵营里的间谍)。参见 The Art of War:A New Translation. Michael Nylan, trans. New York:W.W. North & Company, 2020:74.

enemy's own tactics—that is what the multitude cannot comprehend."(如何基于敌人的战术而取胜,己方士兵不明所以),偏离了前面提到的排兵布阵这一讨论的主题;安乐哲译文在逻辑上与前文一脉相承,更为合理:"I present the rank and file with victories gained through(yin)strategic positioning(hsing), yet they are not able to understand them."(如何靠战略性排兵布阵而取胜,己方士兵不明所以)。但是二者都只提到己方士兵不明所以,与文本的修辞意图有所偏差。原文重点在于基于假想敌立论,要求统帅要在排兵布阵这一修辞行为方面注意自我韬晦(self-effacement),军事修辞策略要深藏不露,就算取得预期目标也要让对手摸不着头脑。以此为参照点,则 Cleary 译文"Victory over multitudes by means of formation is unknowable to the multitudes."(通过布阵制敌而敌人却不明所以)是比较接近原文意图的翻译。Joey Yap 译文"Even if you were to go on to make your tactics public and to explain that you won your victory through adapting your approach to the enemy's ever changing circumstances, they should still not be able to understand how you have achieved it."(即便你公开了所使用的战术,解释说你之所以能够取胜是因为能够顺应不断变化的敌情,他们依然无法理解你究竟是如何取胜的。)固然进一步强化、神化了主帅的修辞人格,却进一步矮化了对手的修辞形象,这种翻译策略固然在主观上有助于放大战果、增强自信,客观上却因为二者过于强烈的智力反差而使读者产生疑虑。但凡是理性的读者都不免会对是否真的批量存在智商如此低下的对手产生怀疑,从而对整个译文的表述失去信心。换句话说,这样夸大其词的翻译其实是译者自我施加的一种修辞伤害(a self-inflicted rhetorical wound),应该尽量加以避免。戴梅可译文"Cleaving to their form, you plant victory in their midst, even before they know what has befallen them."(紧跟敌人阵型,在敌人尚未明白发生什么之前就已一招制敌)更是凸显了高明的排兵布阵艺术所能够达到的出神入化的境界。

**人皆知我所以胜之形,而莫知吾所以制胜之形**

关于句中这个"以"字存留的分歧,笔者赞同杨炳安[①]观点,即删除"以"字。翟林奈把这句话翻译为"致胜的战术、招数有目共睹,但是战略布局却无人能晓",是立意高远的翻译。安乐哲翻译为"人人都看得出致胜的阵型,但是

---

① 杨炳安指出:"此二句乃知其'然'而不知其'所以然'之句型,故上'以'字以无为善。'知我所胜之形,而莫知吾所以制胜之形',言只见我胜敌之状,而不知我所以胜敌之理。制胜之形何以'莫知'?曹注谓'不以一形胜万形',张注谓'因敌形而制此胜',皆得之。"

无人能够参透选用这个阵型的依据以及组构这个阵型的方法",与原文内容高度契合且明白晓畅。戴梅可译文"Others all learn the formulae that supposedly won me victory, yet no one can fathom the process by which I won."（别人都知道我获胜的要素,却琢磨不透我之所以获胜的过程）,使用 formulae（配方）将错综复杂的军事活动要素以非常浅白、贴近日常经验的方式呈现给目标读者,有利于实现受众对译文的迅速认同。

*战胜不复,而应形于无穷*

杨炳安解读本句为"不执故常,不复前谋,随宜制变,即今所谓根据具体情况灵活掌握之谓"。[1] 翟林奈译文"Do not repeat the tactics which have gained you one victory, but let your methods be regulated by the infinite variety of circumstances."（不要重复使用借以取胜的战术,要根据不断变化的情况决定应该采用的方法）不仅逻辑严密,而且完整地实现了原文劝说的修辞话语功能。安乐哲译文意为"军事取胜之道不可重复,因为阵型的形成取决于不断变化的情境"。虽然"不可重复"看起来不无道理,却显得比较绝对。历史不断在重演,在战场上遇到类似的场景也不是完全不可能的,在这个意义上,"故伎重施"是可行的。Stephen F. Kaufman 译文[2]不仅翻译了原文内容,还替读者解释了不可以使用相同的策略的原因。

## 四、无邀正正之旗,勿击堂堂之陈,此治变者也。

—— 《孙子兵法·军争》

To refrain from intercepting an enemy whose banners are in perfect order, to refrain from attacking an army drawn up in calm and confident array:—this is the

---

[1] 杨炳安.孙子会笺.郑州:中州古籍出版社,1986:86.

[2] 译文为:"A clever warlord never repeats his successful actions in the same manner. Variations in the universe are infinite, and so are the methods to be used in any actions. In time, a repeated strategy will be learned by the opposition, and they will be able to prepare defenses against it. If new methods of attack do not work after a second attempt, they must be reevaluated. The warlord must have an alternative method at the ready. Wise warlords always diversify their attacks when necessary."。大意是:久而久之,反复使用的策略必然被敌方所掌握,从而能够准备好防御之道。一个精明的统帅绝不会重复他的获胜方式。世界的变化无穷无尽,军事行动采取的方法也应该相应变化。参见 The Art of War: The Definitive Interpretation of Sun Tzu's Classic Book of *Strategy for the Martial Artist*. Stephen F. Kaufman, trans. North Clarendon: Tuttle Publishing, 1996.

art of studying circumstances.

（翟林奈 译）

　　They do not engage an enemy advancing with well-order banners nor one whose formations are in impressive array. This is control of the factor of changing circumstances.①

（格里菲斯 译）

　　"无邀"，翟林奈译文使用 refrain from（忍住做某件事情的冲动）翻译，形象地表达了克制与对手一决高下的冲动这一心理冲突过程，格里菲斯（Samuel B. Griffith）译文使用 do not engage（不与……交战），和原文的"无邀"（不主动迎战）高度契合，可谓各有千秋。"正正之旗"，两位译者都是对字面进行忠实翻译，Stephen F. Kaufman 则意译为 in prime condition（士气正旺），对原文精神的把握更到位，属于"'得'意'忘'言"的翻译。"堂堂之陈"，翟林奈主要凸显士兵自身的从容与自信，格里菲斯则倾向于形容阵容给对手以深刻印象。对照原文不难发现，格里菲斯的思路更忠实。循着这一思路，不妨将索耶尔注解曾提到的 majestic formations（雄壮的阵容）视为一个重要的备选项。"治变者"，翟林奈翻译为"研究形势"，与前文逻辑不洽。格里菲斯翻译为"控制变量"，比较接近原文意思但是表达显得生硬。安乐哲译为"This is the way to manage changing conditions."（这就是治理变化之道），比较忠实通顺。就"变"的翻译而言，戴梅可的译文 the whole range of contingencies（所有的或然因素）可谓深得"变"之精髓。就本句主旨而言，Cleary 在其译文中翻译何延锡注解"所谓强则避之"②，能够让读者不仅知其然，还能够知其所以然。

　　五、故用兵之法：无恃其不来，恃吾有以待也；无恃其不攻，恃吾有所不可攻也。

——《孙子兵法·九变》

　　The art of war teaches us to rely not on the likelihood of the enemy's not coming, but on our own readiness to receive him; not on the chance of his not attacking, but rather on the fact that we have made our position unassailable.

（翟林奈 译）

---

① 原注为："Or the 'circumstantial factor'. 'They' in these verses refer to those skilled in war."。参见 Sun Tzu: The Art of War. Samuel B. Griffith, trans. Oxford: Oxford University Press, 1963:109.

② 译文为："This is what was earlier referred to as avoiding the strong."。参见 The Art of War. Thomas Cleary, trans. Boston: Shambhala Publications, Inc., 1988.

So the rule of military operations is not to count on opponents not coming, but to rely on having ways of dealing with them; not to count on opponents not attacking, but to rely on having what cannot be attacked.　　(Thomas Cleary 译)

**恃**

翟林奈译文全部使用 rely on（依赖），如"依赖敌人不来或不进攻这种可能性"，比较拗口。Cleary 对 count on（指望）与"依靠"进行区分，使用"指望"搭配不可靠因素，使用"依靠"搭配可靠因素，显得自然地道。

**有以待/不攻/不可攻**

翟林奈译文有"严阵以待"的意涵，比 Cleary 译文所传达的"有办法对付"显得更加积极主动，更能体现稳操胜券的感觉。"不攻"，两位译者译文都很忠实，但是远不如 Yap 的"Do not expect your enemy to hold back or miss an opportunity to attack."（期待敌人退缩或错失进攻良机）生动形象。"不可攻"，Cleary 译文表面上非常忠实（大意为"不能被攻击"），其实语焉不详，不免让读者产生疑问：有（先发制人）不允许被攻击的，有（自己固若金汤）不可能被击破的，"不能被攻击"既不属于第一种，也不属于第二种，是哪一种情况呢？翟林奈译文则很明确指出是"（使己方阵地）牢不可破"之意。闵福德译文 on his own impregnability（依赖己方坚不可摧）最为简约，Chen Song 译文则为读者详细指出 to build an invincible defense（构筑一个不可战胜的防御工事）。索耶尔注解[①]"要做好准备而不是依靠运气或他人的善意，这是军事思想家们的一个基本战略原则"进一步阐明并升华了"抛弃幻想，做好战备"这一务实的军事指导思想。

六、谆谆翕翕，徐（与人）言〔入入〕者[②]，失众也；数赏者，窘也；数罚者，困也；先暴而后畏其众者，不精之至也。

　　　　　　　　　　　　　　——《孙子兵法·行军》

The sight of men whispering together in small knots or speaking in subdued

---

[①] 原注为："Being prepared, rather than having to depend upon circumstances and perhaps the good will of others, was a fundamental aspect of the military thinkers' grand strategy."。参见 Sun Tzu: The Art of War. Ralph D. Sawyer, trans. Boulder: Westview Press, 1994.

[②] 此节各版本有多处出入，"徐（与人）言〔入入〕者"就是一例，本书参照《孙子十家注》版本。

tones points to disaffection amongst the rank and file. Too frequent rewards signify that the enemy is at the end of his resources; too many punishments betray a condition of dire distress. To begin by bluster, but afterwards to take fright at the enemy's numbers, shows a supreme lack of intelligence.　　　　（翟林奈 译）

　　Where, hemming and hawing, the enemy commander speaks to subordinates in a meek and halting voice, he has lost his men. Meting out too many rewards means the enemy is in trouble, and meting out too many punishments means he is in dire straits. The commander who erupts violently at his subordinates, only then to fear them, is totally inept.　　　　（安乐哲 译）

谆谆翕翕,徐（与人）言〔入入〕者,失众也

　　以翟林奈为代表的多数译者将这句话理解为士兵私下非议主帅,安乐哲则认为是主帅与部下打交道时底气不足的表现。基于西方修辞视角,笔者认同杨炳安的观点①,即这里是在讨论修辞者（将帅）在与受众（部众）互动过程中的具体表现以评估二者在特定语境与情形中的相对权力关系。翟林奈译文只提到"窃窃私语",并未提到"抱怨",不如 Christopher MacDonald 译文②既提到"压低声音"又有"抱怨"那么全面且明确地反映基层的不满。安乐哲译文使用 hemming and hawing（"嗯嗯呃呃"）颇为形象地描绘出修辞者说话时为寻找恰当的措辞而踌躇的样态,尤其是在凸显修辞者与受众的身份权势差异之后却使用了与修辞者（主帅）的修辞人格（ethos）不兼容的 meek and halting（卑躬屈节且吞吞吐吐）,不无讽刺意味地暗示读者二者的话语权力关系已然发生反转。

数赏者,窘也;数罚者,困也

　　安乐哲将"窘"理解为"遇到麻烦",不如翟林奈译文"一筹莫展"或 Cleary 译文 impasse（绝境;僵局）更能够体现严峻的形势。安乐哲只是用 mean（意味着）在"数罚"与"困"之间建立逻辑关联进行推理,翟林奈译文使用 betray

---

　　① 原注为:"次乃相将,故所言皆指将帅与部众言谈之情状,非指士卒相与私语以非其上。"参见杨炳安.孙子会笺.郑州:中州古籍出版社,1986:135.

　　② 译文为:"When enemy soldiers cluster in groups, whispering and muttering, it means that their high command has lost control."。参见 Christopher Macdonald. The Science of War: Sun Tzu's "Art of War" Re-translated and Re-considered. Hong Kong: Earnshaw Books Ltd., 2017:182.

(暴露)更能够体现即便主帅想掩盖也藏不住的不利局面。Cleary 翻译杜牧注解①，详尽地为读者解说频繁赏赐、动辄处罚的深层原因，让读者不仅知其然，还能够知其所以然。

**先暴而后畏其众者，不精之至也**

翟林奈译文将本句翻译为"先是虚张声势，然后却害怕敌人数量众多，是极度缺乏智商的表现"。虽然在国内诠释者中也不乏这类观点的同情者(如曹操②)，但他们其实误解了修辞语境与修辞受众③。首先，从行文逻辑而言，前文都是讨论主帅与部众的关系，这里没有理由突然调转话头去讨论主帅与敌人的关系④；其次，这里预期的话语功能是告诫主帅不可因误判形势、前倨后恭而动摇其人格权威，乃至给自己造成修辞伤害。安乐哲翻译为"开始时对部众咆哮，然后又开始害怕他们，这是十分无能的表现"。虽然比较忠实于原文字面意思，在逻辑上依然有跳跃之嫌，读者难免会困惑为什么主帅突然开始害

---

① 杜牧曰："势力穷窘，恐众为叛，数赏以悦之。人力困弊，不畏刑罚，故数罚以惧之。"Thomas Cleary 译文为："DU MU: When the force of their momentum is exhausted, they give repeated rewards to please their soldiers, lest they rebel en masse. When the people are worn out, they do not fear punishment, so they are punished repeatedly so as to terrorize them."。杜牧注解参见孙武.孙子十家注.曹操，等，注.天津：天津市古籍书店，1991：359.Thomas Cleary 译文参见 Sun Tzu. The Art of War. Thomas Cleary, trans. Boston: Shambhala Publications, Inc., 1988.

② 原注为："先轻敌，后闻其众，则心恶之也。"参见孙武.孙子十家注.曹操，等，注.天津：天津市古籍书店，1991：360.

③ 格里菲斯在注解中就曾反对曹操的解读："Ts'ao Ts'ao, Tu Mu, Wang Hsi and Chang Yi all take the chi(其)here to refer to the enemy, but this thought does not follow the preceding verse too well. Tu Yu's interpretation, which I adopt, seems better."。格里菲斯认为若依照曹操的解读，就应该翻译为"at first to bluster but later to be in fear of the enemy's host"，但是他认为杜佑的解读("先行卒暴于士卒，而后欲畏己者，此将不情之极也")更有道理并据此给出自己的译文："If the officers at first treat the men violently and later are fearful of them, the limit of indiscipline has been reached."。格里菲斯的注解与译文均参见 Sun Tzu: The Art of War. Samuel B. Griffith, trans. London, Oxford: Oxford University Press, 1963：122. 曹操、杜佑解读均参见孙武.孙子十家注.曹操，等，注.天津：天津市古籍书店，1991：360.

④ 杨炳安认为曹操的解读不妥，提出"此言将帅对部众先行暴刻，而后畏其散离也"。参见杨炳安.孙子会笺.郑州：中州古籍出版社，1986：135。

怕部众了。在这个方面，MacDonald 的译文①最为周全，尤其是 alternately（变换）的使用，使得主帅摇摆不定的修辞人格跃然纸上。

**七、视卒如婴儿，故可与之赴深溪；视卒如爱子，故可与之俱死。厚而不能使，爱而不能令，乱而不能治，譬若骄子，不可用也。**

——《孙子兵法·地形》

When the general regards his troops as infants, they will be willing to follow him through the greatest threats and gravest danger. When the general treats his troops like beloved sons, they will be willing to support and die for him. An army may be so overly pampered by the general that it cannot be useful, so excessively loved that it cannot be commanded and so disorderly that it cannot be disciplined. Such an army is like a bunch of spoiled and arrogant brats, and cannot be deployed.

(Chen Song 译)

If a general cares for his men in the same way that he would care for his own children, they will follow him through thick and thin. If he loves his men as dearly as he loves his own sons, they will be willing to die with him and for him on the fields of battle. However, if a general indulges his men yet does not know how to challenge them or use their strengths, if he loves them but cannot command them, if he fails to punish them when they transgress or break the rules, then they will become like spoiled children and they will lack the strength required for battle.

(Joey Yap 译)

When a commander is as concerned for his men's safety as if they were infants, they will venture with him into the deepest gorge. When he values their lives as if they were his own sons, they will battle to the death alongside him. On the other hand, if a commander is indulgent and lacks authority, if he cossets the men and fails to enforce orders, if he tolerates indiscipline and does not impose control, then the army becomes as intractable as a spoiled child.

(Christopher MacDonald 译)

---

① 译文为："When officers alternately harangue then plead with the men, it betrays their utter ineptness."（长官若时而斥责部下，时而恳求他们，将会暴露出自己的极度无能。）。参见 Christopher Macdonald. The Science of War: Sun Tzu's "Art of War" Retranslated and Re-considered. Hong Kong: Earnshaw Books Ltd., 2017:182.

### 视卒如婴儿，故可与之赴深溪

Chen Song 的译文对于究竟是要重视婴儿的哪方面特征语焉不详，还有待于进一步补充说明。绕开"赴深溪"的字面意象，使用"赴汤蹈火"进行翻译，则有助于避免引发读者关于"为何要去那么深的溪谷"这样的困惑，是"'得'意'忘'言"的修辞翻译。Yap 译文就很明白地指出要像照顾孩子一样对待他的士兵，凸显了善待相对弱势的群体这一要求；不足之处是把婴儿翻译为儿童，使得其弱势地位打了折扣，反过来也影响了关爱的程度。绕开"赴深溪"字面意象，用带有头韵的"thick and thin"表达不畏艰难险阻，不仅容易让读者接受，还容易被读者记住。MacDonald 译文更是明确指出要像关心婴儿的安全一样关爱自己的士兵，不足之处是对"赴深溪"进行直译却缺乏必要的说明。

### 视卒如爱子

Chen Song 与 Yap 译文虽然忠实地翻译出要像对待自己的孩子那样对待士兵，但是"爱子"容许较大的诠释空间，不如 MacDonald 译文"将士兵视若己出，珍视他们的生命"那么具体入微。

### 故可与之俱死

Chen Song 的译文大意为"心甘情愿地护持主帅并为其献出生命"，强调的是为主献身。MacDonald 的译文大意为"并肩战斗直至死亡"，强调的是不离不弃。Yap 则兼收并蓄，即提到为主而战，也提到共同赴死。格里菲斯译本翻译了杜牧给这一节做注解时提到的吴起与基层士卒平起平坐、同甘共苦的例子[①]，替读者提供了该军事理论的一个鲜活的例子。

### 厚而不能使

Chen Song 译文只是提到部队被娇纵过度而不能使唤，把讨论的焦点放在士兵而非主帅身上，有失焦之嫌。Yap 提到主帅不知道考验士兵或利用其

---

① 格里菲斯译文为："Tu Mu: During the Warring States when Wu Ch'i was a general he took the same food and wore the same clothes as the lowliest of his troops. On his bed there was no mat; on the march he did not mount his horse; he himself carried his reserve rations. He shared exhaustion and bitter toil with his troops."。杜牧曰："战国时，吴起为将，与士卒最下者同衣食，卧不设席，行不乘骑，亲裹赢粮，与士卒分劳苦。"格里菲斯译文参见 Sun Tzu. The Art of War. Samuel B. Griffith, trans. Oxford: Oxford University Press, 1963:128. 杜牧注解参见孙武.孙子十家注.曹操，等，注.天津：天津市古籍书店，1991:391.

优势,MacDonald 提到主帅缺乏威望,均能够体现原文劝导的话语功能。

**爱而不能令**

Chen Song 与 Yap 只是宽泛地提到"爱",MacDonald 使用 cosset(to give a lot of attention to making someone comfortable and to protecting them from anything unpleasant)这个辞屏,将"溺爱"这一负面评价明白无误地传递出来。

**乱而不能治**

"乱"并不是 Chen Song 所理解的"混乱",而是 Yap 与 MacDonald 所表达的"违法乱纪"。"治",Chen Song 所理解的"约束"及 MacDonald 的"控制"都很合理,Yap 译为"惩罚"则有些片面,"罚"毕竟只是管束的一方面。

**譬若骄子,不可用也**

Yap 译文凸显的是士兵缺乏战斗所需要的军事素养;Chen Song 译文大意为"这样的军队就像一帮因为长期被娇惯而目中无人的顽童/淘气鬼,不堪大用",比较接近原文意思;MacDonald 译文主要是强调难以驾驭,最能体现原文要凸显的不良修辞后果;格里菲斯翻译张预注解①,提到为将者应该恩威并施,尤其以曹操割发代首自罚的例子②为英语读者生动地说明了严明的纪律对治军的重要性。

---

① 张预注:"恩不可以专用,罚不可以独行,专用恩则卒如骄子而不能使,此曹公所以割发而自刑……故善将者爱与畏而已。"格里菲斯译文:"Chang Yu:… If one uses kindness exclusively the troops become like arrogant children and cannot be employed. This is the reason Ts'ao Ts'ao cut off his own hair and so, punished himself…Good commanders are both loved and feared. That is all there is to it."。张预注解参见孙武.孙子十家注.曹操,等,注.天津:天津市古籍书店,1991:394.格里菲斯译文参见 Sun Tzu. The Art of War. Samuel B. Griffith, trans. Oxford: Oxford University Press, 1963:129.

② 译文为:"After having issued orders that his troops were not to damage standing grain, Ts'ao Ts'ao carelessly permitted his own grazing horse to trample it. He thereupon ordered himself to be beheaded. His officers tearfully remonstrated, and Ts'ao Ts'ao then inflicted upon himself this symbolic punishment to illustrate that even a commander-in-chief is amenable to military law and discipline."。参见 Sun Tzu. The Art of War. Samuel B. Griffith, trans. Oxford: Oxford University Press, 1963:129.

八、故善用兵,譬如率然。率然者,常山之蛇也,击其首则尾至,击其尾则首至,击其中则首尾俱至。敢问:"兵可使如率然乎?"曰:"可。"夫吴人与越人相恶也,当其同舟而济,遇风,其相救也如左右手。

——《孙子兵法·九地》

Now the troops of those adept in war are used like the 'Simultaneously Responding' snake of Mount Ch'ang. When struck on the head its tail attacks; when struck on the tail, its head attacks; when struck in the centre both head and tail attack.①

Should one ask: "Can troops be made capable of such instantaneous co-ordination?" I reply: "They can. For, although the men of Wu and Yueh mutually hate one another, if together in a boat tossed by the wind they would cooperate as the right hand does with the left."

(格里菲斯 译)

So a skillful military operation should be like a swift snake that counters with its tail when someone strikes at its head, counters with its head when someone strikes at its tail, and counters with both head and tail when someone strikes at its middle. The question may be asked, can a military force be made to be like this swift snake, The answer is that it can. Even people who dislike each other, if in the same boat, will help each other out in trouble.

(Thomas Cleary 译)

**故善用兵,譬如率然**

格里菲斯与 Cleary 译文都把部队比喻为首尾相应的蛇,基于汉简的安乐哲译文②则是将指挥部队的统帅比作反应快捷的蛇。③ 就"率然"的翻译而言,格里菲斯在翻译蛇的名称时就已突出了率然互相呼应这个特征,Cleary、安乐

---

① 原注为:"This mountain was anciently known as Mt. Heng. During the reign of the Emperor Wen(Liu Heng)of the Han(179-159 B.C.)the name was changed to Chang to avoid the taboo. In all existing works 'Heng' was changed to 'Ch'ang'."。参见 Sun Tzu. The Art of War. Samuel B. Griffith, trans. Oxford: Oxford University Press, 1963: 135.

② 译文为:"Therefore, those who are expert at employing the military are like the 'sudden strike'."。参见 The Art of Warfare: The First English Translation Incorporating the Recently Discovered Yin Ch'Ueh Shan Texts. Roger T. Ames, trans. New York: Ballantine Books, 1993:115.

③ 本句的文字有出入:山东临沂银雀山出土汉简《孙子兵法》有"者"字,《孙子十家注》无"者"字。二者大同小异,均能自圆其说。有鉴于下文讨论布阵,出于行文逻辑衔接考虑,笔者赞同无"者"字版。

哲的译文①以及 MacDonald 的 quick-as-a-flash 主要突出反应之快,至于首尾呼应这个特点则主要是通过下文补充的。

*率然者,常山之蛇也*

"常山之蛇",Cleary 没有翻译地点,格里菲斯的注解有提到"恒山",改称"常山"是为了避讳,但是关于避什么讳却语焉不详。安乐哲译文"The 'sudden striker' is a snake indigenous to Mount Heng."(恒山土生土长之蛇),凸显了这种蛇的地域特色并在注解中详细指出是为了避汉文帝的名讳②,有助于解答读者的困惑。

*击其首则尾至*

"至",格里菲斯简单地翻译为攻击,Cleary 翻译为还击,更能够体现各个部分呼应的特点。闵福德译文③ lashes back 不仅译出了反击这一点,其所选择的 lash 这个辞屏自身所带有的鞭状、甩动、猛击这些意涵不仅形象刻画了蛇的动作特点,还有助于在译文读者头脑中重构训练有素的部队协调一致、骁勇善战的意象。

*兵可使如率然乎*

Cleary 只是按字面忠实翻译;格里菲斯译文为读者补充了"即时的协作"这个核心内容。MacdDonald 译文④使用 reflexively(done because of a physical reaction that you cannot control),以条件反射般的本能反应形容部队各个作战单位高度协调,宛如一个有机生命体;加上译者使用了头韵修辞格,比起其他两位译者的译文,更多了一分修辞张力。

---

① 安乐哲译文为:"The 'sudden striker' is a snake indigenous to Mount Heng."(恒山土生土长之蛇)。参见 The Art of Warfare: The First English Translation Incorporating the Recently Discovered Yin Ch'Ueh Shan Texts. Roger T. Ames, trans. New York: Ballantine Books, 1993:115.

② 原注为:"Chang was probably substituted for heng by scribes following the convention of avoiding the given name of the emperor, in this case, Emperor Wen of the Han."。参见 The Art of Warfare: The First English Translation Incorporating the Recently Discovered Yin Ch'Ueh Shan Texts. Roger T. Ames, trans. New York: Ballantine Books, 1993:221.

③ 译文为:"Strike its head, And the tail lashes back."。参见 The Art of War. John Minford, trans. New York: Viking Penguin, 2002:285.

④ 译文为:"The question is: can an army be trained to respond as reflexively as the 'quick-as-a-flash'?"。参见 Christopher Macdonald. The Science of War: Sun Tzu's "Art of War" Re-translated and Re-considered. HongKong: Earnshaw Books Ltd., 2017:194.

**夫吴人与越人相恶也**

格里菲斯翻译为"吴人与越人彼此憎恨对方",但是没有为读者介绍吴越为何交恶。Cleary 的翻译大意为"即便是彼此不喜欢的人",直接略过中国文化细节,阅读起来固然便利,但也错过了向读者介绍中国文化的机会。Yap 译文①(众所周知,吴地与越地人民是宿敌)通过"众所周知"这一提法规避了对中国文化现象加以详细阐释的"举证责任",同时也不无高估受众知识储备之嫌。

**当其同舟而济,遇风,其相救也如左右手**

格里菲斯翻译为"如左右手互相配合",与原文"出手相救"有不少距离。Cleary 也只是泛泛而"译",译为"互助摆脱困境"。MacDonald 译文"They pull together like a pair of hands."(如一双手那样不分彼此地通力合作)更能够体现"遇到外部共同挑战而激发出认同感"的意思,毫无斧凿痕迹地把搁置争议、同舟共济的意象表达了出来。

九、故三军之(事)〔亲〕,莫亲于间②,赏莫厚于间,事莫密于间。非圣智不能用间,非仁义不能使间,非微妙不能得间之实。

——《孙子兵法·用间》

Of all those in the army close to the commander none is more intimate than the secret agent; of all rewards none more liberal than those given to secret agents; of all matters none is more confidential than those relating to secret operations. He who is not sage and wise, humane and just, cannot use secret agents. And he who is not delicate and subtle cannot get the truth out of them. He who is not sage and wise, humane and just, cannot use secret agents. And he who is not delicate and subtle cannot get the truth out of them.

(格里菲斯 译)③

---

① 译文为:"It is common knowledge that the territories of Wu and Yue are sworn enemies."。参见 Joey Yap. Qi Men Dun Jia Sun Tzu Warcraft: For Business, Politics, Absolute Power. Kuala Lumpur: Joey Yap Research International Sdn Bhd, 2014: 366.

② 关于本句的文字分歧及影响,笔者赞同杨炳安观点:"此文字有出入,虽于文意关系不大,然而终以汉简与孙(星衍)校(改'事'为'亲')为善",也就是取"故三军之亲,莫亲于间"这一说法。参见杨炳安.孙子会笺.郑州:中州古籍出版社,1986:203.

③ Sun Tzu. The Art of War. Samuel B. Griffith, trans. Oxford: Oxford University Press, 1963: 147.

Thus, of those close to the army command, no one should have more direct access than spies, ① no one should be more liberally rewarded than spies, and no matters should be held in greater secrecy than those concerning spies. Only the most sagacious ruler is able to employ spies; only the most humane and just commander is able to put them into service; only the most sensitive and alert person can get the truth out of spies.

（安乐哲 译）

故三军之亲，莫亲于间，赏莫厚于间，事莫密于间

与早先的译者翟林奈一样，安乐哲用 spies（间谍）翻译"间"，就字面意义而言是完全正确的，从修辞效果而言，则颇值得商榷。在英语世界中，由于该词与生俱来的贬义色彩，不仅从事这项工作的人不愿意承认自己是 spy，即便是管控与调配情报人员的相关人士也不愿意提及自己日常打交道的是 spy。为了淡化这一负面意涵，往往使用 secret agent（特工）取而代之，格里菲斯便是如此处理。

这一句话到底是描绘一种实然的状态，还是提出应然的建议或者策略，不同译者有不同的解读。格里菲斯的选择显然属于前者：译文描绘了统帅与情报人员的亲密关系、情报人员的优厚待遇以及情报工作的保密级别。② 安乐哲则不然，基本立场是劝说统帅采用如下的做法：给予情报人员最直接接触的便利，给予他们最丰厚的奖赏，对情报相关工作给予最高级别的保密。两种解读旗鼓相当，都站得住脚。如果考虑到本书是关于用兵之法的，也就是给统帅在军事方面提出具体的建议，那么安乐哲的解读可能性更高一些。

Thomas Huynh 的注解不仅替读者解答了为什么要重视情报工作与重赏

---

① 原著为："I have emended this on the basis of the Han strips text. In the received Sung text, it reads: Thus, in the operations of the combined forces, no one should have more direct access than spies, …"。参见 The Art of Warfare: The First English Translation Incorporating The Recently Discovered Yin Ch'Ueh Shan Texts. Roger T. Ames, trans. New York: Ballantine Books, 1993:223.

② 格里菲斯还翻译了梅尧臣注解"入幄受辞最为亲近"与杜牧注解"出口入耳也"："Mei Yao-ch'en: Secret agents receive their instructions within the tent of the general, and are intimate and close to him.

Tu Mu: These are 'mouth to ear' matters."。格里菲斯译文参见 Sun Tzu. The Art of War. Samuel B. Griffith, trans. Oxford: Oxford University Press, 1963:147. 梅尧臣、杜牧注解均参见孙武.孙子十家注.曹操，等，注.天津：天津市古籍书店，1991:510.

情报人员,还就情报工作的具体方法做了说明①。Yap 译文使用定语从句 the spies who risk their lives(出生入死的情报人员)直接对为什么要重赏情报人员做了解释,可谓一目了然。

非圣智不能用间,非仁义不能使间,非微妙不能得间之实

格里菲斯虽然在译文中将"用"与"使"不加区分地合并为"使用"(use),但在引用并翻译的杜牧②与梅尧臣③的注解中倒是对此进行了"择人"与"用人"

---

① 为什么要重视情报工作与重赏情报人员:When compared to the emotional and tangible costs of conflicts, obtaining information that can curtail those costs will be worth your time and effort. Therefore, remain close to your spies. Instead of only calling upon them when you need them, continually build a strong bond with them and help them whenever they need assistance. If you don't have informants who are close to your enemy, you need to seek them out. Earn their trust and build the same tight-knit relationship with them as you do with your existing spies."。大意为:冲突要所耗费巨大的情感与物质代价,获取情报可以显著减少这些成本,与此相比,为情报工作所付出的时间和努力是完全值得的。因此,要与己方间谍保持密切关系。不仅仅是在需要的时候召唤他们,在日常更要不断与他们强化关系、给他们提供及时的帮助。如果没有接近敌方的线人,就要想方设法去找到这样的人,获取他们的信任,与之发展与现有间谍一样的亲密关系。情报工作具体方法:"Secrecy in this verse relates to the formlessness you must maintain in your relationship with each of your spies. Without formlessness your spy may be exposed, and your enemy will be unlikely to share any more information with him."。大意为:与己方每一个情报人员打交道时要注意不露痕迹。如果做不到"无痕",己方情报人员就有可能暴露,敌人很可能不再愿意向他透露信息。英译参考 Thomas Huynh. The Art of War: Spirituality for Conflict Annotated & Explained. Woodstock: Skylight Publishing, 2008:194.

② 原注为:"先量间者之性,诚实多智,然后可用之。""间亦有利于财宝,不得敌之实情,但将虚辞以赴我约,此需用心渊妙,乃能酌其情伪虚实也。"格里菲斯译文为:"Tu Mu: The first essential is to estimate the character of the spy to determine if he is sincere, truthful, and really intelligent. Afterwards, he can be employed ... Among agents there are some whose only interest is in acquiring wealth without obtaining the true situation of the enemy, and only meet my requirements with empty words.(Such agents are now aptly described as 'paper mills')In such a case I must be deep and subtle. Then I can assess the truth or falsity of the spy's statements and discriminate between what is substantial and what is not."。杜牧注解原文参见孙武.孙子十家注.曹操,等,注.天津:天津市古籍书店,1991:512. 格里菲斯译文参见 Sun Tzu. The Art of War. Samuel B. Griffith, trans. Oxford:Oxford University Press, 1963:147.

③ 原注为:"防间反为敌所使。"格里菲斯译文为:"Mei Yao-ch'en: Take precautions against the spy having been turned around."。杜牧注解原文参见孙武.孙子十家注.曹操,等,注.天津:天津市古籍书店,1991:512.格里菲斯译文参见 Sun Tzu. The Art of War. Samuel B. Griffith, trans. Oxford:Oxford University Press, 1963:147.

的区分。安乐哲译文则对二者进行了明确区分,但是对于"择人""用人""得间之实"的原本应该为同一人的主体进行角色分配,一分为三,过犹不及,反而偏离了原文。格里菲斯把原本属于偏正结构的"圣智"翻译为并列结构的圣人与智者,让这一标准显得高不可攀,脱离了实际。安乐哲使用 sagacious ruler (睿智的君主),对"圣智"的理解与表达都是很到位的,但是把主体限定为(远在朝堂的)君主,不仅比较狭隘,而且与军事行动实际脱节。"得间之实"的背景是情报人员获取/提供的往往是半真半假的信息,而不是完全虚假的信息,这样的信息识别起来最有难度,而掌握全面情况必然是与情报人员打交道的统帅的直接目的。相比之下,戴梅可翻译为 get the whole truth out of spies(得到全部实情),要比其他两位译者的译文更符合真实情境,因而更有说服力。

值得一提的是 MacDonald 的翻译①。MacDonald 并没有逐字逐句地进行翻译,而是在把握总体内容之后按照自己的逻辑重新组织语言。如果以修辞效果作为参照点,这样的翻译不仅毫不逊色,还似乎更胜一筹。

## 本章参考的英译本

林戊荪. 孙子兵法:汉英对照. 北京:外文出版社,2016.

Christopher Macdonald. The Science of War: Sun Tzu's "Art of War": Re-translated and Re-considered. Hong Kong: Earnshaw Books Ltd., 2017.

Joey Yap. Qi Men Dun Jia Sun Tzu Warcraft: For Business, Politics, Absolute Power. Kuala Lumpur: Joey Yap Research International Sdn Bhd, 2014.

Shawn Conners. Military Strategy Classics of Ancient China//English & Chinese: The Art of War, Methods of War, 36 Stratagems and Selected Teachings. Chen Song, trans. Texas: El Paso Nortre Press, 2013.

---

① 译文为:"One cannot manage an intelligence network without exceptionally good judgement. One cannot deploy intelligence assets without being humane and principled. One cannot obtain reliable intelligence without great subtlety and discretion."。大意为:没有超乎寻常的判断力无法管控一个情报网络,没有仁爱与道德无法使唤情报精英,没有城府与洞察力则无法获得可靠的情报。参见 Christopher MacDonald. The Science of War: Sun Tzu's "Art of War" Re-translated and Re-considered. Hong Kong: Earnshaw Books Ltd., 2017:206.

Sun Tzu. The Art of War. Thomas Cleary, trans. Boston: Shambhala Publications, Inc., 1988.

Sun Tzu. The Art of War. Ralph D. Sawyer, trans. Boulder: Westview Press, 1994.

Sun Tzu. The Art of War. Samuel B. Griffith, trans. Oxford: Oxford University Press, 1963.

The Art of War/Sun-tzu. John Minford, trans. New York: Viking Penguin, 2002.

The Art of War: A New Translation. Michael Nylan, trans. New York: W.W. North & Company, 2020.

The Art of War: Complete Texts and Commentaries. Thomas Cleary, trans. Boston: Shambhala Publications, Inc., 1988.

The Art of War: The Definitive Interpretation of Sun Tzu's Classic Book of *Strategy for the Martial Artist*. Stephen F. Kaufman, trans. North Clarendon: Tuttle Publishing, 1996.

The Art of War: Spirituality for Conflict Annotated & Explained. Thomas Huynh, trans. Woodstock: Skylight Publishing, 2008.

The Art of Warfare: The First English Translation Incorporating The Recently Discovered Yin Chueh Shan Texts. Roger T. Ames, trans. New York: Ballantine Books, 1993.

Thomas Huynh. The Art of War: Spirituality for Conflict Annotated & Explained. Woodstock: Skylight Publishing, 2008:194.

# 第九章　典故与成语英译比较与评析

## 第一节　《世说新语》典故英译比较与评析

### 一、管宁割席绝交

管宁、华歆共园中锄菜,见地有片金,管挥锄与瓦石不异,华捉而掷去之。又尝同席读书,有乘轩冕过门者,宁读如故,歆废书出看。宁割席分坐,曰:"子非吾友也!"

——《世说新语·德行》[①]

Guan Ning and Hua Xin once hoed in a garden. They saw a piece of gold in the field. Guan Ning did not stop his work, considering gold nothing different from stone, while Hua Xin picked it up and threw it away. Once again they sat on the same mat, reading. A high official in a luxurious carriage passed by. Guan continued reading as before, while Hua went out for a look. So Guan cut the mat in half, and separated himself from Hua, saying, "You are not my friend."

(马照谦 译)

Kuan Ning and Hua Hsin were together in the garden hoeing vegetables when they spied a piece of gold in the earth. Kuan went on plying his hoe as though it were no different from a tile or a stone. Hua, seizing it, threw it away. On another occasion they were sharing a mat reading when someone riding a splendid carriage and wearing a ceremonial cap passed by the gate. Kuan continued to read as be-

---

① 刘义庆.世说新语汇校集注.刘孝标,注.朱铸禹,汇校集注.上海:上海古籍出版社,2002:0011.本节《世说新语》典故引文均出自此书,为节约篇幅,不再一一标注。

fore; Hua, putting down his book, went out to look. Kuan cut the mat in two and sat apart, saying, "You're no friend of mine."

（马瑞 译）

见地有片金

马照谦译文（大意为"看到园地里有一块金子"）是达意的，马瑞（Richard B. Mather）的译文（大意为"突然看见泥土堆里有块金子"）则在逻辑方面更严密，也更有戏剧性。马瑞使用earth（泥土）表明这块金子是锄头从泥里带出来的，与前文"锄草"在逻辑上一脉相承；用spy（突然看见）能够体现这是一个突发状况，在这样的考验下看两人的反应，更能考察其人品。

捉而掷去之

马照谦译文先后使用两个动词（先是捡起，而后又抛掉），准确再现了华歆的价值判断以及内心的挣扎。马瑞的译文却是语焉不详地说金子已在华歆手上，没有明确交代华歆主动去拾取这一重要情节。

乘轩冕过门者

虽然马照谦译文只提到"轩"（马瑞的译文同时还译出了"冕"），使用high official（高官）已经在某种意义上体现了"乘轩冕者"的社会地位，比马瑞泛泛提到某个人能够传达更多有效信息。

歆废书出看

马照谦译文漏译了"废书"这个重要情节，马瑞译文（大意为放下书本）则体现了华歆学习不专注、容易分心的特点。

子非吾友也

在管宁与华歆割席绝交时，管宁表态说"子非吾友也！"，马照谦忽略了这句话其实是典型的"以言行事"的言语行为修辞，而非纯粹地描述两人的关系，因而将其按照字面地翻译为"You are not my friend."（你不是我的朋友），容易让西方读者误以为管宁只是否认与华歆有私交，而未能把管宁对华歆的鄙夷之情表达出来。相比之下，马瑞将其翻译成"You are no friend of mine."（你不配做我的朋友；我耻于与你为友），掷地有声地表现出管宁旗帜鲜明的立场与态度。

## 二、华歆王朗避难

华歆、王朗俱乘船避难，有一人欲依附，歆辄难之。朗曰："幸尚宽,何为不可?"后贼追至,王欲舍所携人。歆曰:"本所以疑,正为此耳。既已纳其自托,宁可以急相弃邪?"遂携拯如初。世以此定华王之优劣。

——《世说新语·德行》

Hua Xin and Wang Lang once rode a boat for refuge. A man asked for a lift. Hua was reluctant to accept him. Wang said, "There is some extra room in the boat. It matters nothing about his boarding". Before long, the enemy approached their boat. Wang wanted to abandon the hitchhiker, but Hua said, "I was reluctant to give him a lift because I am (was) afraid that he would be involved in our trouble. Now that we have accepted him, there is no reason to abandon him in time of danger." So he was still with them and saved. Hua was considered superior over Wang through this incident.

(马照谦 译)

Hua Hsin and Wang Lang were sailing together in a boat fleeing the troubles of war when someone wanted to join them. Hua, for his part, disapproved, but Wang said, "Fortunately we still have room. Why isn't it all right?" Later, when the rebels were overtaking them, Wang wanted to get rid of the man they had taken along, but Hua said, "This was precisely the reason I hesitated in the first place. But since we've already accepted his request, how can we abandon him in an emergency?" So they took him along as before to safety. The world by this incident has determined the relative merits of Hua and Wang.

(马瑞 译)

避难
马照谦忠实直译,没有为读者交代为何避难。马瑞译文点明是躲避战乱。

欲依附
马照谦通过 asked for a lift(请求捎带)将双方不对等的话语权力关系准确呈现出来,马瑞使用 join(加入)则无法精确体现乘船者的弱势地位。

歆辄难之
马照谦翻译成"华歆不乐意接收对方",容易误导读者先入为主地对华歆的人品进行负面评价。马瑞翻译为中性的"不同意",为后面情节反转预留了话语空间。

幸尚宽
马照谦翻译为"还有多余空间",十分地道。马瑞按字面意思把"幸"翻译为"幸运",反而让文本有了斧凿痕迹。

### 何为不可
马照谦将修辞疑问转为肯定陈述,翻译成"让他登船无妨",将斩钉截铁的表态传达出来。马瑞虽然是直译原文修辞问句("这为什么不妥呢?"),但由于措辞的缘故,语气较弱。

### 贼追至
马照谦译为"敌人靠近",不如马瑞的"叛军赶上来了"更能够体现紧张的气氛。

### 本所以疑
"疑",马照谦翻译为"不情愿",不利于构建华歆正面的修辞人格,马瑞使用中性的 hesitated(犹豫)则能够体现华歆当时的顾虑以及长远眼光。

### 遂携拯如初
马照谦译为"于是那人得以留了下来",不如马瑞译文"于是他们一直带着那人,直到找到安全的地方"更能够体现收留者的修辞人格与美德。

### 世以此定华王之优劣
马瑞以模糊的方式翻译原文模糊的表达,将对二者人品高下的评判权交给了读者。马照谦则使用 superior over(优越于)替读者给出结果,虽然失之含蓄,倒也替读者省了不少力气。如果能够在前面加个限定语,比如 morally(道德方面),译文会更加明晰。

## 三、王祥事后母

王祥事后母朱夫人甚谨。家有一李树,结子殊好,母恒使守之。时风雨忽至,祥抱树而泣。祥尝在别床眠,母自往,暗斫之,值祥私起,空斫得被。既还,知母憾之不已,因跪前请死。母于是感悟,爱之如己子。

——《世说新语·德行》

Wang Xiang was an obedient son to Zhu, his step mother, and he was careful in serving her. There was a plum tree yielding rich fruits in the garden. Zhu left it to his care. When a storm came, he would embrace the tree, crying. Wang once slept in another bed. One night Zhu went to kill him with a knife, but she stabbed only the quilt. Wang was lucky to miss the killing, because he happened to be absent for washing his hands at that moment. Later he learnt that Zhu regretted having done this, so he knelt down before her, asking for being killed. She was greatly touched and thereafter treated him as her own son. (马照谦 译)

Wang Hsiang in serving his stepmother, Mme. Chu, was extremely conscientious. There was a plum tree in their home whose fruit was exceptionally good, and his stepmother always had him protect it. Once when a storm of wind and rain came up suddenly, Hsiang embraced the tree, weeping. On another occasion Hsiang was sleeping on a separate bed when his stepmother herself came over and slashed at him in the dark. As it happened, Hsiang had gotten up to relieve himself, and her vain slashing struck only the bedclothes. After Hsiang returned to the room he realized his stepmother bore him an implacable resentment, and kneeling before her he begged her to end his life. His stepmother then for the first time came to her senses and loved him ever afterward as her own son. （马瑞 译）

谨

马照谦拆开翻译为 obedient（顺从）以及 careful（认真），虽然失了简约，倒是为下文王祥主动请死埋下伏笔。马瑞翻译为 conscientious（勤勉认真），则不仅忠实而且简约。

母恒使守之

马照谦翻译为"让他照看"是比较妥当的，马瑞翻译为"派他去保护"颇为生硬。

时风雨忽至，祥抱树而泣

这一句讲的是有那么一回发生的事情，而非每每如此。马照谦翻译为"一旦风雨来临，王祥就抱树而泣"，过于夸张且不合常理，有可能招致读者反感。马瑞翻译为"曾经有一场突如其来的狂风暴雨，王祥（因护树心切而）抱树哭泣"，相对而言更合理，译文容易获得读者认同。

暗斫之

马照谦翻译为"持刀欲杀王祥"，忽略了"在黑暗中行刺"这个重要细节；马瑞译文提到了"在黑暗中"这个要素，为下文情节发展做了充分铺垫。

#### 私起

马照谦翻译为"洗手",比较口语化,远不如马瑞的 relieve himself(解手)端庄得体。

#### 知母憾之不已

关于"知母憾之不已",在这个故事中,王祥以至孝事后母,后母却对其虐难有加,当王祥意识到后母因刺杀他未果而懊恼不已时,竟主动请死,引颈待戮。因此,"憾"并非后母良心发现,而是因错失良机而遗憾、懊恼。马照谦译文"Zhu regretted having done this."(懊悔自己所作所为)会让西方读者误以为后母良心未泯,对自己的恶行感到懊悔。而原文作者的写作意图则是通过后母因图谋不遂而悻悻然以反衬王祥的"视死如归"的至孝精神。因此,译者对原文存在比较明显的误读。马瑞译文("王祥意识到后母对他的恨无法调和")虽然不准确,逻辑上还不至于与前文自相矛盾。从西方修辞的修辞人格建构角度而言,原文若将后母描绘成自行悔过,则王祥的修辞人格固然高尚,故事却并不十分感人,将会因为缺失应有的修辞张力而很难流传久远。通过一个"憾"字,原文将后母的修辞人格进一步矮化,同时也可以进一步巩固王祥舍命尽孝的修辞人格。因此,不妨将这句话翻译为"Zhu regretted having failed to get rid of him."。

#### 感悟

马照谦翻译为"受到触动",依然停留在直观感受浅层,不如马瑞译为"(从恨令智昏的状态中)恢复了理智",能够体现后母主动反思此前行为的荒谬,比单纯的"感动"境界更高。

## 第二节 《韩非子》典故与成语英译比较与评析

### 一、守株待兔[①]

宋人有耕田者,田中有株,兔走触株,折颈而死,因释其耒而守株,冀复得兔。兔不可复得,而身为宋国笑。今欲以先王之政,治当

---

① 《韩非子》原文中这个寓言并非独立故事,而是其论证的一部分,因此没有标题。"守株待兔"系后人在该寓言广泛流传中提炼出来的。本文为讨论方便,特意添加这一标题。下文"自相矛盾"等情况相同,不再一一说明。

世之民，皆守株之类也。

——《韩非子·五蠹》

There was a farmer of Sung who tilled the land, and in his field was a stump. One day a rabbit, racing across the field, bumped into the stump, broke its neck, and died. Thereupon the farmer laid aside his plow and took up watch beside the stump, hoping that he would get another rabbit in the same way. But he got no more rabbits, and instead became the laughing stock of Sung. Those who think they can take the ways of the ancient kings and use them to govern the people of today all belong in the category of stump-watchers!

(华兹生 译)

Waiting for a Hare to Turn Up

There was a peasant in the state of Song. One day a hare dashed up, knocked against a tree in his field, broke its neck and fell dead. Then the peasant put down his hoe and waited by the tree for another hare to turn up. No more hares [①]appeared, however; but he became the laughing-stock of the state.

(杨宪益等 译)

关于标题的翻译，乔车洁玲译文 The Vigil by the Tree Stump(守株)，杨宪益等译文 Waiting for a Hare to Turn Up(待兔)，两个译文都只有译者各自要凸显的那一半内容。唐再凤译文 Waiting by the Stump for a Hare to Crash into It(守在树桩旁等着兔子撞死在树桩上)与尹斌庸译文 Sitting by a Stump, Waiting for a Careless Hare(在树桩旁边等待粗心的兔子)都比较全面地体现了字面内容，但是对于成语的隐喻意义并没有足够的提示。《汉英双解成语词典》[②]译文 to trust to chance and windfalls 跳过主要情节的具体信息，对寓意进行了提炼，若是稍加调整，比如变为 trusting to chance and windfalls(指望意外之财)，倒是不错的标题。《汉英·英汉习语大全》[③]翻译为 to watch the stump and wait for a hare—to stick to old practice and refuse to have a change(守着树桩等兔子——执着于过去的做法，不愿改变)，使用头韵修辞格(watch 和 wait)点明典故的核心要素，令人耳目一新且过目不忘，不足之处是稍显冗长。

---

① 中国古代寓言选.杨宪益,戴乃迭,译.北京：外文出版社,2001:88.

② 《汉英双解成语词典》编委会.汉英双解成语词典.北京：商务印书馆国际有限公司,2005:872.

③ 张学英,张会.汉英·英汉习语大全.北京：清华大学出版社,2005:1516.

《汉英双解成语词典》注解提到该成语原来的比喻意义是指"to sit idle and enjoy the fruits of others' work"（坐享他人的劳动成果）[①]，或许本意是要表达"企图不劳而获/坐享其成"，但是这一译文容易将读者的注意力导向主人公的懒惰与贪婪这类品格缺陷，反而忽略了其不知变通的智力缺陷这一核心问题。有鉴于典故原文并没有提到占有他人劳动成果这个问题，这一译文还有待商榷。词典中对该成语的当代隐喻意义的若干解读之一 to stick to old experience without considering the circumstances（拘泥于旧有经验而不知变通）则十分契合这个成语的实际意涵。

宋人有耕田者

"宋"，杨宪益等使用 the state of Song（宋国）比华兹生的译文更能给读者传递文化信息。"耕田者"，华兹生使用 farmer（someone who owns or takes care of a farm），大意是农场主或者农夫，不如杨宪益等译为 peasant（a person who owns or rents a small piece of land and grows crops, keeps animals, etc. on it, especially one who has a low income, very little education, and a low social position. This is usually used of someone who lived in the past or of someone in a poor country）准确，后者主要是指旧时或贫穷国家的农民或者农夫，不仅能够表明职业，还能够暗示其社会地位不高以及接受的教育有限，有利于为下文故事做铺垫。

株/兔

"株"，杨宪益等译为 tree 并没有错误，但是不够精确，华兹生的译文使用 stump（树桩），能给读者提供更具体的信息。"兔"，华兹生译文使用的 rabbit（a small animal with long ears and large front teeth that moves by jumping on its long back legs, or the meat of this animal eaten as food）主要是指人类驯养的家兔，不够准确。杨宪益等译为 hare（an animal like a large rabbit that can run very fast and has long ears），也就是野兔，是很准确的翻译。

兔走触株，折颈而死

这是原文的亮点，也是翻译的难点，华兹生、杨宪益等对于这里的汉语意合文字都基于形合语言规则进行了精心处理。杨宪益等译文连用四个动作，一气呵成，生动地描绘出兔子从出现到死亡的全过程。华兹生的译文使用了

---

[①] 《汉英双解成语词典》编委会.汉英双解成语词典.北京:商务印书馆国际有限公司,2005:873.

一个伴随状语,使得句子比较紧凑,更符合英语读者的阅读习惯。

耒

耒是犁的前身,华兹生翻译为 plow(a large farming tool with blades that digs the soil in fields so that seeds can be planted)比较接近;杨宪益等译文使用的 hoe(a garden tool with a long handle and a short blade used to remove weeds and break up the surface of the ground)则是锄头,虽然二者功能有交集,但还是有些差别的。从修辞角度而言,农夫拿的究竟是什么农具并不重要,重要的是要表达他因为一个偶然的机遇而产生了企图长期不劳而获的思想,就此而言,两个译文修辞效果大同小异。

冀复得兔

潘智丹译为 in the hope that the miracle would happen again so that he could get another hare[①](希望奇迹再次发生,再得到一只兔子)。兔子出现并一头撞死在树桩上并非完全不可能,只是概率较小罢了,使用 miracle(奇迹)与实际情况有偏差。周仪翻译为 just wait there for more suicidal hares to come[②](在那里等待更多自杀的兔子的到来)。虽然从结果看来这只兔子确实是自取灭亡,但是兔子触桩而亡纯属偶然事件,并非主动选择结束自己的生命,因此使用 suicidal(自杀的)是值得商榷的。华兹生译为"以相同的方式再得到一只兔子"是十分准确的,杨宪益等翻译为"等待另外一只兔子出现"也含蓄地表达了相近的意思。

身为宋国笑

大部分译者翻译为"成为笑柄",唐敦燕等译为"The people in the village laughed at him for taking the accidental for the inevitable.[③]"(乡亲们因为他把偶然发生的当作不可避免会发生的事情而笑话他),不仅解释了农夫被群嘲的原因,还提炼并升华了主题。值得商榷的是 the inevitable 的使用,它主要是指"不可避免的情况"或"逃避不了的事实"(something that is certain to happen and cannot be prevented),是人们主观上想避免、客观上却往往不可抗拒的事情,与农夫希望坐享其成相龃龉。

---

① 姚萱.韩非子智慧故事.潘智丹,译.上海:上海外语教育出版社,2010:230.
② 周仪.中国文化故事.上海:同济大学出版社,2012:165.
③ 朱一飞,佘长茂,朱瑛,等.英译中国文化寓言故事.唐敦燕,蔡文谦,译.上海:上海外语教育出版社,2007:132.

**以**

华兹生译文使用 take(采取),不如布莱恩·布雅(Brian Bruya)译文 sticking to(固守)形象生动。与多数译者不同,布雅在翻译完主体内容后,还替读者解释说为什么固守先王之道行不通:某些政策之所以能够奏效,只是因为当时的偶然因素起作用,并不具有普世意义。①

**先王**

华兹生使用 the ancient kings(古代帝王),考虑到原文中韩非子这段话的开头是"上古之世"以及前文中提到"是以圣人不期修古",从时间上看是翻译得很准确的。而后出的 Sahleen 译文使用 the former kings(先前的帝王),读起来更像是因为前后任政见分歧而不能"以先王之政",而非因为难以跨越的时代鸿沟而不能"以先王之政",无法明确表达出"过时的政策要被淘汰,国家管理者要学会与时俱进"这个修辞主旨。

**政**

华兹生的译文使用 the ways(方式)比较宽泛,如果能够翻译为 the policies(政策)反倒更具体明晰。

尹斌庸译本对这个成语有不同的解读,认为"守株待兔"这个成语讽刺的是那些不想经过努力,存在侥幸心理,希望得到意外收获的人。② 撇开语境,就这个典故本身而言,任何读者做出这样的理解都是无可非议的。这一解读的关注点在于这个农夫,尤其是对他品性的评价。假如重新语境化(recontexualize)这个典故,则显然原作者韩非子的修辞意图在于劝阻人们千万不要像这个农夫一样墨守成规、不知变通。这个农夫只是韩非子阐发道理的手段或工具而非目的,因此,对农夫的道德评价并非这个故事的题中应有之义。

## 二、自相矛盾

楚人有鬻楯与矛者,誉之曰:"吾楯之坚,物莫能陷也。"又誉其

---

① 其译文为:"The fact that it worked once was just a chance occurrence."。参见蔡志忠.列子说·韩非子说.布莱恩·布雅,译.北京:现代出版社,2019:260.

② 其补充说明:"This idiom satirizes those who just wait for a stroke of luck rather than making efforts to obtain what they need."。参见尹斌庸.成语100:汉英对照.北京:华语教学出版社,1999:119.

矛曰："吾矛之利,于物无不陷也。"或曰："以子之矛陷子之楯,何如?"其人弗能应也。夫不可陷之楯与无不陷之矛,不可同世而立。

——《韩非子·难一》①

## The Self-contradiction of Spear and Shield

Once there was a man selling spears and shields in the State of Chu. One day he went to the market to peddle his wares. He first bragged about his shield, "This shield of mine is the most solid in the world that nothing can pierce it." He then bragged about his spear, "This spear of mine is the sharpest in the world that it can pierce through anything." Hearing his words, someone in the crowd refuted him at once, "What will happen if we thrust your spear at your shield? Will your shield be hard enough to withstand your spear or will your spear pierce into your shield? The man selling spears and shields suddenly became dumbfounded, unable to utter a single word. After telling this story, Han Feizi says in conclusion, "Logic dictates that the shield that can withstand anything and the spear that can pierce through anything can't exist at the same time."

(潘智丹 译)

关于标题,杨宪益等译为 The Man Who Sold Spears and Shields②(卖矛与盾的人),凸显的是人而非其话语内在逻辑冲突的特征;唐再凤译为 Self-contradiction③(表述自我冲突),把这个故事的修辞要旨提炼出来,是典型的得鱼忘筌的翻译方法,遗憾的是遗失了这个故事中最经典的要素——矛和盾。乔车洁玲译文 His Spear Against His Shield④(以彼之矛,攻彼之盾)描绘了这个故事的主要情节,具体逻辑冲突交由读者去想象。潘智丹译文 The Self Contradiction of Spear and Shield⑤(矛和盾的表述上的自我冲突)从表面上看,囊括了所有的要素,即矛、盾以及逻辑冲突,但从语言应用的实际而言,contradiction(of statements or pieces of evidence to be so different from each other that one of them must be wrong)主要是指以语言为代表的象征意义上

---

① 王先慎.韩非子集解.钟哲,点校.北京:中华书局,1998:350.
② 中国古代寓言选.杨宪益,戴乃迭,译.北京:外文出版社,2001:81.
③ 张雪彬,刘士毅.中国传统民间寓言选.唐再凤,译.天津:百花文艺出版社,2003:128.
④ 中国古代寓言一百篇.乔车洁玲,选译.北京:中国对外翻译出版公司,香港:商务印书馆(香港)有限公司,1991:113.
⑤ 姚萱.韩非子智慧故事.潘智丹,译.上海:上海外语教育出版社,2010:292-293.

的陈述或事实性的证据在逻辑上相抵触,并不适用于矛与盾这类具体事物的实力比拼或冲突。

**鬻**

廖文奎使用 selling(卖)翻译"鬻"自然是中规中矩的翻译。唐敦燕等译为 hawked his wares at the market[①],其中,hawk(to sell goods informally in public places)表达沿街兜售、叫卖不仅准确,而且形象生动。潘智丹译为 peddle[②](to sell things, especially by taking them to different places)的主要意思是兜售,(尤指)巡回销售;考虑到矛和盾的体积和重量,这个不太现实,因此比起 hawk 略逊一筹。

**或**

尹斌庸把"或"翻译为 a passer-by(路人),虽然很有新意,却在逻辑上有欠缺。路人听到的极有可能是只言片语,未必能够获得足够信息进行严密的推理并对卖家进行反驳。潘智丹译为 someone in the crowd(人群中有个人)、周仪译为 on-looker(旁观者)、杨振刚等译为 a voice was heard from the audience(观众中有个声音传出来)都能够重构现场,让读者身临其境。

**曰**

潘智丹译为 refuted him at once[③](当场质疑),比其他大多数译者的 asked(问)更鲜明地体现了原文预期的驳斥话语功能。

**以子之矛,陷子之楯,何如**

原文"以子之矛,陷子之盾"强调的是一种尝试的过程,潘智丹译文"What will happen if we thrust[④] your spear at your shield?"使用 thrust(而不是用更强调"刺穿"这一结果的 pierce),更好地体现了(结果尚在未定之天)的"刺"这一过程。

**其人弗能应也**

潘智丹译为"The man selling spears and shields suddenly became dumbfounded, unable to utter a single word."(卖矛和盾的人目瞪口呆,无言以对)

---

① 朱一飞,佘长茂,朱瑛,等.英译中国文化寓言故事.唐敦燕,蔡文谦,译.上海:上海外语教育出版社,2007:91.
② 姚萱.韩非子智慧故事.潘智丹,译.上海:上海外语教育出版社,2010:292-293.
③ 姚萱.韩非子智慧故事.潘智丹,译.上海:上海外语教育出版社,2010:292-293.
④ 姚萱.韩非子智慧故事.潘智丹,译.上海:上海外语教育出版社,2010:292-293.

固然形象生动,唐敦燕等译为"The man was so embarrassed that he could not utter a single word①."(尴尬得无言以对),不仅语言简洁且与上文逻辑联系紧密,因而比潘译更有修辞张力。

韩非子原文在这个故事后附加了一句评论:"夫不可陷之楯与无不陷之矛、不可同世而立。"潘智丹译文不仅忠实于原文,还通过添加 logic dictates(根据逻辑)这个导语,让寓言故事隐含的道理充满理性之光,客观上也进一步增强了译文的说服力。

### 三、买椟还珠

楚人有卖其珠于郑者,为木兰之椟,薰以桂椒,缀以珠玉,饰以玫瑰,辑以翡翠。郑人买其椟而还其珠。此可谓善卖椟矣,未可谓善鬻珠也。

——《韩非子·外储说左上》

A man of Chu, who lived in the State of Zheng, had a beautiful precious pearl and wanted to sell it. In order to get a good price, he racked his brains to dress up the pearl. He made a casket of a rare aromatic "magnolia wood" and perfumed it with cinnamon and spice. The outside of the casket was inlaid with pearls, jewels and jades as ornaments and edged with emeralds. The whole casket glittered with gems and was indeed a beautiful and delicate work of art. Then, the man of Chu carefully put the pearl inside the casket and took it to the market. A man of Zheng liked this casket very much, so he bought it. When he found the precious pearl inside the casket, he returned the pearl to the man of Chu. The man of Chu can be said to be good at selling the casket instead of the pearl.

(潘智丹 译)

这个故事最吊诡(paradoxical)的地方就在于原作者的修辞意图往往与实际流传中接受者重新赋予的话语价值南辕北辙:原作者韩非意在讥讽卖家修辞过度而适得其反,而读者往往将批评的焦点放在买家不识货而舍本逐末这个方面。

---

① 朱一飞,佘长茂,朱瑛,等.英译中国文化寓言故事.唐敦燕,蔡文谦,译.上海:上海外语教育出版社,2007:91.

关于标题的翻译,乔车洁玲译为 The Casket and the Pearl(匣子与珍珠)①,呈现了故事里最重要的元素,虽然有无限想象空间,但是因为缺乏具体情节与发展脉络提示,显得过于简单。杨宪益等译为 Selling the Casket without the Pearl(只卖不带珍珠的匣子或卖了匣子,却没给珍珠)②,如果读者做前一种理解,还算合理,如果做后一种理解,则不免对商人的修辞人格产生怀疑。潘智丹译为 Keeping the Glittering Casket and Giving Back the Pearl(留下了闪光的匣子,退回了珍珠),不仅译出了买家的取舍有违价值阶共识的意思,还以修辞凸显策略,即通过使用 glittering(闪光的,夺目的)在极其有限的文字空间里巧妙传达了买家舍本逐末的根本原因。

### 楚人有卖其珠于郑者

"楚人",王雷翻译为 a jewelry dealer(珠宝商),杨振刚等译为 a merchant(商人),给读者的印象是这个楚国人做的不是单一货品的一次性买卖,而是大量售卖珍珠这种商品甚至长期以此为业。③ 这与原文后文提到的无比精细又极其烦琐的修饰程序不相符,读者很难想象一个珠宝商会如此不惜成本、大费周章地去以手工方式批量为每一个珍珠制作流光溢彩、香气四溢的包装匣子。

潘智丹译为"一个住在郑国的楚国人有一个漂亮又贵重的珍珠要拿去卖"④,明确了卖家只有一个珍贵的珍珠可卖,并非以此为业,这为下文卖家不厌其烦从多维度包装修饰匣子奠定了坚实的话语基础。

### 为木兰之椟

潘智丹在译文前面加了一句这样做的原因,即"为了卖个好价钱,他绞尽脑汁想把珍珠装饰起来",属于合理补充,无可厚非。但是对于木兰的翻译,加了个"稀罕"的限定语,于理不通。这个故事中卖珍珠的人固然情商不高,智力却是完全正常的,没有理由认为他会不以营利为目的而去花血本装饰珍珠,从而出现成本与售价倒挂的情况。从理性角度而言,卖家用于装饰之物固然可

---

① 中国古代寓言一百篇.乔车洁玲.选译.北京:中国对外翻译出版公司,香港:商务印书馆(香港)有限公司,1991:103.
② 中国古代寓言选.杨宪益,戴乃迭,译.北京:北京外文出版社,2001:95.
③ 王雷译文参见王雷.汉英对照中国成语1000.北京:北京大学出版社,2011:112. 杨振刚等译文参见中国成语故事:汉英对照.杨振刚,郑分,译.成都:西南交通大学出版社,2020:191.
④ 关于楚国人居所的内容是译者自己想象补充的,谈不上忠实,但是属于合理想象,无碍于行文。

以美、可以巧、可以新、可以奇,独独不可以贵。rare 这个辞屏给读者极强烈的价值引导,让读者不由自主地靠近故事中的买家立场,这一话语效果与文本预设的读者会理性地与买家拉开距离的修辞效果大相径庭,因此有待商榷。

**薰以桂椒,缀以珠玉,饰以玫瑰,辑以翡翠**

"桂椒"是肉桂①与花椒两种香料,潘智丹译文使用并列结构进行翻译,比较忠实于原文。"缀以珠玉,饰以玫瑰,辑以翡翠",潘智丹译为"匣子外头镶嵌了许多珍珠、宝石、玉石,并以祖母绿镶边",对装饰工艺的翻译是很细致的,但是没有对所选用装饰材料与待售珍珠的相对价值差进行明确提示,不免让读者觉得这琳琅满目的珠宝玉石本身就价值不菲,"买椟还珠"也就顺理成章了。这一译法可能产生的修辞效果与文本的预期修辞效果恰好背道而驰,因此有过犹不及之嫌。

**郑人买其椟而还其珠**

潘智丹译文首先增补了一句原文没有的"整个匣子珠光宝气、精彩夺目,俨然是一件精美的艺术品",渲染了匣子的价值,为下文买家的选择做了充分铺垫。潘译还增补了卖家慎重打包、运输、展示以及买家对匣子的喜爱之情,这些皆属于原文所无但是又都在情理之中的合理想象。对于核心情节"买椟还珠",潘译为"当他发现里面那颗珍贵的珍珠时,把它还给了楚人"。虽然总体忠实于原文,但是多出的这个 precious(珍贵的)难免让读者犯疑:既然是珍贵的,也就是有价值的,为什么(在自己已经支付购买费用的情况下)还要还给卖家?这里所谓"珍贵",只是听故事、读故事的人以"上帝视角"/"全知视角"提前知道的信息,故事中的买家因为信息差并不知情,因此有蛇足之嫌。杨振刚等的译文对这一处的处理②尤其富有戏剧性,用对话的方式再现了充满反讽意味的修辞场景。

---

① 两个译本对"桂"所用的词不同,属于专业细微区别问题,不影响整体译文走向,亦非笔者所长,姑且存而不论。

② 译文为:"But he came back after a few steps later and said, 'Sir, it seems that you left a pearl in the box and here you are.'"。大意为:买家走了几步后又折回来了,说"先生,你好像把一颗珍珠落在匣子里了,拿回去吧"。杨振刚译文参见中国成语故事:汉英对照.杨振刚,郑分,译.成都:西南交通大学出版社,2020:191.

此可谓善卖椟矣,未可谓善鬻珠也

"此",潘智丹译为"这个人",与前文衔接比较紧密。杨宪益等对这一句的翻译①无论是行文措辞还是语气都很有修辞冲击力。

杨振刚等译文结尾总结说"买椟还珠这个成语指的是那些做出错误选择且缺乏判断的人"②,如果不考虑原作者使用该寓言的语境及其原初修辞意图,这一总结无疑是正确的。唐敦燕等的译文结尾也补充了"过于追求形式就有如喧宾夺主,结果只会适得其反"③,清晰地点明了原文本的修辞意图④。究竟哪一种解读更适切,译者完全可以在完整传递文本基本信息之后将判断的权力交还读者。

### 四、三人成虎

庞恭与太子质于邯郸,谓魏王曰:"今一人言市有虎,王信之乎?"曰:"不信。""二人言市有虎,王信之乎?"曰:"不信。""三人言市有虎,王信之乎?"王曰:"寡人信之。"庞恭曰:"夫市之无虎也明矣,然而三人言而成虎。今邯郸之去魏也远于市,议臣者过于三人,愿王察之。"庞恭从邯郸反,竟不得见。

——《韩非子·内储说上》

---

① 译文为:"This fellow may be considered a skilled casket seller, but deserves no credit at all as a seller of pearls."。大意为:这个家伙在兜售匣子方面可以说是很有营销技巧的,但是在卖珍珠这个事情上可就令人不敢恭维了。杨宪益等译文参见 中国古代寓言选.杨宪益,戴乃迭,译.北京:北京外文出版社,2001:95.

② 杨振刚译文中评论部分为:"This idiom refers to people who make a wrong choice and lack sound judgment."。严格来说,应该是指那种行为而不是指人。杨振刚译文中点评部分参见中国成语故事:汉英对照.杨振刚,郑分,译.成都:西南交通大学出版社,2020:191.

③ 译文为:"To go too far in the pursuit of form just like letting a presumptuous guest usurp the host's role, which brings about opposite results."。唐敦燕等译文参见朱一飞,佘长茂,朱英,等.英译中国文化寓言故事.唐敦燕,蔡文谦,译.上海:上海外语教育出版社,2007:123.

④ 遗憾的是在译文主体部分,对于装饰物与珍珠本身的价值差异并未以醒目方式为读者加以呈现,因此读者难以自行做出结尾增补的这个与原文本一致的判断。

## Three People Are Enough to Fabricate a Tiger

In the Warring States Period, the states often attacked each other. In order to make every one truly abide by agreements of truce, the states usually sent their own crown princes to each other as hostages. Pang Gong, a minister of the state of Wei, was going to accompany the crown prince of Wei to the State of Zhao as the hostage and the date had been settled for them to go to Handan, the capital of Zhao. Before their departure, Pang Gong asked the King of Wei a question, "If a man comes to tell Your Majesty now that he saw a tiger in the bustling crowd in the market, will Your Majesty believe it?" The king said, "I certainly won't believe it." Pang Gong asked again, "What if a second man comes to tell Your Majesty the same thing?" The king said, "I won't believe it, either." Pang Gong then pressed the question, "If three men claim to have seen a tiger in the bustling market in person, will Your Majesty still disbelieve it?" The king said, "Since so many people all say they have seen the tiger, it must be true. I have to believe it." At these words, Pang Gong mused and said, "As expected, this is where the problem lies. In fact man and tiger both fear each other to some extent. Specifically speaking, whether man are afraid of tiger or vice versa depends on the balance of the strengths of the two parties in the specific situation. As we all know, a tiger dare not break into a bustling downtown area with a lot of people. However, now three men's words create a tiger. The distance between the capital of Zhao, Handan, and the capital of Wei, Daliang, is much longer than that between the palace and the market. Besides, there will be more than three people who will talk about me. If you hear them speak ill of me, won't you develop the idea that I'm an evil man? Therefore, I tell you about my doubts before my departure, in the hope that you won't easily place trust in others' words." When Pang Gong left, some people who had harbored grudge against him started to speak ill of him. As time went by, the King of Wei really believed their false accusation. When Pang Gong came back from Handan, the King of Wei was no longer willing to see him. （潘智丹 译）

关于标题,潘智丹译为"三个人就足够编造出一只老虎(的谣言)",信息的焦点偏离到究竟多少人才可以编造出一只老虎这个问题上。周仪翻译为How a Lie Becomes a Truth(谎言是怎样变成真理的),虽然其字面意思恰好就是对故事核心情节与主旨的概括,但细察之下其实不然。就这个故事而言,谣言只不过是因为多人的修辞人格叠加形成的合力而获得免于事实核查

(factual check)的话语红利,从而暂时获得了"事实"的身份,这一所谓"事实"与真理、真相相去甚远。除了故事中被定向投喂误导性信息的目标受众魏王之外,其余在街上的人以及造谣、传谣者都知道实际情况究竟是怎么回事,因此不能说这个信息是普世真理,只能说被某个特定受众在特定情境中接纳为"事实"。从哲学角度而言,谎言就是谎言,无论重复多少遍都改变不了其虚假的本质属性。只有通过修辞干预,通过使用诸如本例中的证人证言、利用受众一贯特有的或恰好处于其中的某种特殊情感状态等修辞手段才可以让受众接受由谎言改编的所谓"事实"。但是即便是这些获得被蒙蔽的受众认可的事实,其时效性也是非常有限的,其持续存在是有严苛条件的。就以本案例而言,倘若魏王愿意到现场(街市)走一遭,则谎言必然不攻自破。张学英等主编的《汉英·英汉习语大全》给出了几个翻译,译文之一 A Repeated Slander Makes Others Believe[①] 被杨振刚等采纳为标题。就对应程度而言,传言街上有老虎并不以伤害特定个体名誉为目的[②],因此以此为标题尚需斟酌。词典给出的另外两个译文,其中一个[③]大意是"三个人的证言捏造出市场上有一只老虎(这种事)——重复的虚假报告会把人带偏、使人误入歧途",就前半句而言,总体已经是比较成功的翻译了,后半句则未免过度强调其话语后果,使得译文重心偏离了原初修辞意图,从而忽略了对修辞人格在说服中的重要性的关注。这个寓言原本是一个关于修辞人格及其叠加效应的代表性例子,翻译时理应凸显数量的叠加使得话语产生质的变化这一点,也就是使得原本完全不信或者半信半疑的受众接纳缺乏根据的话语,从而实现预期的告诫话语功能。

译文之二[④]是"三个人传播老虎的消息使你相信附近真的有虎——谎言如果重复足够多次,就会被接纳为真理"。考虑到句子长度问题,如果去掉后面半个句子,这一译文基本可以当作"三人成虎"的寓言标题了。首先,这个故事的大部分修辞要素(相关人物,主要话语事件,话语后果等)都体现出来了。

---

① 意为"诋毁的话重复多次,人们就信以为真了。"

② 究竟是什么目的我们不得而知,或许是为了制造恐慌情绪以达到其他不可告人的目的,又或许是为了通过谣言削弱某个君主亲近的人的修辞人格。无论如何,有一点十分清楚,那就是故意无中生有、说闹市有虎本身不属于诽谤这个范畴。

③ 译文之一:"The testimony of three men creates a tiger in the market—repeated false reports will lead one astray."。引自:张学英,张会.汉英·英汉习语大全.北京:清华大学出版社,2005.

④ 译文之二:"Three people spreading reports of a tiger makes you believe there is one around—a lie, if repeated often enough will be accepted as truth."。引自:张学英,张会.汉英·英汉习语大全.北京:清华大学出版社,2005.

其次,译文特别指明是"使你相信",而不是说"事实就是这样",为后续真相被披露后受骗者恍然大悟预留了足够的话语空间。

### 庞恭与太子质于邯郸

关于庞恭与太子为何主动去邯郸做人质,潘智丹译文在这个故事之前通过导论进行介绍。译文通过补充"战国时期互相攻伐的各国为了确保彼此守信,通常都会以太子作为人质交给对方看管",为读者提供了充分的文化背景知识。

### 市有虎

潘译并不是简单地翻译为"市场里有老虎",而是将场景具象化,译为"在熙熙攘攘的市场里,人群中出现了一只老虎",通过增补原文没有的"熙熙攘攘"和"人群",让这个初听之下就不可信的说法更加不可信,修辞效果明显可感。

### 不信

第一个"不信",潘智丹通过加入一个副词 certainly 让人物的表态更加立场鲜明,方便与后文态度转变形成对照。周仪将这一个"不信"译为"It's mere nonsense."(这纯属胡说),别具一格,有很强的修辞张力。

### 二人言市有虎,王信之乎/不信

"二人言市有虎",潘智丹处理为"又来了一个人跑过来告诉你同一件事情",译文语言比较活泼且富有概括力。第二个"不信",潘智丹则译为"我也不会信",照应了前一回的对话。周仪将这一个"不信"译为"I'll begin to wonder."(那我可要有点怀疑了),把受众开始有些动摇表现了出来,让两个"不信"产生明显的渐退梯度,也给读者进行了心理预构筑。

### 三人言市有虎,王信之乎

潘智丹并未照本宣科进行直译,而是根据实际修辞场景添加了一个"追问",并将"言"翻译为"宣称/宣认",能够体现出报信者一副言之凿凿的样态。

### 寡人信之/夫市之无虎也明矣

"寡人信之",潘智丹译文呈现了相对完整的三段论推理过程[①]:"既然这

---

① 这个三段论只呈现了小前提和结论,大前提(很多人相信的事情大概率是真的)被隐去了。所谓"真理有时候掌握在少数人手中",从逻辑角度而言,众人相信之事未必是真的,这个推理逻辑存疑。

么多人相信,应该就是真的,我也不得不信了",虽然文字稍显烦琐,但是"不得不信"很明显传达出勉强接受这一点,符合人的认知规律,从话语修辞角度而言可信度极高。"夫市之无虎也明矣",潘智丹增补了大量关于"虎畏人"的常识以及为何闹市区极不可能出现老虎的论证,为读者补充了动物习性的背景知识,让论述显得有理有据。

然而三人言而成虎

潘智丹译文"三个人的话语就创造出一只老虎"读起来似乎是话语直接催生了老虎在物理世界中的出现。如果能够调整为"三个人的话语就使得人们相信真有老虎"(because three men allege the presence of a tiger, a lie is taken as a truth),在逻辑上会更容易为读者所接受。

议臣者过于三人,愿王察之

潘智丹依然没有选择直译,而是详尽展开论述,补充了很多原文没有提到但是完全合乎情理的细节,比如"如果有人说我坏话,您会不会渐渐开始怀疑我是个坏人?",又如,"我之所以在临行前把我的顾虑向您坦白,是希望您不要轻易相信别人对我的非议"。这些话语都充满了现场感,让人物变得栩栩如生,给读者较强的修辞感染。

庞恭从邯郸反,竟不得见

潘智丹在译文中再次施展修辞想象力,补充构想了庞恭离开宫廷之后,对其心怀不满者如何诽谤他,随着时日推移,魏王也就听信了这些莫须有的指控。"不得见",潘智丹译为"当他回来时,魏王已经不再愿意与他见面了",这一译法与前文叙事一脉相承,具有很强的修辞说服力。

## 第三节  其他来源的典故与成语英译比较与评析

### 一、画蛇添足

楚有祠者,赐其舍人卮酒。舍人相谓曰:"数人饮之不足,一人饮之有余。请画地为蛇,先成者饮酒。"

一人蛇先成,引酒且饮之。乃左手持卮,右手画蛇曰:"吾能为之足。"

未成。一人之蛇成，夺其卮曰："蛇固无足，子安得为之足！"遂饮其酒。

为蛇足者终亡其酒。

——《战国策·齐策》①

Drawing a Snake and Adding Feet to It

In the Warring States Period(AD 960-1279), a man of the State of Chu gave his retainers a beaker of liquor when the sacrificial rite was over. Obviously a beaker of liquor was not enough to go around. So the retainers started a discussion among themselves and one of them suggested, "Since there is no enough liquor for all of us, why not draw a snake to decide who has the priority to enjoy it? The one who finishes the drawing first will sample it. OK?"

One retainer finished his drawing quickly enough and grabbed the beaker with his left hand, while his right hand continued to draw. Seeing the others were still busy drawing, he said euphorically: "See, I can add feet to it." At this moment, another man finished his drawing and snatched the beaker, and alleged: "Snakes have no feet at all. How can you add feet to it?" With this he gulped down the liquor. The man who added feet to the snake lost the chance to drink the liquor. This idiom means "Don't gild the lily" or "Don't carry coal to Newcastle".

(杨振刚等 译)

关于标题的翻译，杨振刚等译为 Drawing a Snake and Adding Feet to It，是很忠实于原文的，成功体现了该成语所有的要素。唐再凤的译文使用 Adding Claws to a Snake(为蛇添爪)，虽然典故中这个蛇足究竟是什么样已经无从可考，从动物学的角度而言，claw(one of the sharp curved nails at the end of each of the toes of some animals and birds)也就是爪，应该是足的延伸部分，为了在逻辑上更严密，恐怕还是用 feet 更合适。乔车洁玲译为 The "Finishing" Touch，虽然没有提到蛇这个具体对象，但是使用引号修辞性地提醒读者添足是成事不足败事有余的一笔，读者从这个翻译很容易关联到"画龙点睛"这个与"画蛇添足"语义相对的成语。通过引发读者头脑中呈现的正面形象与眼前的负面形象形成强烈反差，译文更好地传达了原作的态度与情感。

---

① 参见战国策.缪文远,缪伟,罗永莲,译.北京:中华书局,2018:168.

### 楚有祠者

大部分译者选择使用 a man(就说有这么一个人)一语带过;乔车洁玲基于文本中含有"舍人"(古代豪门贵族家里的门客)这个元素,对主人身份进行合理推测,翻译为 aristocrat(贵族),对于建构具体修辞场景、设定人物身份及分配修辞话语权力等都有积极意义。

### 赐其舍人卮酒

"舍人",尹斌庸翻译为 servants,杨宪益等译为 steward(a person whose job is to organize a particular event, or to provide services to particular people, or to take care of a particular place),相当于管家;唐再凤译为 attendant(a person who takes care of and lives or travels with an important person or a sick or disabled person),即侍从;杨振刚等译为 retainer(a servant who has usually been with the same family for a long time),也就是仆人。这些译文与语境都不太兼容,因为即便是管家,也只是仆人的领班,与主人的话语权严重不对等;特别在等级森严的中国封建社会,大部分时候仆人都是噤若寒蝉,我们很难想象他们敢在主人面前喧哗逞能。门客则不然,虽然也是寄人篱下者,但是往往有一技之长,享有一定的自由。为了获得主人赏识(也是在主人默许下),他们往往各逞其能,热衷于比拼才艺,斗智斗勇。或许是基于这样的认识,乔车洁玲翻译为 the gentlemen who worked for him(为他工作的绅士)以体现主人对门客某种程度的尊重。这一译文因为婉转而显得模糊,不妨考虑使用 hanger-on(a person who tries to be friendly and spend time with rich and important people, especially to get an advantage)进行翻译。

### 先成者饮酒

大部分译者都是直接翻译为"速度快的先得",唐敦燕等的译文"Whoever draws fastest and most lifelike will get the pot of wine."(画得快且最像的喝酒)则增设了一个被许多人忽略的重要条件——画的质量,在逻辑上滴水不漏,增强了故事的可信度。就"饮酒"的翻译而言,杨振刚等的译文"享有饮酒的特权"最为生动,把一人独享的排他性凸显了出来。

### 乃左手持卮,右手画蛇曰

或许是因为原文这句话逻辑比较松散,杨振刚等的译文也如实翻译为"拿到酒后右手还在画",读者自然感到不明就里。虽然后文有补充说是因为看到时间很充裕才继续画,在逻辑上却形成了一个断层。唐再凤译文①基于受众视角,为读者进行合理拓展,活灵活现地展现了画蛇足者的个性特征,让译文既可信又可读。

  尹斌庸译文结尾指出这个成语的意思是因为节外生枝或多此一举而坏了正事②,是很精辟的提炼。杨振刚等的译文结尾指出这个成语的寓意是"Don't gild the lily."(别给百合花上色),也就是不要多此一举的意思,这个是很正确的。同时还指出"Don't carry coal to Newcastle."[不要把煤运到煤都(不要做徒劳无功的事)],虽然大方向接近原来成语的意思,实际上二者还是有区别的:给百合花上色就像画蛇添足一样效果适得其反,而把煤炭运到盛产煤的纽卡斯尔,并不会给纽卡斯尔造成明显可感的损害,反倒是运送者白费力气,修辞意图主要在于提醒当事人要了解情况后再做决策。

## 二、失斧疑邻

  人有亡铁者,意其邻之子。视其行步,窃铁也;颜色,窃铁也;言语,窃铁也;动作态度,无为而不窃铁也。俄而抇其谷而得其铁。他日复见其邻人之子,动作态度无似窃铁者。

——《列子·说符》③

  There was a man who lost an ax and suspected that the boy next door stole it. For the next few days he watched the boy's movements and decided his behavior and looks were like those of a guilty person.

  Later, the man found the ax in a deserted area in the woods. When he got

---

  ① 译文为:"There was one who drew most quickly and he seemed to have finished it in a blink of the eye and then he thought the jar of wine belonged to him. When he looked around, he saw nobody finished the drawing. Taking the wine in his left hand and the stick in the right, he said proudly, 'You are drawing too slowly, I can still add some claws!'"大意是:有一个人眨眼间就把蛇画好了,他觉得这酒归他了。四处张望了一下,他发现大家都没有画完。于是左手拿着酒,右手继续画蛇,得意洋洋地说:"你们画得太慢了,我还能再给它添上几只脚呢!"参见张雪彬,刘士毅.中国传统民间寓言选.唐再凤,译.天津:百花文艺出版社,2003:161.

  ② 尹斌庸译文评论部分为:"This idiom refers to ruining a venture by doing unnecessary and surplus things."参见尹斌庸.成语100:汉英对照.北京:华语教学出版社,1999:42.

  ③ 杨伯峻.列子集释.北京:中华书局,2012:260-261.

home, his neighbor's boy no longer looked like a thief.

Whether someone is guilty or not depends on your opinion of them in the first place. (Eva Wong)[①]

唐敦燕等将标题直译为 Suspecting Others of Stealing the Hatchet,虽然内容比较全面,作为标题则稍欠简约。杨宪益等用 Suspicion(怀疑)作为标题则比较简约且颇具修辞吸引力。Suspicion 内在的否定意涵很容易吊起读者的胃口,为了满足好奇心,读者难免会去一探究竟,于是在不知不觉间就完成了全文阅读。唐再凤译文 The Neighbor is Under Suspicion(邻居被怀疑)信息量更大,无疑是个优点,但是反而可能会因为太过直白而减弱对读者的吸引力,反观杨宪益等的译文,不难体会到标题翻译少胜于多(less is more)的艺术。乔车洁玲译作 In the Eyes of the Beholder(取决于旁观者)也颇有修辞兴味:一是从互文(intertexuality)角度而言,很容易使读者联想到 Beauty is in the eye of the beholder(审美是言人人殊的事情),因此提示读者这是关于从不同视角看同一个问题而产生不同结论的一个范模(form)。二是这里缺失主语,根据格式塔完型心理机制,读者自然会想方设法去寻找答案。

无为而不窃铁也

葛瑞汉译为 everything about him betrayed that he had stolen the axe(一切无不表露出是他偷了斧头),"表露出"是很精彩的措辞,如果能够加上"他(主观上)觉得"逻辑就更加严密了。Eva Wong 的译文便是说他观察后觉得对方很像是嫌疑人。杨宪益、戴乃迭的译文[②]用 proclaim(表明;宣布)更是形象,让读者有呼之欲出的观感,仿佛就只缺将罪行写在脸上了。

俄而扬其谷而得其铁

葛瑞汉译文"Digging in his garden and found the axe."(在菜园刨出斧头),Cleary 译文 found the axe as he was digging in the valley(在山谷中刨出来斧头),Wong 译文 found the ax in a deserted area in the woods(林中空地里找到斧头),虽然都有自行发挥的成分,但是都在合理范围内。乔车洁玲译文 found his axe while digging in his cellar(地窖里刨出来斧头)则有些勉强,因为地窖主要是用于贮藏的空间,而非耕耘的场地,"刨"在这里并不是很

---

[①] Eva Wong. Lieh-Tzu: A Taoist Guide to Practical Living. Boston: Shambhala, 2013.

[②] 译文为:"All his gestures and actions proclaimed him guilty of theft."。参见中国古代寓言选.杨宪益,戴乃迭,译.北京:北京外文出版社,2001:7.

恰当。

唐敦燕等的译文增补为"After a few days, the hatchet was found. It turned out to be that when he went up the hill to cut firewood a few days ago, he left his hatchet there."(大意为"发现斧头是砍柴时落在山上了"),对丢失的原因与场所进行合理重构,有利于增加故事的现场感与可信度。

王雷译本在结尾补了一段疑邻者内心独白①,对话内容十分精彩(个别措辞如 small 等有待商榷),固然可以丰富人物形象,但是从修辞角度而言,译文有些地方于理不合,比如"我不是早就说过这小孩肯定不会做这样的事情吗?"这样的话语,虽然当代修辞学已经接纳自我作为受众(self as audience)这样的概念,但是如此自我谴责的场景也是十分罕见的。若能将其纳入具体对话场景中,译文会更加真实动人。与多数译者不同,周仪在结尾进行修辞升华②,将这个貌似平淡无奇的故事提升到了哲学的高度。

## 本章参考的英译资料

蔡志忠.列子说·韩非子说.布莱恩·布雅,译.北京:现代出版社,2019.

《汉英双解成语词典》编委会.汉英双解成语词典.北京:商务印书馆国际有限公司,2005.

刘义庆.绘画世说新语:评点·英译珍藏本.张澍助读、陈力农,绘画.马照谦,译.上海:上海古籍出版社,2004.

王雷.汉英对照中国成语 1000.北京:北京大学出版社,2011.

姚萱.韩非子智慧故事.潘智丹,译.上海:上海外语教育出版社,2010.

尹斌庸.成语 100:汉英对照.北京:华语教学出版社,1999.

张雪彬,刘士毅.中国传统民间寓言选.唐再凤,译.天津:百花文艺出版社,2003.

张学英,张会.汉英·英汉习语大全.北京:清华大学出版社,2005.

中国成语故事:汉英对照.杨振刚,郑分,译.成都:西南交通大学出版社,2020.

---

① 译文中该独白为:"'It is after all,' he thought, 'but a small axe. Who will steal such a cheap thing? Didn't I say long ago that this boy wouldn't do that at all?'"。参见王雷.中国成语 1000:汉英对照.北京:北京大学出版社,2011:172.

② 结尾提到"Prejudice stands farther from truth than ignorance"(偏见比无知离真理更远)。参见周仪.中国文化故事.上海:同济大学出版社,2012:126.

中国古代寓言选.杨宪益,戴乃迭,译.北京:北京外文出版社,2001.

中国古代寓言一百篇.乔车洁玲,选译.北京:中国对外翻译出版公司,香港:商务印书馆(香港)有限公司,1991.

周苓仲,何泽人.典故100.北京:华语教学出版社,1998.

周仪.中国文化故事.上海:同济大学出版社,2012.

朱一飞,佘长茂,朱英,等.英译中国文化寓言故事.唐敦燕,蔡文谦,译.上海:上海外语教育出版社,2007.

Han Fei Tzu: Basic Writings. Burton Watson, trans. New York: Columbia University Press, 1964.

Lieh-Tzu: A Taoist Guide to Practical Living. Eva Wong, trans. Boston: Shambhala, 2013.

Liu I-ch'ing. Shih-shuo Hsin-yu: A New Account of Tales of the World. Richard B. Mather, Trans. 2nd ed. Michigan: Center for Chinese Studies, 2002.

P. J. Ivanhoe, Bryan W. Van Norden. Readings in Classical Chinese Philosophy. New York: Seven Bridges Press, 2001.

The Book of Lieh-Tzu. A. C. Graham, trans. New York: Columbia University Press, 1990.

Thomas Cleary. The Book of Master Lie. https://archive.org.

# 后　记

　　正如书名《中国文化英译探索》所提示的，本书的写作是一场中国文化探索之旅。通过选择以先秦诸子百家学说为主的中国文化片段，首先确定了讨论的话题。其次通过比较各家译本，"邀请"了相关学者"各抒己见"，贡献自己的视角。在此基础上对各家译本做出探讨。从这个意义上说，这是一场虚拟的文化对话。中国经典文本的作者开启了话题，译者们前赴后继给出了自己（不无互文关联）的译本，本书作者参与这场对话，提出了自己的见解，同时期待学术同仁纠偏乃至斧正。这一情形正如伯克所言，是一场"永不停歇的学术对话"。

　　本书有若干明显的不足：一是中国文化博大精深，浩如烟海，所选材料不过是海边几枚赏心悦目的贝壳。二是译者、译本数量众多，选择难免受到客观条件（如获取途径、篇幅限制、处理文本所需要的时间等）及主观因素（如学科视野的局限）所制约。本人因所接受的西方修辞学术训练所形成的职业心理（occupational psychosis）难免使本研究在选材与解读时带有修辞滤镜。从积极的一面而言，西方修辞视角或许可以说是本研究在同类研究中的差异性特征；从消极的一面而言，正如伯克所言，"见即有所不见"，这同时意味着其他同样有价值，甚至更有见地的视角被忽略了。所有这些缺憾与不足，只能期待其他学科的同仁以及方家指正了。